Implementing Application Solutions in a Client/ Server Environment

Robert L. Koelmel

A Wiley–QED Publication

John Wiley & Sons, Inc.

New York • Chichester • Brisbane • Toronto • Singapore

Publisher: K. Schowalter
Editor: R. O'Hanley
Managing Editor: M. Frederick
Editorial Production & Design: Publishers' Design and Production Services

Designations used by companies to distinguish their products are often claimed as trademarks. In all instances where John Wiley & Sons, Inc. is aware of a claim, the product names appear in initial capital or all capital letters. Readers, however, should contact the appropriate companies for more complete information regarding trademarks and registration.

This text is printed on acid-free paper.

This publication is designed to provide accurate and authoritative information in regard to the subject matter covered. It is sold with the understanding that the publisher is not engaged in rendering legal, accounting, or other professional service. If legal advice or other expert assistance is required, the services of a competent professional person should be sought.

Library of Congress Cataloging-in-Publication Data
Koelmel, Robert L.
   Implementing Application Solutions in a Client/Server Environment /
   Robert L. Koelmel.
       p.   cm.
     "A Wiley–QED publication."
     Includes index.
     ISBN 0-471-06068-2 (alk. paper)
     1. Client/server computing.   2. Application software.   I. Title.
   QA76.9.C55K64   1995
   004'.36—dc20   94-12961
                                                                    CIP

Printed in the United States of America
10 9 8 7 6 5 4 3 2 1

To Karen, Rob, Eric, and Alison

Contents

4   DATABASE SERVERS **77**

Preface

This book was written for the business professional, data processing manager, systems analyst, application developer, programmer, and production system user who will be developing or utilizing application solutions in a client/server environment. The reader is exposed to the potentials and limits of client/server technology. Real-life examples demonstrate how client/server technology can be used to increase user productivity significantly. The transition issues and the risks in implementing large-scale client/server systems are examined.

The data processing industry has changed dramatically in the last 15 years. Before that time services were supplied exclusively by mainframe-based technologies. With the introduction of the PC in the early 1980s we started to experience the potential offload of mainframe services, but the alternative environment was still its namesake: the *personal* computer. In the last five years the PC has evolved into a workplace platform. These new powerful workstations, joined together by a network with even more powerful servers capable of mainframe processing, make up the base platform for client/server solutions.

Client/server architecture differs extensively from mainframe architecture because the application is divided between the client and the server. The client typically is responsible for the application presentation, editing, and some processing, whereas the server provides data management, shared resource facilities (for example, printing), and the remaining processing. The server is connected to the client via a network. Any single user request can be processed on the client alone or split between the client and the server(s).

This processing can take place on a single LAN platform that contains all the clients and servers necessary to support the application. The application may require access to mini-computers or mainframes acting as servers. Yet more complex are requirements to link together geographically disbursed LANs, especially if they have different network operating systems, workstation operating systems (both clients and servers), and database management software.

If one were to believe the advertising and the available product literature that focuses on client/server solutions, one could easily assume that implementing client/server solutions is as simple a process as upgrading existing hardware, adding some new hardware, purchasing some new tools, and providing training to a few IS professionals. In a few months the first client/ server application will be ready and thereafter application development will be a snap. Unfortunately, the hype is different from the reality. The right client/server platform for one organization can be significantly different for another organization. Additionally, client/server solutions may not be the most cost-effective solution in all cases. However, if the question is "Should the organization enter the client/server arena?" the answer is **yes**.

Most industry analysts agree that client/server-based application solutions are here to stay because there are many significant benefits once the client/server development platform is in place and developers have experience with the platform:

- *reduced development costs:* reduced mainframe usage-related costs and easier development requiring less staff.
- *quicker development:* more dynamic response to business needs.
- *data availability:* users have simplified access to information via locally distributed data and user-friendly query and report writing tools.

- *flexibility:* new technologies continue to appear at a rapid rate. The client/server platform is adaptable and accommodates integration with these technologies.

Managing development and production of enterprise-wide client/server computing architecture necessitates a comprehensive systems integration and systems management strategy. Support is needed from many vendors because the platforms will be composed of numerous products from varied vendors. Hardware reliability is a factor also; servers in general should be viewed as analogous to mainframes: they require security, backup, disaster recovery, redundancy, and environmental considerations. The client/server solutions run on networks which are prone to traffic problems and therefore require consideration during design and regular tuning during production. Software is spread throughout the organization because each workstation is an intelligent device with its own storage and stand-alone processing capability. Use of the new platforms for both development and production requires that both the information systems professional and the user be trained.

This book provides management with an overview of what considerations client/server applications place on training, change management, testing, performance (system response time), backup and recover, problem management (help desk), vendor relations, software distribution, standards and guidelines, security and auditing.

TEXT PURPOSE

Client/server technology will be a major information system technology during the 1990s. Most organizations will move from mainframe-based technology to some form of mainframe and LAN-based or exclusive LAN-based client/server platform.

Current available sources of information about the client/server environment include trade publications, vendor publications, standards organizations, and a limited number of books. The amount of literature is diverse and voluminous. These sources of information generally do not agree on what client/server is, nor do they agree on a common direction.

Experience with numerous clients and exposure to many students over the past two years has revealed the need for a book that would

- introduce mainframe developers, management, and users to the advantages and complex issues of the client/server paradigm.
- provide ideas for implementing client/server solutions.
- consolidate information relating to products, platforms, and directions within this environment.

THE TARGET AUDIENCE

This book draws upon personal experiences in implementing large-scale systems using mainframe, cooperative, distributed, and client/server technologies. These experiences traverse planning, analysis, design, implementation, production support, administration, and performance tuning and include teaching courses that introduce mainframe technologists to client/server concepts and facilities.

The book assumes that the reader has little or no prior knowledge or exposure to client/server architecture and builds on the basics. The book is intended to both educate and enlighten. Many questions concerning the client/server environment and associated technologies will be answered and, hopefully, many questions will also be raised.

This book can be used by all mainframe-based technologists, including managers, analysts, database administrators, production support personnel, programmers, and *users* who are looking for an understanding of client/server concepts and how to use those concepts to best implement and maintain client/server solutions.

PRESENTATION STYLE

This book has two significant features: (1) numerous illustrations, diagrams, figures, and examples and (2) hundreds of alternative software products. The illustrations, diagrams, figures, and examples are used to simplify the material, which is presented for readers with varied backgrounds. Illustrations have frequently been used to define the responsibilities of the server versus the client in the numerous examples of client/server solutions given.

The client/server marketplace has grown and now has many new development tools and tool features. The features and functions that distinguish tool types are described, as well as the framework for evaluating them. Included in the materials are lists of hundreds of alternative software products which can be used within the client/server solution arena. Products include those available to implement client/server architecture, such as front-end tools, back-end server products, applications development tools, networking software, gateway software, security and system management tools, and off-the-shelf client/server solutions.

The reader should note that although there are several hundred products listed in this text, this is not intended to be a comprehensive shopping list. The products listed in each category have been provided to give the reader a sense of what types of products are available and a starting point for further research. Since the client/server arena is still in its infancy, new solutions and alternatives come to the market every month. However, the products listed herein provide an excellent basis to choose from to construct simple client/server solutions, as well as platforms to build and maintain enterprise-wide mission critical client/server applications.

WHAT THE TEXT ADDRESSES

The book has been structured to address the following client/server subjects:

- *The Client/Server Platform:* What is the basic platform on which client/server solutions will operate? What are the basic components of LANs and WANs and how do they provide services to client/server applications? The first two chapters include discussions of topology, cabling, types of LANs, protocols, print, file and database servers, repeaters, gateways, bridges, routers, network operating systems, and so forth.
- *What is Client/Server?:* An introduction to client/server technology and concepts. What is client/server and why is it so popular? Chapter 3 includes examples of database, transaction, and application client/server solutions.
- *Database Servers:* One of the major components of the client/server environment is the database server. Chapter 4

discuss the features required in a robust client/server database server. Additionally, "industrial strength" SQL server software products are listed.

- *Simplified Client/Server Solutions:* How can available shrink-wrapped software be applied quickly and inexpensively to develop client/server applications? Included in Chapter 5 are numerous software products which can be used to create client/server solutions in areas such as imaging, multimedia, presentation graphics, spreadsheets, database software, word processing, E-mail, fax, single image, calendaring, and text retrieval.

- *Design Considerations:* This section is an overview of numerous design issues which must be addressed during client/server development. An emphasis is placed on GUI design. Chapters 6 and 7 cover design issues, including GUI, database, program, operating system, performance, and security design issues.

- *Developing Applications in the Client/Server Environment:* Client/server development concepts and tools are discussed, including prototyping, rapid application development, EIS (Executive Information Systems), GUI development tools, report writers, and CASE facilities. Chapter 8 includes software products that provide GUI development, Executive Information System development, and CASE.

- *Client/Server Implications During the Project Life Cycle:* What considerations do client/server applications place on training, change management, testing, performance (system response time), backup and recovery, problem management (help desk), vendor relations, software distribution, standards and guidelines, security and auditing. Chapter 9 includes software products that address testing, change management, software distribution, performance tuning, and so forth.

The index at the end of the text is preceded by a list of abbreviations and a list of trademarks used in the text.

About the Author

Robert L. Koelmel (Huntington, New York) has more than 25 years of experience as a programmer, analyst, systems architect, manager, consultant, and instructor. His broad background includes the design and implementation of mainframe, distributed, cooperative, LAN based, and client/server applications. He developed client/server courses which he currently teaches throughout the country and is the president of R.L. Koelmel & Associates which specializes in implementing client/server solutions.

LAN Component Overview

This introduction to LANs is not intended to be a comprehensive discussion of LANs. It has been included in this text to provide you with a broad background of the special environment that you will be using to develop and then run your client/server applications.

1.1 INTRODUCTION

LAN technology originated in the early 1970s, when computing began to move away from large centralized mainframes toward smaller departmental minicomputers. With this introduction of micro-computing and later the development of less expensive and more powerful machines, single-user workstations became a reality.

The initial disadvantages of single-user workstations were that the facilities available on larger, centralized systems were lacking on the single-user workstation. Sharing information, sharing access to peripherals such as printers and disks, and sending messages from one computer to another could not be done; these workstations were strictly stand-alone devices.

At about the same time, advances were made in communications technology. A new generation of networks emerged which operated in a limited geographical area but much more reliably and at a higher data transmission rate than previous networks.

These high speed Local Area Networks (LANs) opened up the possibility of attaining the advantages of single-user workstations, without losing those of centralized mainframe systems.

1.1.1   What is a Network?

A network is a group of interconnected autonomous computers. Two computers are considered to be networked if they are capable of exchanging information. Note that the key point in this definition of a network is that the computers are autonomous; this is different from the traditional definition of a network, which includes IBM 3270 terminals connected to a mainframe as peripheral non-autonomous computers or "dumb" terminals.

1.1.2   Difference Between LAN, MAN, and WAN

All three networks differ simply in the geographical area they cover (see Figure 1.1). A Wide Area Network, or WAN, spans a large geographical area: cities, states, countries, continents. A Local Area Network, or LAN, is confined to a relatively small area, such as a floor of a building, a building, or group of buildings in close proximity, where wires can be run between all locations. A Metropolitan Area Network, or MAN, is somewhere between a WAN and a LAN in size; for example, it may span a small city or a town. This distinction in the size of the three networks is emphasized because each has different connectivity needs and facilities.

Some of the more specific differences between a LAN and a WAN are as follows:

- The distance between nodes (for example, workstations) on a LAN is limited. There is an upper limit of approximately 10 km and a lower limit of 1 meter.
- WANs usually operate at speeds of less than 1 mbps (megabits per second). LANs normally operate at between 1 and 10 mbps.
- Error rates on LANs are much lower than those on WANs due to shorter distances and fewer electronic connections. This additional reliability has an impact both on the proto-

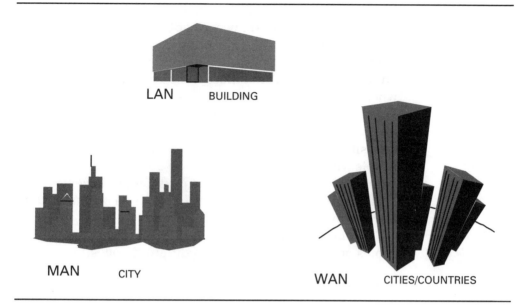

Figure 1.1   LAN, MAN, WAN

cols used in their operation and on the range of applications that they can support.

- The limited distances associated with LANs usually imply that the entire network is under the ownership and control of a single organization. WANs typically use telephone lines, which means the involvement of telephone companies. If they span countries, they are further complicated because they must meet the regulations of the telecommunications authorities of those nations.

1.1.3   Advantages and Disadvantages of LANs

The advantages include:

- *sharing:* the ability to share resources between users of the network. Ideally each user has access to all resources on the network: hardware, software (programs), and data. This is the most attractive advantage of the LAN.
- *incremental growth:* a computing system based around a LAN

has the ability to expand and contract easily. New resources can be added as they are needed or become available.

- *placing a resource where it is required:* processors or peripherals can be physically placed where they are needed and will be used. This differs from a mainframe operation where print facilities, for example, are usually centralized and the output requires delivery facilities.
- *autonomy:* placing resources where they are used gives responsibility for their control and administration to the people who use them. These are the people with the most to gain and lose. This local autonomy differs from centralized systems where decisions on availability and resource quantity are made in a broader framework.
- *redundancy:* easily built into the system. For example, two copies of a file can be stored on different nodes.

The disadvantages include:

- *backup:* there is no centralized control in LAN based systems. Taking backups requires specialized procedures. Do you backup each node or just the LAN servers?
- *security:* centralized systems have their own security concerns (usually satisfied by available and mature software), but using a LAN introduces additional security concerns. Distributed data at each workstation presents a new concern: it creates a new window of vulnerability to confidential data while it is being transmitted over the network; "listening" can take place. Encryption may be necessary.
- *creation of standards:* standards must be imposed across all networks to reduce complexity of interconnection and maintenance.
- *system failure:* failure is a problem in any system, but particularly in a network. Each node is intelligent and can potentially operate independently, but the node is dependent because it shares programs, data, and devices.

The next three topics examine the basic components of a LAN:

1. Topology: how the cabling is laid out
2. Transmission medium: cabling that carries the information

3. Access to the medium: algorithms used to send information across the cabling

1.2   LAN TOPOLOGIES

Topology is the method by which the LAN nodes are connected. The wiring can be run a number of different ways, each having certain advantages and disadvantages. Generally, the most important factors to consider in choosing which method to use to interconnect are:

- *reliability:* numerous types of failures can occur on a LAN, workstation, medium, network, servers, etc. The topology chosen for the network can help by assisting in fault detection and minimizing the impact of that fault.
- *flexibility:* benefits of a LAN include having workstations and peripherals around a given area close to the ultimate users. Because office layouts often change, the topology should allow for easy reconfiguration of the network. Adding new nodes and moving existing nodes should be done easily.
- *cost:* the LAN must be physically installed in a building in cable ducts and raceways, and this is ideally done during construction prior to completion of the inner walls and ceilings. Minimizing distances and the number of cables run will minimize costs, especially in a building already completed.

There are three major topologies currently in use:

- *star:* looks like a star—that is, the center of a circle with many radii.
- *bus:* straight line with many perpendicular lines attached.
- *ring:* looks like a ring—that is, a circle with all nodes on the circle.

Hybrid topologies take advantage of the strong points of the above topologies.

The following is a discussion of the three basic topologies and one hybrid that is currently popular; in each case, the discussion focuses on both the advantages and disadvantages.

1.2.1   Star

The Star topology (see Figure 1.2), as the name indicates, consists of a central node called a hub, to which all other nodes are connected. Each node has a single direct connection. This topology is commonly used in voice communications and is typical of IBM 3270 terminals connected to a host. In the case of IBM 3270 terminals, each unit is connected to a controller via a single coax cable. Sometimes a building is wired with feeder cables from the center to intermediate concentration points called wiring closets (see Figure 1.3). From there additional cables are run to individual locations.

The advantages include:

- *one node per connection (wire):* generally, all cables are potential points of failure; this is especially true of connection points. In this topology, failure of a single connection affects that node and only that node.

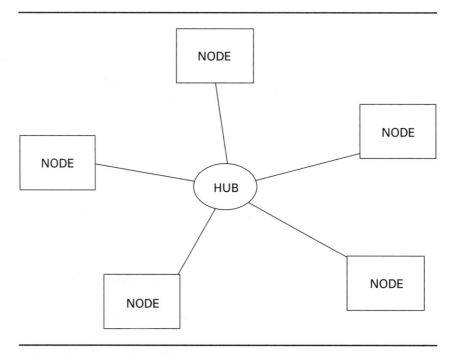

Figure 1.2   Star Topology

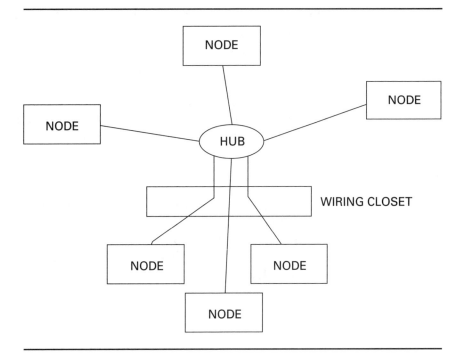

Figure 1.3   Wiring Closet

- *easier service:* this topology has a number of concentration points. The central node, or hub, and the intermediate wiring closets provide easy access for service.
- *simple access protocols:* contention for who has control of the medium for transmission purposes is easier because access to the wire is limited to two nodes: the central and the peripheral. However, if a hub is used instead of a central node, contention protocol is more complex.
- *centralized problem diagnosis:* since the central node is connected directly to every other node in the network, faults are easily detected and isolated.

The disadvantages include:

- *central node / hub dependency:* if the central node in a star network fails, the entire network fails.
- *high cost of expansion:* since each cable must be run from

the central node, expansion is always difficult. Sometimes wiring is done with many more wires than required from the central node and then workstations connected as necessary. However, each termination point must be determined in advance.

- *extra cable length:* Star topology necessitates a full length cable for each node. Cable is generally cheap, but running the cable, especially in completed buildings, is usually expensive.

1.2.2   **Bus**

The bus topology (see Figure 1.4) consists of a single length of transmission cable, to which various nodes are attached. Typically there is a central computer on one end and terminals attached along its length. This is also known as a multi-drop line. It is also the topology used in ethernet.

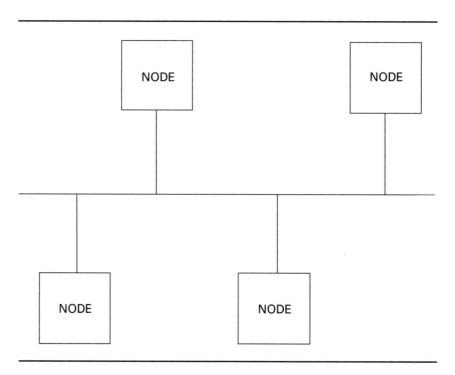

Figure 1.4   Bus Topology

The advantages include:

- *easier to expand:* additional nodes can be connected directly anywhere along its length. Additionally, a signal amplifier, called a repeater, can be used to add more extensive segments and segments of long length.
- *less cable length:* the single common data path connecting all nodes allows for shorter cable length. This decreases the installation cost, and also leads to simple, easy-to-maintain wiring layout.

The disadvantages include:

- *may require repeaters:* because the bus is a single length and may be very long, the signal may require a boost by a repeater. Repeaters require a special configuration, including tailoring cable lengths and adjusting terminators.
- *difficult problem diagnosis:* in most LANs based on a bus, control of the network is not centralized in any particular node. This means that detection of a fault may have to be performed from many points in the network.
- *problematic fault isolation:* if a node is faulty on a bus, the node can simply be removed. In the case where the fault is the network cable itself, an entire segment of the bus must be disconnected.
- *nodes must be intelligent:* each node on the network is directly connected to the central bus. This means that some way of deciding who can use the network at any given time must be performed in each node by hardware or software.

1.2.3   Ring

In the ring topology (see Figure 1.5) each node is connected to two and only two neighboring nodes. Data is accepted from one of the neighboring nodes and is transmitted onward to another. Data travels in one direction only, from node to node around the ring. After passing through each node, it returns to the sending node, which removes it. Data passes through, rather than travels past, each node. The recipient can easily mark a message as read before resending it, so when it arrives at the sender, he knows it has been successfully read.

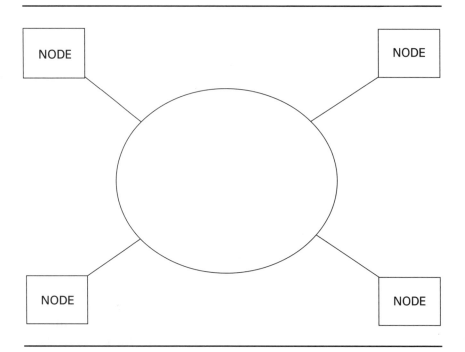

Figure 1.5   Ring Topology

The advantages include:

- *shorter cable length:* length similar to that of a bus. The single common data path connecting all nodes allows for short cable length. This decreases the installation cost, and also leads to simple, easy-to-maintain wiring layout.
- *no wiring closet:* single cable negates possible use of a wiring closet.
- *optical fiber cable possible:* optical fiber cable offers the possibility of very high-speed transmission. Since traffic on the ring travels in one direction, optical fiber can be used as a medium of transmission. This may be a critical concern in any environment where electrical interference might disrupt transmission, such as a factory floor that uses large machines run by electricity.

The disadvantages include:

- *network reconfiguration difficult:* it is not possible to shut down only a segment of the ring and keep the majority working during an installation. The whole ring is affected. Also the location of each new node is dependent upon the location of two existing nodes since the new mode will be wired between two existing nodes.
- *node failure disrupts network:* since the transmission of data on a ring goes through every connected node on the ring before returning to the sender, one node malfunction can cause network failure.
- *problems difficult to identify:* since a single node failure affects all nodes, diagnosing the defective one is difficult. Diagnostic facilities may be required in each node.

1.2.4   Star-Ring Hybrid Topology

The star-ring topology (see Figure 1.6) has combined the two topologies to achieve the best of both. The configuration consists of a number of concentration points connected together in a ring. These concentration points consist of wiring closets located on the floor, or at one or two points on a large floor, of a building. From each closet, nodes are connected in a star configuration, with some or all of the connection points used up. Electrically, the star-ring operates in the same way as a normal ring. The difference is that the physical wiring is arranged in a series of interconnected stars.

The advantages include:

- *easier expansion:* the network can be designed with extra built-in connections at each concentration point or star. Additional growth can be accomplished by adding more concentration points.
- *easier cabling:* concentration points are connected via a single cable; this simplifies extension of the network from floor to floor. Also the wiring techniques used are similar to those of a telephone system and are usually well understood by building engineers.

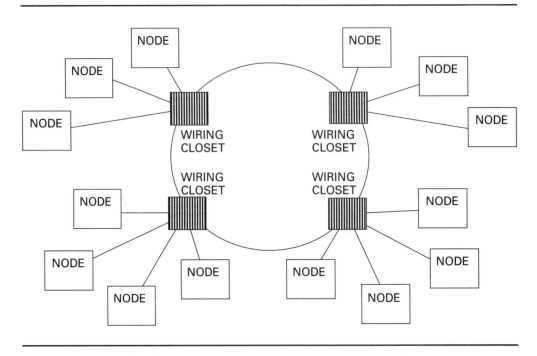

Figure 1.6   Star-Ring Hybrid Topology

- *problem diagnosis and isolation:* if a fault is detected, isolate the problem to one concentration point on the ring.
Since the ring is small in relation to the total number of
nodes on the network, the problem is much more manageable than with a simple ring topology. The faulty concentration point can be disconnected, leaving the network in a
fully functional state. Further diagnosis can then be carried out on the defective star node.

The disadvantages include:

- *cabling vulnerability:* cabling between points of concentration is critical to its operation; one outage in this ring
causes the entire network to fail. This may mean that redundant cabling in the form of one or more backup rings
will be needed to meet reliability requirements. The points

from the concentration point to the nodes is a star topology and may mean extra cable lengths.

When choosing a topology for a LAN, consider whether it is

- easy to install both in existing buildings and those that can be pre-wired
- easily expandable to meet growth requirements, with minimal disruption of users of LAN

Breakdowns in a LAN are to be expected. It is desirable to have a system where faults can be detected quickly and subsequently isolated, leaving the main section of the network operating normally.

The choice of topology can affect the range of possible media and the access method used to share it. Both of these can in turn affect the complexity and speed of operation of the individual nodes.

The star topology is historically of the most interest and is usually the topology against which all others are measured, but it is more appropriate for host and terminal connectivity than for a large LAN.

1.3   TRANSMISSION MEDIUM—CABLING

The medium, or cabling, connects the nodes on the LAN. This medium should be immune to natural and environmental hazards, for example, electrical noise, lightning, and other forms of electromagnetic interference (EMI). For maximum availability of the network, the system should be serviceable; cable breaks and node failures must be easily repairable or bypassed.

Transmission speed is an important component of LAN design. First review the applications that will be running, and then estimate their transmission requirements. Host-to-terminal traffic for terminal emulation or cooperative processing is typically a low traffic user, whereas graphic applications, especially imaging, are a high traffic user. The medium should be chosen based on projecting its use for a least 5 to 10 years since the cost of replacement is significant.

Several different types of media are currently in use. Copper wiring is the most common and exists in the form of twisted pair or coaxial cable. Optical fiber technology has recently become another medium of choice.

Since copper has been used for many years, more experience with this technology has accumulated. Connectors, a variety of cabling, terminators, receptacles, and so forth are all available as high-quality and cost-competitive items.

Optical fiber transmits a modulated light beam through a glass fiber connecting nodes with each other or connecting segments of a LAN (backbone). The major concern with this medium is that no reliable, low-cost method exists to date to connect one fiber segment to another.

The major concern with data transmission is electrical noise. This noise can be generated by the environment outside the cable or by the cable itself. Noise from the environment is usually caused by sources of electromagnetic radiation in the vicinity, for example, electrical equipment, lightning, and radiation from other cables. The radiation emanating from the cable itself can also cause problems within the cable. For example, if the cable contains multiple pairs of wires and more than one pair is used for transmission, electrical noise can be generated.

1.3.1   Twisted Pair

The most common form of wiring in data communication applications is twisted pair cable. Its name describes the telephone wire consisting of separate copper wires in pairs of 2 or 4 wires that was run in offices and homes in the past. These were twisted together to make a common cable. This wiring is not used for data communications.

Problems can occur due to differences in the electrical characteristics between the pair of wires (for example, length, resistance, inter-pair capacitance). Care is taken during production to make the wires uniform in length and thickness. LAN applications use a higher-quality cable known as data grade; currently this is 10 BaseT cable data grade 4 or 5. Capacitance problems can be minimized by using a high-quality insulation material. External noise can be reduced by using a shield made of copper foil or wire braid.

10 BaseT cable is physically flexible, has a low weight, and can be easily spliced or connected. As a result, this cable is easy to install.

1.3.2 **Coax**

This cable consists of a solid wire core surrounded by one or more foil or braided wire shields that are separated by some kind of plastic insulator. The inner core carries the signal; the shield provides the ground. At one point it was widely used as LAN cabling, but it is currently more frequently used to carry television signals.

Coaxial cable varies in its characteristics, all the way from the light and flexible CATV cable to the heavily shielded low-loss cable that is very rigid and quite heavy. The heavy cable is used to connect segments of LANs that are separated by significant distances (for example, floors in a building); the heavy shielding helps to reduce electrical noise in any part of the run. The type used has a major impact on the ease and cost of installation.

1.3.3 **Optical Fibers**

There are two major advantages of optical fibers. The first is that they are a medium which can run at very high transmission speeds and carry a large amount of traffic. The second is their immunity to noise. Because the information is traveling on a modulated light beam, electromagnetic interference has no effect. This means that inter-building connections do not need lightning protection. It is also an excellent media for industries that use heavy machinery run by electric motors.

The major problem encountered in using optical fibers is the difficulty of connecting two fibers together or a light source to a fiber. Special equipment is required to align the fibers before joining them, and therefore installation is more expensive than it is when copper wire is used. Additionally, if the nodes on a LAN are connected in a ring configuration by optical fibers, bypassing a defective node is more difficult because the fiber ring must be disconnected and reconnected.

1.3.4 **Other Media**

Since LANs require high speed and reliable data transmission, the above medium are used most often. Sometimes another medium, such as phone system wiring, is used to reduce installation time and cost.

Most existing office buildings, as well as new office buildings, have wiring to accommodate telephone systems. The wiring is called voice grade and generally has a high noise-sensitivity level. At the hub of the system is usually something known as a private (automatic) branch exchange (PBX or PABX). Using this existing wiring, along with hardware and software to share the wiring or split its usage, may be an option for some applications that are low traffic based and can tolerate errors caused by noise on the cabling.

1.4   ACCESS TO THE MEDIUM

We have now introduced LAN cabling (medium) and the design for the cabling (topology). Next we discuss how to send the data through the cabling.

1.4.1   Lan Interface/Adaptor Cards

First we should consider the connection of the nodes to the cabling. This is done by the LAN interface, or adaptor card, which provides the direct interface between the LAN wire and the computer (node) itself. They are installed in the computer in one of the expansion slots within the CPU cabinet of the PC.

The cards interpret the electronic signal and have programs built into their computer chips that provide the necessary interface to run on the network. These cards, together with the network operating system, provide all the software necessary to run the network and individual nodes on it.

1.4.2   Packet Switching

Packet switching is a means of transferring chunks of data from one node to another. Computers tend to communicate with each other in bursts of activity followed by periods of no activity. A more efficient way of utilizing the communications channel is to use a technique known as packet switching.

In this scheme the data to be sent is wrapped in a packet and placed on the network. Stations have access to the medium when they are sending a packet. During periods of no activity, other nodes can transmit. Sharing access to the network can then be reduced to a technique with some rules that allow each node to place a packet on the network.

Although packet formats vary according to the software used on the LAN, the following are the general elements (see Figure 1.7):

- *packet prefix:* a start of packet indicator for all nodes on the LAN to recognize. It is important that the packet prefix be unique, to differentiate it from data which may be transmitted normally and also from noise sometimes found on the LAN medium.
- *addressing information:* nodes on the network identify each other by means of an address unique by node. This is done most often via a software identifier loaded as part of the LAN workstation configuration. Typically a node sees all traffic passing by or through it and retrieves only packets containing its own address.
- *control information:* states the purpose of the packet (for example, packets may be sent for network management purposes as a broadcast message or to determine whether a workstation is operational).
- *data:* actual data to be transferred between nodes. The data may either be fixed or variable in length, depending upon the protocol. Some LAN protocols divide data into multiple fixed-length packets.
- *error checking:* is usually done to detect errors during transmission. This error detection may take the form of a simple parity bit or more extensive cyclic redundancy checking (CRC).

PREFIX	ADDR. INFO.	CNTRL. INFO.	DATA	ERROR CHECKING

Figure 1.7   Packet

1.4.3   **Sharing the Medium—Contention & Non-Contention Methods**

The packets previously described must be sent throughout the network. A single node transmitting at the high speed at which the network operates does not create a problem, but as the number of nodes on a network increases, the contention for that network increases. The possibility that two or more nodes might attempt to use the network simultaneously becomes a real concern. Therefore, some mechanism must be in place to provide orderly use of the network.

The software resident on each node uses this agreed-upon mechanism to transmit. This mechanism or procedure is one of two kinds: contention and non-contention.

- *contention:* this method checks the network to see if it is idle and then transmits. The general term associated with this mechanism is Carrier Sense Multiple Access (CSMA). If two or more nodes find the network idle and then transmit, something called a crash will occur. If this happens they will need to retransmit. The mechanism with this extra facility is called Carrier Sense Multiple Access with Collision Detect (CSMA/CD). If a collision occurs, the mechanism is designed to wait some small amount of time and then retry the transmission. After a predefined number of retries, the transmission is aborted.
- *non-contention:* this method has each node wait until they have permission to transmit. At that point they transmit and then give control back so that another node can transmit. The token ring mechanism is a good example of non-contention. This works by passing a unique transmission sequence called a token. The token circulates around the ring being passed by each node to the next. If a node has data to transmit, it will remove it from the network, build its packet, and then transmit. The receiving node will remove the packet and return the token to its non-busy state. This gives every node an opportunity to transmit after each packet is sent.

The two most popular methods of sharing the medium are CSMA/CD and token ring. When the two methods are compared, it becomes apparent that they have the following pros and cons:

- *pro CSMA/CD:* this technology or algorithm is simple to implement. This simplicity is important in the design of network adapter cards because it makes them less expensive. A second advantage is that the topology can be either star or bus. Additionally, the amount of traffic that can be sent is simply a matter of the availability of the medium. This technology can sustain a higher traffic rate than a token ring, provided that the packet size is kept large.
- *con CSMA/CD:* since any traffic mix can be on the LAN at any time, a guaranteed minimum level of response time cannot be provided. The response time is directly dependent upon the activity present on the LAN.
- *pro token ring:* collisions do not occur and therefore collision detection and retransmission are unnecessary; this overhead reduction makes its performance at low loads reasonable. This technology can give the best results with heavy loads that are well distributed over stations on the network.
- *con token ring:* this technology is more complex to implement and thus involves a more expensive interface that includes the network interface card. Another drawback is that it can only be implemented as a ring. Additionally, although minimum response time can be guaranteed, this method cannot support as high transmission volumes as CSMA/CD.

1.5 TYPES OF NETWORKS

The following are a few of the more popular types of LANs.

1.5.1 Ethernet

Ethernet is one of the oldest LAN technologies available. It was originated and marketed by three large corporations: Digital, Intel, and Xerox. The original intent was to establish it as the industry standard. However, today several other technologies are competing to be that standard.

Described simply, Ethernet is a baseband network, with a bus topology and a data transmission rate of 10 mbps. The access method is CSMA/CD. Two types of cabling are normally used:

thin and thick ethernet. Thin is used because it is easier to run and manipulate. Thick is used because it can cover greater distances; it is often run between floors in buildings as the leg that joins two segments of a bus.

1.5.2   Token Ring

IBM introduced the Token Ring Network in the mid 1980s. The hardware consists of token ring wiring, with connectors and adapter cards for the PCs. The network topology is a ring or star ring. Electrically the nodes are wired in a ring configuration, with each node having connections to the prior and subsequent nodes.

The token is the crucial component of this type of LAN and provisions must be made for three types of conditions that can occur: no token, multiple tokens, and unprocessed tokens. A token monitoring station is responsible for correcting all three of these conditions.

- *no token:* this condition occurs when power is first applied to stations on the ring. It may also occur due to noise damaging the active token. If a predefined period of time expires without a valid token on the ring, the monitor clears the circuit and issues a new token.
- *multiple tokens:* this can occur when noise creates a token in addition to the one already circulating. Usually the receiving station will identify this noise token as invalid and delete it from the ring. If the original valid token is also deleted in the confusion, the situation is handled in the same way as for no token above.
- *unprocessed token:* transmits a packet and if some failure causes it not to be removed (for example, the receiving station has been turned off), the packet will continue around the ring. When the sender receives the token unprocessed, it issues a new token.

1.5.3   Applebus

This is Apple's LAN facility. It is inexpensive to implement and is suited for an office situation that has Macintosh and Apple computers and peripherals all located in close proximity. The transmission medium is unshielded twisted pair with a bus topology. A maximum of 32 nodes can be connected to a single network and the cable must be less than 300 m in length. The transmission speed is 230 kbps. These limits are considered to be shortcomings since most other networks can handle hundreds of nodes, and have maximum cable lengths in kilometers and transmission speeds in megabits.

1.5.4   PBX Systems

PBX systems or telephone networks function by using techniques different from those used in LANs, but the services they provide correspond to those provided by LANs. PBX systems provide LAN-type connectivity and reliability of transmission at a very low cost. The type of wiring used is more susceptible to noise, but since the transmission is often limited to voice, this noise is not a significant factor. These systems, however, are sometimes used for data transmission (for example, dial-up). In this kind of application, the noise level and transmission speeds become a concern.

1.6   LAN PROTOCOLS

We have now covered LAN technology at its most basic level. Consider the simple example of a file transfer. This process consists of one node reading a file and transmitting that file to another node which then stores it. This process creates several concerns which must be addressed. For example,

- *breaking up the data:* the file or set of records is too large to fit into a single packet. This means that it will have to be broken up into pieces to be sent over the network. Apart from the actual data, additional information will have to be transmitted to indicate the start of each record, the number of records, and the end of each record.
- *receiving node processing:* once a packet is received it must be processed. The time taken to do this can be significant. If the rate of processing received packets is slower than the rate at which they are arriving, the packets cannot be processed properly. One solution to this problem of controlling the rate of transfer is to have the source delay transmis-

sion of the next packet until it receives an explicit acknowl-edgment (ACK) from the receiver.

- *packets can get corrupted:* no network is completely reliable; packets may get corrupted or lost during transmission. This can happen if there is noise on the communication medium or a malfunction in some component. Again, explicit ac-knowledgments can be used to inform the source that a packet was received.
- *transmission path:* a decision must be made in a wide area network as to which route is best; this is not easy since not all connections may operate at the same speed, nodes may become congested if there is too much traffic through them, and links between network segments may fail.
- *different network requirements:* transferring files between nodes on different networks with varying interfaces will require alternative "hand shaking."
- *one or both nodes crash:* if either the sending node or re-ceiving node crash, the other node must halt processing, back out what has been done, and then begin other func-tions before retrying the operation.

1.6.1   Layered Protocols

To address the concerns in a basic file transmission and other transmission within a network, layered protocols have been de-signed that remove the application from most of these concerns. Successful use of wide area networks has been based upon the use of these layered protocols. LANs use the same software to make use of its full features and in anticipation of connecting to a WAN.

The basic layers of a protocol are outlined in Figure 1.8. At the lowest level, a LAN consists of a piece of cable and some circuitry to send an electrical signal over the cable. The physical layer applies a transmission technique to the cable to implement a bit transmission function.

The data link layer utilizes this transmission technique to concentrate on solving the problems associated with packet for-mats and sharing the network capacity. Users of the data link layer are provided with a packet transmission.

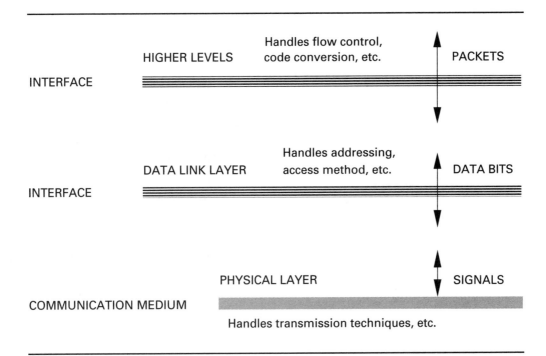

Figure 1.8   Layered Protocols

The remaining layers provide additional functionality until the application (for example, file transfer) can be performed with minimal interface requirements and transparent to the actual hardware and software doing the work.

1.6.2   Nonproprietary Standards

A nonproprietary layered protocol model has been developed by the International Standards Organization. This standard, called Reference Model for Open Systems Interconnection (RM/OSI), is more commonly known as OSI. It runs independent of the network architecture.

The seven-layer OSI reference model (see Figure 1.9) can be divided into three sections. The lower three layers are the communications component, the upper three layers are the host pro-

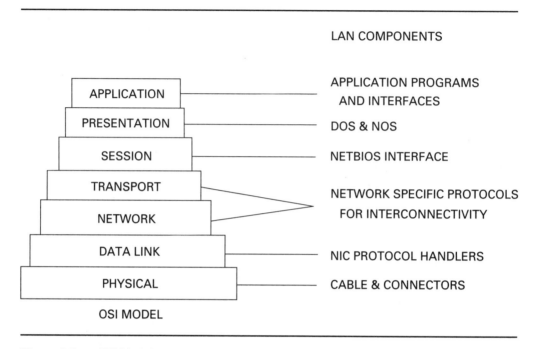

Figure 1.9   OSI Model

cess component, and the middle layer, called the Transport Layer, acts as an interface between the other two components.

The seven layers perform the following functions:

- *Physical Layer:* this layer is responsible for transmission between nodes. It interfaces with the transmission media, the topology, connectors, and generally anything associated with the physical transmission.
- *Data Link Layer:* this layer is responsible for providing reliable communication between nodes. It assumes that the physical layer is noisy or error prone. The Data Link Layer provides a mechanism to transmit the frames of data and assures reliable delivery to the next node. This requires a means of addressing both the source and the destination, as well as providing error control.
- *Network Layer:* this layer is responsible for switching, routing, and controlling the congestion of packets on the lower two layers.

- *Transport Layer:* this layer provides for delivering host messages originating at Layer 7 (Application Layer) similar to the way the Data Link Layer is responsible for delivering data between adjacent nodes. The Transport Layer, however, is responsible for message integrity across the entire network. For example, the Transport Layer segments a long message into smaller units prior to transmission and is responsible for reassembling those packets into the original message at the receiver.
- *Session Layer:* this layer establishes and terminates processing communication sessions between hosts.
- *Presentation Layer:* this layer operates on the data and is responsible for the syntax at the sending and receiving nodes. Data compression and data encryption are two examples of Presentation Layer services.
- *Application Layer:* this layer provides end user services such as file transfer, electronic mail, terminal emulation, remote database access. The Application Layer is the user interface.

A practical example of how the OSI model applies to a LAN is represented in Figure 1.9 as follows:

- *Physical Layer:* this layer is implemented with the cable, connectors, and the circuitry of the Network Interface Card (NIC).
- *Data Link Layer:* this layer's functions are performed with protocol handler integrated circuits in the NIC. An example of these protocols is Intel Corp 82586 (which is for IEEE 802.3 networks).
- *The Network and Transport Layers:* these layers are necessary for interconnecting multiple LANs. They may have minimal responsibilities for a single LAN since there is only one route, which is the cabling itself, and therefore there are no routing, switching, or communication reliability issues. An example of a protocol that is implemented at these layers is Novell's Sequenced Packet Exchange/Internetwork Packet Exchange (SPX/IPX).
- *Session Layer:* this is typically implemented with NetBios (Network Basic Input/Output System), developed by IBM.

- *Presentation and Application Layers:* the functions of these layers are performed by a combination of the workstation operating system (for example, DOS) and the Network Operating System (NOS).

1.6.3   Proprietary Standard Protocols

IBM has been manufacturing telecommunication computer equipment since the 1950s. Communications between much of the equipment in the early product line did not follow a single standard. To resolve this problem IBM designed an architecture for all future development called Systems Network Architecture (SNA).

In SNA architecture the high-level layers are referred to as the logical unit and low layers take care of the actual transmission. Figure 1.10 shows how the individual layers relate to the OSI mode. As it applies to the LAN, the lower layers will be fulfilled by the topologies, transmission methods, and access methods of the LAN

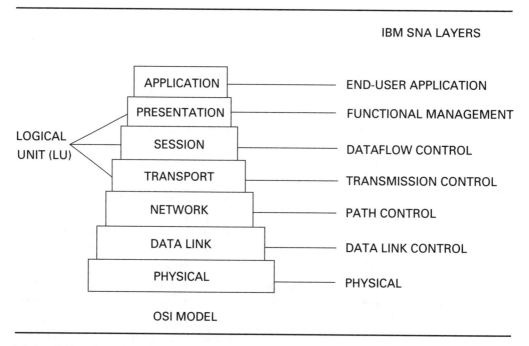

Figure 1.10   SNA Layered Protocol

in use. As indicated, SNA communicates using logical units (LU). Sessions are established between LUs by using facilities provided by the path, data link, and physical layers of SNA. The specific protocol LU2 communicates between a host and 3270 controller (dumb terminal). This communications protocol is frequently used on a LAN to emulate host communications and therefore let the PC operate as a dumb terminal; this communications protocol is also used to accomplish data and file transfers. However, since it operates by emulating an IBM 3270, the data is passed in less than 2,000 byte increments, the buffer size for IBM 3270 operation. Additionally, this process is slowed by the hand shaking that must be done to emulate the IBM 3270 in operation.

To address this problem IBM implemented a generalized program-to-program communication facility called LU6.2 Advanced Program to Program Communications (commonly referred to as APPC or LU6.2), which focuses on volume and high-speed data (information) transfers. Figure 1.11 shows how the individual

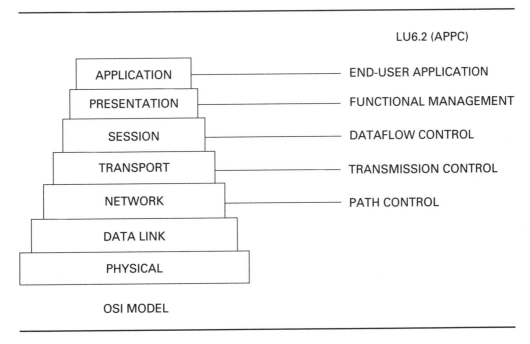

Figure 1.11   LU6.2 Layered Protocol

layers of LU6.2 or APPC relate to the OSI mode. The APPC token ring program provides the functionality of LU6.2 built on top of the data link and physical layers that are provided by the adapter card, token ring, and connectors.

By implementing both SNA and OSI like architecture, IBM has provided a base of network connectivity that can be used with LANs and also interface with OSI-based applications.

1.6.4   LAN Protocol Implementations

The Protocol Implementation chart (Figure 1.12) provides an example of two different LAN protocols and how they fit into the OSI model discussed.

The lower two layers, Physical and Data Link, are hardware

	NOVELL NETWARE	BANYAN VINES
APPLICATION	APPLICATION PROGRAMS AND INTERFACES E-MAIL, CLIENT SERVER APPS, ETC.	
PRESENTATION	NOVELL NETWARE CORE PROTOCOLS (NCP)	REMOTE PROCEDURAL CALLS (NET RPC)
SESSION	NETBIOS	
TRANSPORT	NETWARE SPX	VINES INTERPROCESS COMM. PROTOCOL (VIPC)
NETWORK	NETWARE IPX	VINES INTERNET PROTOCOL (VIP)
DATA LINK	NETWORK INTERFACE CARDS ETHERNET, TOKEN RING	
PHYSICAL	TRANSMISSION MEDIA TWISTED PAIR, COAX, FIBER OPTICS	

Figure 1.12   Protocol Implementation

dependent. They define the type of transmission medium (twisted-pair, coax, or fiber-optic cable), the network topology (bus, star, or ring), medium-access technique (CSMA/CD or token passing), and the transmission frame format.

Starting at the Network layer and extending to the Application layer are the various protocols associated with each NOS, in this case with Novell's NetWare and Banyan Systems' VINES.

Not all network operating systems implement each layer. The strengths and weaknesses of each protocol suite are defined by their protocol solution in relation to the OSI model.

2

Network Functionality

LANs can be used to provide a mechanism whereby potentially expensive peripherals can be shared between a number of users. For example, a printer is usually not necessary for each PC. Sharing peripherals can result in substantial savings since some peripherals, such as high speed multi-tray laser printers, are very expensive.

To share these resources, additional software on the server and sometimes hardware on the print device to be shared (for example, stand-alone printers) is necessary. Moreover, the use of these shared peripherals on the LAN can cause performance problems that must also be considered. One example would be the large amount of print traffic that would be generated, particularly for graphics, which require high volumes of bit patterns to define an image.

2.1 SERVERS

Network servers store data and programs and can manage access to attached printers and communications equipment. The server is typically a networked PC equipped with file, database, or facsimile server software, but it can also be a stand-alone device bundled with software or a mainframe or a minicomputer converted to a server.

The device used as a server must possess a microprocessor (for example, Intel 80286, 80386, or i486 chip) that can handle a heavy workload, as well as fast mass-storage devices. Server software can provide control of the network, file services, print services, and additional features such as electronic mail, security, and network diagnostics.

All workstations provide their own processing power and make use of the network connection to transmit, store, and receive data from other computers and to access shared peripherals.

All server functions can be performed by a single node on the LAN. This usually occurs with small LAN configurations (under ten nodes). As the LAN requirements increase, it is no longer possible for a single machine to service all requirements and still perform well. Therefore individual servers are added with unique responsibilities: network server, database server, print server, gateway, and so forth. See Figure 2.1.

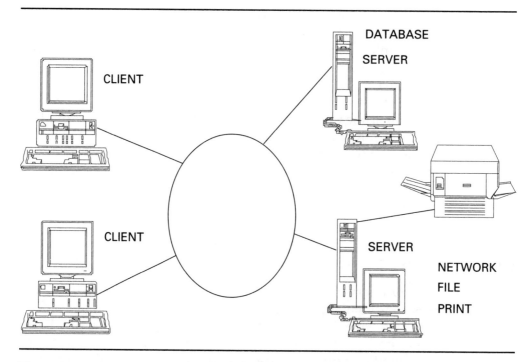

Figure 2.1   File, Print, and Database Servers

2.1.1　　Print Server

On a host computer system, terminals have access to various printers that are all connected to the host computer, thereby sharing the cost of these printers.

A LAN provides a means by which printers can be shared by connecting them to the network server, a separate node whose sole responsibility is to provide print capability (for performance reasons) or, more recently, a stand-alone printer with a network interface card. The print server and printers are usually located at a central site for maximum convenience (security or sensitive material may dictate otherwise).

The following is generally true of print servers:

- Communication is via a predefined protocol.
- Packets addressed to the print server are either commands or data.
- LAN management facilities exist to control the printer (for example, a cancel request deletes a file from the print queue or stops the current file being printed).
- Data blocks are treated as part of the current file being transmitted and are either stored or printed immediately.
- Invalid or erroneous packets from the client are rejected with or without an error response being returned to the sender, depending upon the protocol used.
- More than one printer can reside on a print server and more than one print server can reside on the LAN.

2.1.2　　File Server

Large amounts of disk space can be expensive on a LAN. Additionally, if each individual node has disk space, it would be the responsibility of each user to back up that disk file. If these disk files were large, each node would have to be equipped with backup tape facilities. To avoid these expenses and complications, sharing disk space on the network and providing common backup facilities reduces hardware costs and man hours spent in maintaining disk facilities. Disk space is typically carved out per node by providing each node with a home directory on the LAN where it can store data that pertains to that node only.

This is different than file sharing, during which the information will be read and updated by many nodes. The networking software running on the file server controls data transfer, data access, and file or record sharing. All standard file services are provided: create, delete, open, close files, as well as add, delete, read, and update records. These can be done from any authorized node (create, delete, read, and update access is provided on a file, not on a record, basis).

Potential file access response concerns include:

- the data transmission speed of the network
- the speed of the CPU and disk on which the server is implemented
- the level of disk activity generated by each client

2.1.3   Database Server

Database servers provide similar basic services to the file server functions available on the LAN, but they are provided as a database facility (for example, SQL) with full database functionality provided through programming languages and associated utilities. We will focus on these database servers in another section of this book.

2.2   OTHER FACILITIES

The following additional hardware facilities are an integral part of most networks.

2.2.1   Gateways

Gateways connect LANs to mid-range or mainframe hosts in wide area network environments (see Figure 2.2). In order to initiate the micro host connection, the gateway must either emulate the functions of a dumb terminal (for example, IBM 3270 running IBM LU2) to be recognized by the host, or provide other compatible host connectivity (for example, IBM LU6.2 program-to-program communications).

When running emulation, the functions of the PC keyboard must be mapped or must correspond to the functions provided by

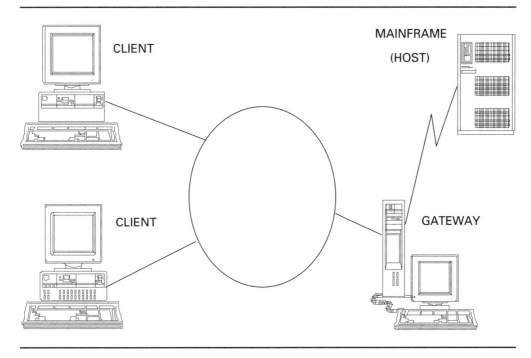

Figure 2.2   Gateway

the emulated terminal. The network connections are made via adapter boards that reside in an available PC and connect to the network via standard network cables. The gateways use a combination of hardware and software to provide the required emulation. This emulation may be as a single stand-alone device directly connected to a live controller of dumb terminals (no gateway necessary), or a gateway (PC workstation) may emulate the live controller itself. In the latter case, all PCs with the same emulation software can be connected to the gateway. The gateway provides intelligent connections with diagnostic capability. For 3270 connectivity, IBM (3270 Emulation), Rabbit [Rabbit Software, Malvern, PA 19355 (800) RABBITC] and Attachmate [Attachmate Corp. Bellevue WA 98006 (800) 426-6283] provide the emulation required at the terminal and controller level as LU2 devices.

These vendors also supply LU6.2 connectivity. LU6.2 provides the protocols to support distributed processing between intelligent workstations. Within the IBM communications umbrella the other types of LU (logical unit) communications that are used frequently in SNA include LU1, LU2, and LU3. LU1 is used for non-display devices such as Remote Job Entry (RJE) attached printers. LU2, as indicated, supports IBM 3270-type display terminals and LU3 is used for IBM 3270 printers. LU6.2 communicates from one Transaction Program (TP) to another TP. These TPs can be a mainframe host, a PC, a mini (for example, IBM AS400), or any other device capable of running the required protocol.

The functionality in LU6.2 provides for parallel sessions between two LUs. This means that a LAN gateway and mainframe or mini can be servicing multiple file transfers, database requests, and so forth, simultaneously. It means that data can travel in both directions and the session can be initiated by either TP. Advanced Program to Program Communication (APPC) or LU6.2 protocol supports client/server and open systems functionality in IBM SNA. It is inherently platform independent and can support mainframe applications that run on any platform, control data across platforms, and provide access to transactions from any network.

2.2.2   Repeaters/Hubs

These devices generally link together parts of a LAN (see Figure 2.3). The hub is used in a star topology to join together all nodes on the LAN; the repeater in a bus topology joins segments of the LAN together. Repeaters/hubs are used to:

- boost the electronic signal
- provide a focal point for trouble shooting
- join parts of a LAN

In the case of ethernet bus topology, the repeater consists of a rack of individual repeater cards containing one or more ports on each, or a panel of fully integrated ports. The wiring can be ethernet or 10BaseT with each wire terminating in a connector that is attached to the repeater.

Both repeaters and intelligent hubs usually have diagnostic capabilities. Each port (sometimes a group of ports if cards are used) has an indicator that is either a light or an LED readout. In the case of lights, on/off or green/red indicates whether the connection is OK/NG.

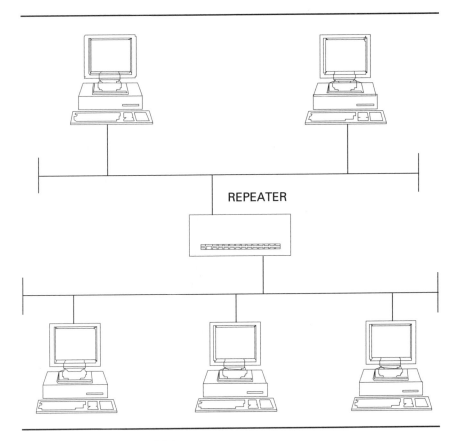

Figure 2.3   Repeaters/Hubs

The recommended approach is that each node be attached via a single cable and that there never be 2 or more nodes per cable. The following basic diagnosis can be done:

- If the light on the card is solid green (on), the attached node is OK.
- If the light is a solid red (off), the attached node is defective or improperly connected (for example, the cable is broken or has a short). Simply disconnect the node to reduce potential impact on the LAN and then diagnose the problem.
- If the light is flashing, traffic is present. If the associated node is inactive, this may be an indication that there is "error traffic."

2.2.3 Bridges

Bridges connect two or more LANs in local or remote locations. A bridge, unlike a gateway, does not have to ensure the integrity of transferred LAN data. It must only establish a viable connection between multiple LAN users. Local bridges (see Figure 2.4) connect geographical close networks, whereas remote bridges (see Figure 2.5) connect LANs through dial up or leased lines or via a wide area network (for example, X.25). Although the distance between LANs is a factor, the distinction between local and remote bridges is based more on the manner in which they are configured.

Local bridges are generally one of two types: hardware or software installed on a microcomputer that resides on both LANs, or a stand-alone device with direct connections to both LANs. A stand-alone local bridge generally allows no more than

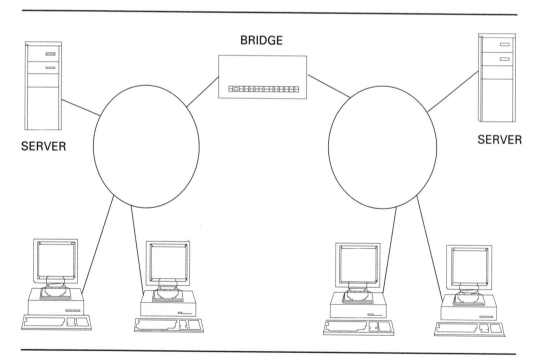

Figure 2.4   Local Bridge

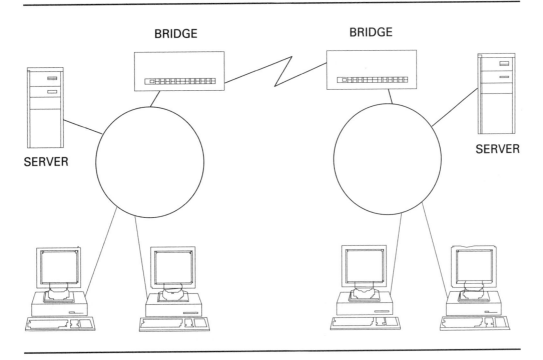

Figure 2.5   Remote Bridge

100 meters between each LAN, although a few allow distances of up to two kilometers. Although stand-alone bridges are generally faster and more powerful than microcomputer bridges they are also more costly.

Remote bridge connections require the installation of bridge software and hardware on a LAN microcomputer or the configuration of a stand-alone device on each network. A bridge system in each LAN is linked by a wide area transmission medium such as a modem and a leased or dial-up line.

Most bridges today support Ethernet to Token Ring bridging. The bridge converts the Ethernet packet frame into the Token Ring frame format.

Although bridges tend to be simpler to install and maintain than routers, they also offer fewer management features. They have the following characteristics:

Pros
- easy to install
- network configuration changes are simple
- low cost compared to cost of routers
- transmission speed no problem since the data is simply passed through

Cons
- cannot distinguish between multiple network paths
- cannot isolate traffic: all traffic travels on all LANs
- some protocols cannot be bridged
- bridge is part of a single network approach, therefore problem diagnosis is more complex

2.2.4   Routers

Routers (see Figure 2.6) function in the OSI Network Layer. They have more intelligence than bridges and logically link separate networks. They are better suited to complex systems in which members of a subnetwork are located in several geographically dispersed locations.

Routers allow users to stop traffic going to network segments, for both security and network efficiency purposes. Routers are intelligent and can determine alternate routes in case of network failures. They also provide the ability to translate between different protocols used on subnetworks.

Routers receive only packets destined for them and network nodes located downstream from them. They then append the appropriate addressing information to each packet to continue routing the packet. This approach gives routed networks more flexibility by allowing multiple routes and least-cost routing to occur.

Routers offer considerably more filtering capabilities than bridges and can be programmed to selectively analyze network packets and addresses. Routers, for example, can allow electronic mail to pass through them, but restrict file transfers from one subnet to another based on addressing and node account information. As a result, they can dramatically limit the traffic that would normally travel throughout the network to only that segment of the network that needs the data.

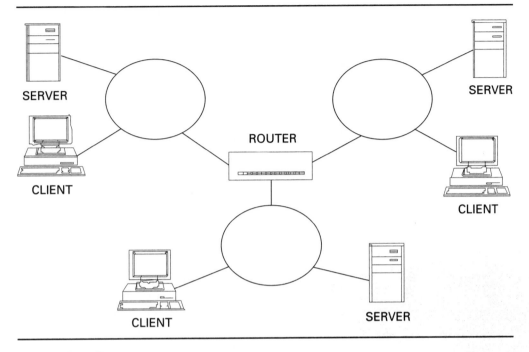

Figure 2.6   Router

Routers have the following characteristics:

Pros
- can be reconfigured
- can partition networks into subnetworks
- can support complex networks

Cons
- difficult to install
- not all protocols available
- substantially higher cost than the cost of bridges

2.3   NETWORK OPERATING SYSTEMS

Network or LAN operating systems (NOS or LOS) grew from a set of utility functions to manage file sharing to more extensive operating systems with responsibilities similar to mainframes.

As such they typically provide database management, development languages, real time interactive transaction processing, and security facilities.

Network Operation Systems provide functions such as:

- network usage management reports
- assignment of work to servers (nodes) (for example, direct print requests)
- remote administration of network (access from any node on the network, provided you have authorization)
- inter LAN communications and processing
- access to all servers on the LAN
- security over access to LAN facilities
- monitoring performance
- audit trails

File and print services, which are a major reason for installing NOS on the LAN, can just as easily be provided by client/server operating systems. Client/server operating environments such as Windows for Workgroups, OS/2 with peer services, and many types of UNIX operating systems provide these services. NOS are therefore moving to provide additional service and facilities.

NOS are moving in the direction of interconnecting disparate client operating systems and providing transport level support for enterprise-wide needs such as database and messaging to increase their functionality. In addition to DOS, NOS vendors have added support for Macintosh, OS/2, NT, UNIX, and NeXTstep. NOS vendors must also address LAN administration by simplifying the creation of user ids and defining their access to resources across servers and multiple LANs.

The most-used Network/LAN Operating System products are provided by Novel, IBM, Banyan, and Microsoft. The following sections briefly describe some of the special features and concerns of each product and also summarize the connectivity and server requirements.

2.3.1   Novell NetWare

Novell NetWare has about a 50 percent share of the current network operating system market. It addressed the office-systems environment and particularly printer and file-sharing requirements while minimizing network usage when it was introduced over 10 years ago; at that time one of its major selling points was response time. As mentioned, hardware improvements and other NOS vendor improvements have substantially narrowed or eliminated the response-time gap. At the same time Novell has upgraded its server facilities. With their new release, they are moving into the high-end WAN technology.

Connectivity capability and server requirements are as follows:

- dedicated server—yes
- minimum memory configuration—6Mb
- native protocols—IPX/SPX
- client file system support
      DOS
      Windows
      Macintosh
      OS/2
      UNIX (optional)
      Windows NT
- disk space used by NOS—12–60Mb

Novell NetWare 4.01
Novell Inc.
Provo, UT 84606
(800) 453-1267

2.3.2   IBM LAN Server

IBM's LAN Server runs on top of OS/2. This means that you have to have the OS/2 graphical interface as the user interface to LAN Server; it also means that the server can operate in a nondedicated mode since OS/2 is a multi-tasking operating system.

IBM's OS/2 is the basis for many of its downsizing products, such as Data Manager to run DB2 applications on the LAN, Communications Manager to provide LU6.2 connectivity to the mainframe and also as a basis to run such products as CICS/OS2, a full service CICS environment on a PC. If you are headed in this downsizing direction, IBM's LAN Server fits well in the environment.

The concern expressed by most users is the installation of LAN Server. You first must install OS.2 and then the LAN Adapter Protocol Support (LAPS); each is a separate program with its own options and manuals for installation. Then you install LAN Server with its own options and manuals.

Connectivity capability and server requirements are as follows:

- dedicated server—no
- minimum memory configuration—8Mb (including OS/2)
- native protocols—NETBIOS, TCP/IP
- client file system support
    DOS
    Windows
    Macintosh (optional)
    OS/2
    UNIX (optional)
    Windows NT
- disk space used by NOS—40Mb

IBM LAN Server 3.0
IBM Corp.
Armonk, NY 10504
(914) 765-1900

2.3.3   Banyan VINES

Banyan VINES is known as a high-end enterprise NOS that has a good reputation in WAN implementation. It is integrated with UNIX, which makes installation simple; the network operating system and the server operating system load at the same time.

Connectivity capability and server requirements are as follows:

- dedicated server—yes
- minimum memory configuration—8Mb
- native protocols—VINES IP, NETBIOS, TCP/IP, AFP, IPX
- client file system support
    DOS
    Windows
    Macintosh (optional)
    OS/2
    UNIX
    Windows NY (optional)
- disk space used by NOS—80Mb

Banyan VINES 5.52
Banyan Systems Inc.
Westboro, MA 01581
(508) 898-1000

2.3.4 Microsoft Windows NT Advanced Server

Microsoft Windows NT Advanced Server is a newcomer to the NOS market. It has geared itself to connect to all possible environments. The earlier Microsoft NOS product, LAN Manager, will probably be phased out.

Connectivity capability and server requirements are as follows:

- dedicated server—no
- minimum memory configuration—16 mb
- native protocols—NETBEUI, TCP/IP, IPX/SPX, DLC, Appletalk, ASYNCBEUI
- client file system support
     DOS
     Windows
     Macintosh
     OS/2
     UNIX
     Windows NT
- disk space used by NOS—90 mb

Microsoft Windows NT Advanced Server 3.1
Microsoft Corp.
Redmond, WA 98052-6309
(206) 882-8080

2.4 LAN SUMMARY

The following material recaps the software and hardware components of the LAN. It represents the basic environment on which client/server platforms are built.

2.4.1 LAN Software Review

Figure 2.7 displays the software components in a typical LAN configuration. Each node (client and server) has the following

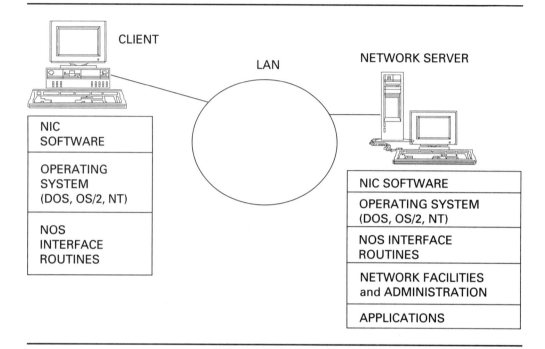

Figure 2.7 LAN Software Components

basic components to interface with other nodes, including servers on the LAN:

- *NIC software:* software on the NIC (Network Interface Card) that provides the hardware-level communications on the LAN.
- *operating system:* software to run each node itself. Examples include DOS, OS/2, and NT. This provides each node with autonomy. The node can function as a stand-alone workstation or communicate with the LAN.
- *NOS interface routines:* NOS (Network Operating System) on the node itself to provide the following:
  packeting of data
  protocol interface
  network interface layering technology
  error detection

Servers themselves contain additional software provided by the NOS, including:

- file sharing
- printer sharing
- network administration
- security access

They also are the repository for networked applications such as shrink-wrapped word processing, spreadsheet, and database programs.

2.4.2   LAN Hardware Review

Figure 2.8 displays the hardware components in a typical LAN configuration. Let's recap what these components are and how they interface with your application.

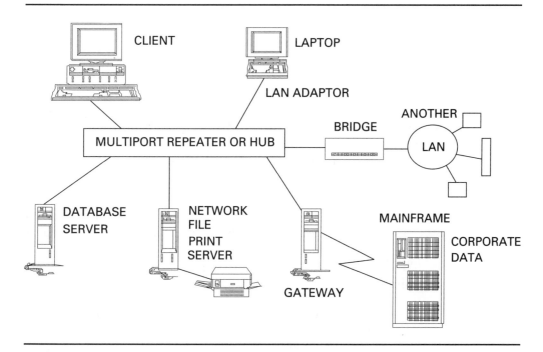

Figure 2.8   LAN Hardware Components

The LAN is connected through hardware with the following:

- *LAN wiring:* ethernet (coax), twisted pair, optical fiber.
- *network interface cards (NIC):* in each node.
- *repeaters:* join nodes together or join segments of LANs together.
- *bridges and routers:* join LANs together.
- *gateways:* join mainframes and minis to LANs.

Servers provide functionality available to all nodes on the LAN. This functionality consists of print, file, network, database, and application sharing.

How does your application program run on the LAN?

- It runs on a node.
- It calls software to interface with the mainframe to retrieve data not available on the LAN.
- It uses interface routines to access the LAN-based database servers (code written in line).
- It uses standard code and interface routines to access files on the LAN.
- You can route reports to the LAN printer by writing standard code and pointing to the LAN printer(s).

2.4.3   Problem Diagnosis in a Complex Environment

Although LAN software and hardware provide built in hardware diagnostic facilities, often when a problem occurs it is not isolated and diagnosed by these components. The most frequently occurring problems are related to the connection between the work station (node) and the LAN.

Hardware (see Figure 2.9) and software components: work station software, LAN adaptor card, connectors, wires, repeater port, network servers.

The LAN workstation connectivity is provided by the following components:

- software in the workstation that describes the workstation to the LAN and prepares information for shipping to the LAN or storing on the workstation once it has arrived from the LAN. This software interfaces with the LAN adaptor card.

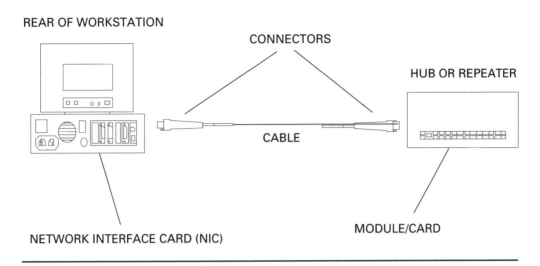

REAR OF WORKSTATION

CONNECTORS

HUB OR REPEATER

CABLE

NETWORK INTERFACE CARD (NIC)

MODULE/CARD

Figure 2.9   Problem Diagnosis

- the LAN adaptor card has software in the form of micro chips that interface with the LAN itself. It uses the workstation identifier passed to it by the workstation software to identify incoming and outgoing packets of data on the LAN.
- the connectors physically connect the LAN adaptor cards to the cable/wire. On the other side of the wire they connect to the repeater card.
- the wires connect between the workstation and the repeater.
- the repeater card connects a single workstation or multiple workstations to the rest of the LAN.

The repeater or hub often has intelligence and attempts to diagnose a problem with a specific connection. As we have already discussed, it is often supplied with lights that can indicate that a problem exists. The repeater or hub attempts to establish a specific resistance on each of the ports that relates to a specific wire and node on the LAN; if it is present, a connection is presumed; if absent, no connection.

Types of problems:

- *workstation cannot sign on:* most of the time this problem is generated by the physical connection on the LAN. The LAN wiring (connectors and the wires) is most often at fault. However, diagnosis is not necessarily simple. If a single problem exists in the connectivity above, the workstation will not be able to sign on. For example, the workstation connector can simply be detached from the LAN adaptor card; the repeater cannot detect this and will continue to signal "good wire connection" because the resistance on the wire remains the same.

LAN software does not always make a distinction between workstation improperly defined on the LAN server and workstation not connected to the LAN. This also makes the diagnosis more difficult.

Additionally, if the workstations have been chained together in such a way that several are connected to a single repeater port, they must somehow be isolated in order to diagnose which one may be at fault.

* *poor response time:* frequently due to error traffic (bad packets) riding the LAN wiring and not the software on the LAN or very high traffic volume on the LAN. Sometimes the repeater will identify the error traffic and signal that a problem exists. At other times no alert will be given by any of the LAN components that a problem exists. Specialized hardware and software can be purchased that will assist in the diagnosis, but these are usually too expensive to have at each LAN site. Knowledge of the components and a good sense of problem diagnosis are often the only tools available.

The following is an example of how difficult this kind of diagnosis can be: The LAN adaptor cards or NICS for thin ethernet wire have BNC connectors that look the same as a standard coax cable connector for non-intelligent 3270 terminals. There have been cases of a user attempting to "connect" their PC to a LAN by simply placing a live LAN wire on a 3270 emulator card in their PC (the card looks very similar to the LAN card). This creates so much error traffic that the *entire* LAN cannot function. Worse than that, the offending station may not be isolated without disconnecting each workstation individually.

3

Client/Server— The Basics

The client/server buzzword has come to mean any process that involves more than one computer. The following chapter provides a more definitive understanding of client/server.

3.1   OVERVIEW

Let's answer some of the basic questions about client/server.

3.1.1   What Is Client/Server?

In its simplest terms, client/server means two intelligent computers connected via a network that have a working relationship. Both the client and the server must be intelligent machines, so this definition does not apply to dumb terminals. An example is two nodes, A and B. Node B holds the data and node A wants the data. Node B is the server providing the data requested by other nodes. Node A is the client requesting the data (see Figure 3.1).

The client is sometimes referred to as the front end, whereas the server is called the back end. There is a one-way communication between each end. The front end makes a request to the back end; the back end processes the request. Each part of the architecture has specific functions; the client is proactive and the

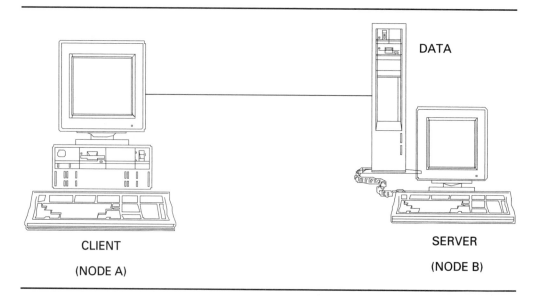

DATA

CLIENT

(NODE A)

SERVER

(NODE B)

Figure 3.1 Client/Server

server is reactive. While both ends do not normally run on the same machine, they do have to be connected by a network.

3.1.2 What Are Their Characteristics?

Generally, client/server systems have the following characteristics:

- *service:* the server is a provider of services. The client is a consumer of services. Client/server provides a clear separation of function based on the idea of service.
- *shared resources:* a server can service many clients at the same time and regulate their access to shared resources.
- *platform independence:* the ideal client/server software is independent of the hardware or operating system software platforms. One should be able to mix and match client and server platforms.
- *message-based interface:* clients and servers communicate through a message-passing mechanism. The message is the delivery mechanism for the service requests and replies.
- *server transparency:* the server is a specialist. A message

tells a server what service is requested and it is then up to the server to determine how to get the job done. Servers can be upgraded without affecting the clients as long as the message interface does not change.

- *scalability:* client/server systems can be scaled horizontally or vertically. Horizontal scaling means adding or removing client workstations with negligible performance impact. Vertical scaling means migrating to a larger and faster server machine or multi-servers.
- *separate responsibilities:* the server code and server data is centrally maintained, which results in cheaper maintenance and the guarding of shared data integrity. At the same time the clients remain independent.
- *many-to-one relationship:* there is a many-to-one relationship between clients and server. Clients initiate the service request. Servers are passively waiting for requests from the clients but can handle many clients.

3.1.3   What Functions Do Servers Perform?

The following functions can be performed, each on an individual node dedicated to that function or as a combination run on a single or series of machines:

- *database:* full-function database servers. The functions include add, delete, inquiry, update, security access, database definition functions, utilities, etc. This is perhaps the single most important server function in the client/server environment. The server should be responsible for activities such as executing the SQL code, business rule enforcement, stored procedures and triggers, security (of data), logging, and recovery.
- *file:* add, delete, inquiry, update, open and close files, multiple node access, and access authorization.
- *print:* share printers on a network, on another LAN, on a mini computer, or on a mainframe.
- *gateway:* access to mainframes, databases, etc. that require highly sophisticated software and hardware to interface with them. This is usually a dedicated machine.
- *network:* the LAN itself must have a network operating sys-

tem that is responsible for controlling traffic on the LAN. This server typically runs other functions listed previously (for example, file).

- *applications:* applications can be run on a server, for all nodes on a LAN. Typically such applications include E-mail, word processing, spread sheet, and simple applications developed by using relational DB packages such as FoxPro, Dbase (Clipper), etc., as well as OS/2 and Windows developed applications.
- *routines:* programmed functions can be placed on the server to perform any desired action. These programs or routines would be called by an application running on some node, for example, a specialized calculation routine resident on the server; the application program passes data to the routine and the server passes back the results.

3.1.4   Types of Servers

The following types of computers can all potentially be servers:

- *mainframe:* typically is used as a data repository (file and database), to run applications (transaction processing), to print, to run routines, etc.
- *mini-computer:* typically is used as a data repository (file and database), to run applications (transaction processing), to print, to run routines, act as a gateway to mainframe or database, etc.
- *LAN server:* typically is used as a data repository (file and database), to run applications (transaction processing), to print, to run routines, act as a gateway to mainframe or database, provide LAN networking and operating system, etc. The LAN server can perform these exclusively (dedicated server) or may perform several functions, as long as performance of these services is not degraded.
- *LAN node:* could be a client station serving a user but which in its "free" time acts as a server to other nodes on the LAN. In theory it could provide any of the services that a server might, but it is unlikely to provide most of these services because performance of both the workstation itself and LAN service response might be adversely affected. A likely prospect is that it would be a part-time print server.

The printing would be done at a low priority, thereby limiting the effect on the workstation itself. Print requests from other nodes would be handled at a low priority as well.

3.1.5   Types of Clients

The client process can be almost anything, from simply sending an E-mail message to a complex transaction routed to a host. The key is that it does not perform the process. Instead, it prepares the request, sends it, and then reviews and presents the result on behalf of the user.

A client workstation typically provides the following services:

- *format/presents data:* the client workstation typically is the user's interface to the entire LAN world and beyond. No matter where resources reside (LAN servers, mainframe, etc.) this node presents the information or runs the activity to gather the data as if it were done on that node. The location of the actual data is transparent to the user.
- *friendly user interface:* the presentation should be user friendly. Even if the client machine must do a complex sequence of events, that sequence should be transparent to the user. Additionally, traversing all activities on the client machine should be user friendly.
- *user's access to all services:* the client machine is the user's window to all the activities that are possible. The client machine can do these activities itself or can call other server resources to accomplish them. These activities include, but are not limited to, printing, routines, applications, gateway (mainframe access and dumb terminal emulation), and so forth.

A server can be a client of services as well. A database server may go to the mainframe to get data. In this case the server is a client of the mainframe but also a server to the node on the LAN requesting the database service.

3.2   WHY CLIENT/SERVER?

Client/server solutions that are implemented on the LAN is the end point of the downsizing trend that data processing has witnessed in the past few years. Business applications have been placed on PCs, and on Macintosh and Unix workstations. Generally, downsizing takes large mainframe applications and divides them into smaller entities that can run on a LAN. At the same time, the applications take advantage of the Graphic User Interfaces (GUI) available on the PC to provide much more friendly user interfaces, as well as field sensitive help, information windows, and so forth.

Client/server solutions on low-cost standard PC/LAN hardware dominate the downsizing trend. Client/server technology can create an integrated environment out of autonomous desktop workstations. The client/server solution combines the best of two worlds: low-cost development and production platforms and the high-tech power of desktop computers. They also provide a flexible environment with many devices and programs to choose from.

> . . . Forrester Research Inc., a market researcher, projects that the client-server market will account for $29 billion worth of sales by 1993 with the big losers from these sales being minicomputer-based solutions. (Client Server Programming with OS/2 EE by Robert Orfali, p. 3)

The overall objective of client/server solutions, from a justification point of view, is to combine mainframe reliability with PC productivity.

3.2.1   Reduce Hardware and Software Costs

Client/server architecture can reduce significantly the hardware and software costs of developing and running production applications.

* *processor costs:* the largest segment of development and production costs for mainframe activity is usually based on the CPU cycles used. Since applications that are completely LAN based will eliminate those costs, an entire LAN hardware and software environment can sometimes be cost justified in less than one year. Even if the mainframe remains as a server (for example, print, database server/repository or software library management and distribution) the majority of costs can be reduced by off-loading 60–70 percent of the CPU costs.

- *network costs:* mainframe development and production is often done at sites that are outside the building that houses the mainframe. This requires lines (probably dedicated) to be run between the mainframe and all user sites. These lines incur initial installation fees, monthly lease fees, and so forth. With LANs most activities are local and many of these lines and the associated overhead is reduced. The total costs will probably never be eliminated because even LANs frequently require connection to the mainframe. Depending upon the client/server design, the line traffic requirements can be substantially reduced. However, it is possible that this cost will increase. If the client/server application has been designed to use the mainframe as a repository for most or all databases, then the data traffic could exceed the traffic normally associated with a mainframe and a large number of dumb terminals that are attached.
- *development costs:* the two key elements of the development costs are (1) processor costs discussed above and (2) staff costs. Because the nature of client/server is quick development and the facilities provide immediate turnaround, developers are often 50 percent more productive, which in turn means a significant reduction in development costs.

  Downsizing projects by using COBOL compilers, PC editors, CICS/OS2, and the like normally results in a payback of investment in the development workstation of under 1 year.
- *operational costs:* mainframe support requires a staff to run the computer 24 hours a day. The client/server environment does not require a regular operations staff. However, a LAN administrator is necessary. This function can be performed by as little as one-half a person to as much as one person or more per LAN. The person is typically the focal point of all software and hardware changes and problem resolution. So depending upon how many and how varied the software products and vendors are, the job can be time consuming and complex. This cost, although potentially a "wash," is most likely less than the pro-rated mainframe operational cost because the mainframe equipment is so expensive.

- *system software costs:* mainframe software tends to be very expensive to purchase or lease and usually carries an annual maintenance fee of 15–20 percent of the annual license fee or purchase price. PC software tends to be a single purchase price and has no annual maintenance fee. Upgrades can be purchased and are usually less, on average, than 15–20 percent of the original purchase price annualized. Volume discounts and corporate licenses are readily available.
- *maintenance costs:* Mainframe hardware typically has a regular annual (monthly) maintenance fee associated with it. 15–20 percent of the purchase is normal. PC hardware can be purchased without a maintenance contract. Individual nodes can be replaced or fixed as needed without a service contract. LAN servers, however, should be covered by a maintenance contract to avoid significant outages. Also, the original purchase decision should take into account that the servers and certain other equipment are critical. They therefore should be purchased from a top-of-the-line manufacturer.

3.2.2   Autonomy and Flexibility

Autonomy is another benefit of the client/server environment. The mainframe technology in place at most installations is so vast and complex that the developer controls only a small part of the environment and must depend on others for many activities. The user competes with many other users who each have their own needs, priorities, and so forth. Mainframe development is subject to reaching a consensus of opinion regarding prioritization, configuration, and system software.

The client/server environment is different. Within the cost constraints that are applied by most management on projects, you can choose more freely in the client/server environment.

Most LAN-based hardware configurations can be more cost effective than the equivalent mainframe facilities. Therefore, you have a choice (and probably many choices) on the LAN, for example:

- *LAN:* the LAN equipment itself, the capacity, speed and reliability of all LAN components wiring, NICs, servers, repeaters, bridges, etc.

- *nodes:* the CPU capacity and speed, the hard disk capacity and speed, where the devices are located, small, large "footprint or tower," and how the node components are located on each workstation table.
- *printing:* what types of printers (laserjet, inkjet, matrix, graphic, plotter), how many, where to locate them (localized print services).
- *servers:* servers can be implemented to be redundant for fault tolerance purposes. For example, a second database server can be added for crucial applications and a duplicate write performed. If the primary DB server goes down, processing can switch exclusively to the redundant server while the primary is being repaired.

You can pick from the available functional and stable environments. They are not as costly as the mainframe and provide many more user-friendly facilities and interfaces. For example:

- *operating systems:* choose the fastest/easiest to maintain. The operating environments include the node (DOS, OS/2, NT) as well as the network (IBM LAN Server, Novell Netware, Banyan VINES).
- *applications:* choose among spreadsheet, word processing, E-mail, graphics, and other generic software for the user community.
- *development environment:* create one that can be highly productive. Immediate turnaround using tools available for interactive debugging, prototyping, etc. and GUI interfaces and database server interface tools to build applications quickly.
- *tools:* development, LAN Troubleshooting, etc. They are available; simply select the best according to need and go!

All this control and flexibility does not come without a price. The price is that the developer and user must be more responsible than in the mainframe situation. All the functions performed on the mainframe by operations and software support are still required on the LAN level: for example, hardware maintenance, troubleshooting, repair and upgrades, software upgrades, debugging, fixes, application library management and software distribution. This subject is covered in more detail in the last chapter.

3.2.3 Maximize Use of Intelligent Workstations

PCs are very powerful workstations. They are not just intelligent workstations capable of running sundry shrink-wrapped software packages; they can also provide graphic presentation, windows, hot fields and help facilities, all without degrading response time. Client/server applications can take advantage of all this intelligence.

3.2.4 Scalability

Client/server systems can be scaled (enlarged or diminished) in size both horizontally and vertically. See Figure 3.2.

Horizontal scaling means adding or removing client workstations. This can be done with minimum impact on the daily operation or system performance. If a work load doubles and twice as many personnel are required, client/server can simply be expanded to double the client workstations.

Vertical scaling means migrating to a larger and faster server machine or multi-servers:

- If the server is a shared operation on a PC and it is running too slow, it can be moved to a dedicated PC.
- If the server is dedicated but does not have enough disk space to hold the data, increase the disk size on the server.
- If the server is dedicated but cannot service all users adequately, add another server.
- If the LAN server cannot hold the amount of data required or it does not have the computing power required (for example, there are too many clients, too much transaction processing), move the data and/or application up to a mini-computer or mainframe.

3.3 CLIENT/SERVER ARCHITECTURE

Systems with very different architectures have been called "client/server." Vendors often use the "client/server" phrase to attract people to their product because the term is *hot*. Other vendors may try to convince you that their, and only their, soft-

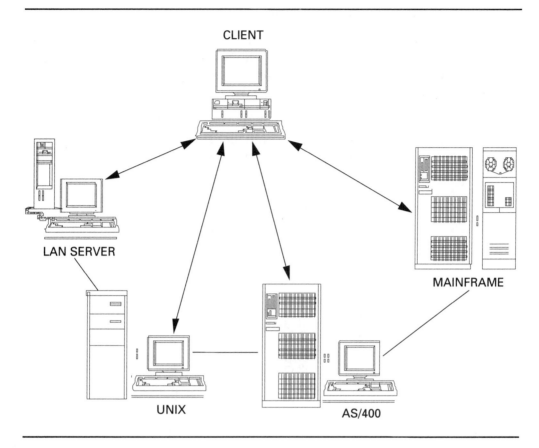

CLIENT

LAN SERVER

MAINFRAME

UNIX

AS/400

Figure 3.2   Scalability

ware is truly the client/server architecture. For example, file server vendors may indicate that they invented client/server, and DB server vendors may claim that they are the only genuine client/server vehicle.

Actually, all of these environments are really client/server. The idea of splitting an application along client/server lines has been used over many years in distributed processing (downsizing). Typically, distributed processing moves segments of the application including data from the mainframe to minicomputers and finally to LANs and PCs on the LAN. Shrink-wrapped software products (word processing, spreadsheet, applications, and so forth) can be client/server applications as well.

3.3.1 Mainframe Architecture

This architecture is composed of non-intelligent ("dumb") terminals connected to a mainframe. See Figure 3.3. A PC running in emulation mode is also a dumb terminal for this purpose. Generally, this technology

- is mature and, as such, is very reliable
- provides for a large number of concurrent users, very large databases, and high transaction rates per second

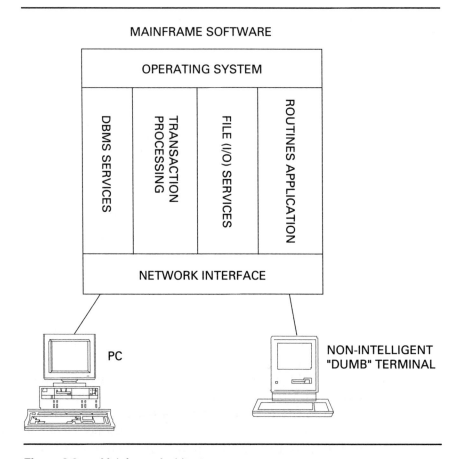

Figure 3.3   Mainframe Architecture

- is full featured to support the environment with facilities such as:
  - TP communications management
  - Security facilities
  - Task and job management
  - Backup and recovery

The architecture consists of:

- *the operating system:* controls all functions, including printing, concurrent running of jobs and applications, etc.
- *network interface:* provides all dumb terminals that are connected directly or remotely with access to various running applications.
- *file servers:* in essence, the mainframe provides all applications and programs with access to files that are resident on the mainframe.
- *DBMS servers:* for example, IBM's DB2, IMS, etc.
- *transaction servers:* software such as IBM's CICS provides an environment to run real-time transaction processing.
- *application servers:* applications written for mainframe: batch or online.

3.3.2 Client/Server Architecture

Let's contrast this architecture with that of the mainframe. The basic LAN technology provides complete processing for the applications, but with intelligent terminals. These terminals, workstations, or nodes are capable of GUI and user-friendly interfaces not available on the mainframe-connected terminals.

The LAN is tied together by hardware and software, as we have discussed. The network operating system, in addition to providing the LAN connectivity and management software, also provides file-sharing facilities.

With a file server, the client (typically a PC) passes requests for file records over a network to the file server (see Figure 3.4).

These file-sharing facilities, together with program language interfaces provided by vendors [for example, Computer Associates (Realia COBOL), Microfocus (Microfocus COBOL)], allow

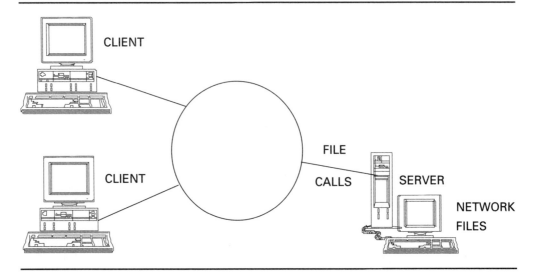

Figure 3.4   File Server

the programmer to access and share files on the LAN by using standard COBOL programming and file access techniques (for example, VSAM, SAM). The overall architecture reduces costs, as we mentioned earlier, because mainframe costs are bypassed and development as well as production is done on a system with a one-time cost expense.

Data transfer in this environment is done fast enough to appear to be at mainframe speed. Since the number of users on a LAN is typically smaller than the number on a mainframe, disk access speeds and data transfer rates are not as critical. However, since the LAN's disk access and data transfer rates are slower than the mainframe's, disk access requirements should be considered when designing the application.

3.3.3   Database Servers

The client passes database requests as messages to the database server; the results of the data search are returned to the client (see Figure 3.5). The code that processes the database request and the data both reside on the same machine. The server pro-

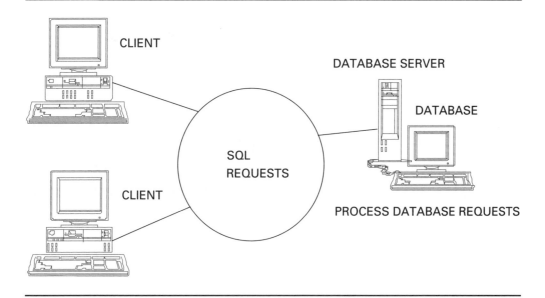

Figure 3.5   Database Server

cesses the inquiry or update request instead of sending the data to the client for processing. This type of processing is a much more efficient use of distributed processing and the network. The server is usually a shrink-wrapped solution purchased from the vendor; the application developer must write applications code on the client or purchase a shrink-wrapped solution that interfaces with the server.

3.3.4   Transaction Servers

The client calls remote procedures resident on the server (see Figure 3.6). For example, on an SQL transaction server, the database engine is on the server which executes remote procedures. These procedures consist of a group of SQL statements that perform a complete transaction. This transaction either completes or fails and is backed out.

The developer creates applications that are sometimes referred to as OLTP (Online Transaction Processing) by writing

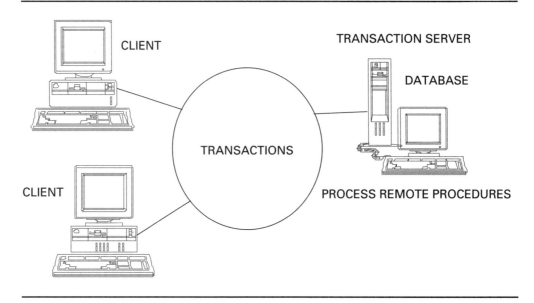

Figure 3.6   Transaction Server

the server remote procedures and the user front end on the client workstations. OLTP applications are usually mission critical and require response time under 3 seconds, with an average between 1 and 2 seconds.

Since they are mission critical, security and database integrity are issues of concern. Application design usually limits the remote procedures to one per transaction. If the database is SQL based, the server is usually a shrink-wrapped solution purchased from the vendor; the application developer must write applications code for both the server and the client.

3.3.5   Application Servers

Application servers place additional application responsibility on the server itself. They combine database and application requirements (see Figure 3.7). The client can invoke the application, not wait for a response, and continue to service the user. The server processes the activity requested and marks the process com-

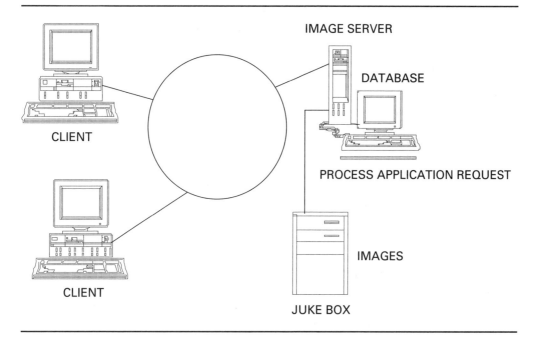

IMAGE SERVER

DATABASE

CLIENT

PROCESS APPLICATION REQUEST

IMAGES

CLIENT

JUKE BOX

Figure 3.7   Application Server

pleted. This can be done by actively notifying the client or passively marking the activity completed on the server. At some later time, the client checks the results of the request.

One example of an application server occurs within imaging technology. The imaging server may be responsible for accessing data contained on multiple CDs that must be retrieved from a juke box, loaded, searched by using indices resident on the server, and stored on the server, ready for transmission to the client. The client does not want to wait for this lengthy request to be completed, so the process is off-loaded to the server and the client interrogates at a later time to determine whether the process has been completed. In this example, the server may or may not be a shrink-wrapped solution purchased from the vendor; the application developer must write applications code for both the server and the client.

3.4   CLIENT/SERVER ENVIRONMENT

Chapters 1 and 2 reviewed the basic environment on which client/ server applications will run. The following section covers some of the environment components in greater depth.

3.4.1   Server Hardware and Software

What is the hardware platform for servers in the client/server environment? The basic focus should be on CPU speed, disk speed, and disk capacity. The following are alternative server solutions:

- *386:* for certain servers (for example, gateways, print servers) this will do the job. This can be a method of putting existing equipment to good use.
- *486:* based on current PC hardware prices, all new servers should be 486s. Execution speed should vary according to the functions to be performed and the system throughput requirements. If the LAN has a large user base, needs a high-capacity, high-speed database server, and has numerous and large applications that run off a server, this machine configured at the highest speed could do the job.
- *mini-computers:* these are more powerful but also more expensive. They are mini-computers with mainframe capabilities.

What is the software platform for servers in the client/server environment? The basic focus is on questions such as: Can they run applications in protected mode? Do they provide paging? What kind of task management facilities do they provide? The comparisons are made with mainframe facilities in mind:

- *DOS:* a single tasking operating system that cannot run concurrent activities. No paging facilities are available, which means that even if you could run multiple applications concurrently, if they did not fit in memory together, they could not be swapped out. DOS runs basically out of 640K base memory, with all programs running together in the same memory base without protection from one another. This should be rejected as an alternative unless it is used in conjunction with another software level such as Microsoft's Windows.

- *OS/2:* IBM's OS/2 has paging facilities for multiple activities (applications) running simultaneously that occupy memory not large enough for all to be resident simultaneously. OS/2 makes use of all memory available on the machine—no constraints. OS/2 is moving in the direction of full mainframe features and currently is close. The number of current users is small despite the fact that IBM has been pushing the product for many years; reduced pricing and Microsoft's marketing of their own version has made it more popular. This software platform is the only way to use certain IBM products such as CICS/OS2 in downsizing projects.
- *NT:* Microsoft's alternative to OS/2. It has much of the functionality of OS/2; however, it currently requires substantial server memory and disk resources.
- *Netware:* Novell's Netware is both an operating system and a network operating system. It is popular and has been installed on many LANs, but it lacks some of the strengths of OS/2 as an operating system for a client/server platform. For example, it does not currently provide protected mode running of applications and it does not have paging facilities.
- *UNIX:* has greater capacity than most operating systems. It is upward compatible to larger machines. It is multiuser, and has protection mode and paging facilities. The software environment, although expensive, is more comprehensive and has more features to assist in the development process. If interfaces to database and application servers can be provided, the environment can be excellent.
- *other alternative server platforms:*
  SunOS
  IBM VM via CMS, CICS, etc.
  IBM MVS via TSO, CICS, APP/MVS, IMS/DC
  IBM OS/400
  NCR 3000 Unix

3.4.2   Workstation Hardware and Software

What is the hardware platform for workstations in the client/server environment? The basic focus is on CPU speed, disk speed, disk capacity, and type of monitor. Minimally, the client should be a 16 MHz machine; depending upon the application, the disk size varies, but for development 80–100 meg is a starting point and the monitor should be a VGA. The following are alternative client solutions:

- *286:* there are plenty of them around; however, their base architecture is not the same as the 386 and 486. The type of memory expansion is unique and requires specialized programming. Their speed at 8–12 megahertz is just not enough for a typical client/server application. They can be used for certain shrink-wrapped software in the office, such as word processing, but not as a client.
- *386:* could be the machine. The 386 is popular and has the 32-bit architecture which is the current accepted norm. It starts minimally at 16 MHz but can go higher. If the equipment already exists it may be the solution, but upgrading existing equipment or purchasing new 386 machines is not cost effective in the current market.
- *486:* may appear to be overkill, but the low-end 486 is price competitive when compared to the upper-end 386. You are buying CPU speed, disk capacity, and disk speed, all of which are necessary to maximize productivity in development. The 486 is also the machine of choice for production because the client/server front end facilities for GUI, reporting, and so forth require significant resources.
- *CAM workstations:* these are more powerful and more expensive. In the case of CAM (Computer Assisted Manufacturing), for example, the stations may have to be more powerful to get the job done. But this is a specialized requirement and not necessarily a normal client/server application.
- *Macintosh:* made by Apple, these machines are moderately priced and popular. However, both their architecture and the LAN environment on which they operate are totally different than the PC. As a result they do not readily interface with other server platforms. Apple is trailing other vendors in addressing client/server development.

What is the software platform for workstations in the client/server environment? The basic focus is on the workstation operating system, as follows:

- *DOS:* popular and inexpensive, but memory limitations and protection are a concern.
- *OS/2:* IBM's Presentation Manager is the GUI interface. Writing applications code is difficult. Also the number of shrink-wrapped solutions available is limited. It offers the best means of developing client/server solutions via tools available from many vendors; these tools are discussed in a later section. The overhead of OS/2 on the client machine (both memory and disk usage) may make it less desirable than other alternatives.
- *Windows:* Microsoft's GUI interface, based on a DOS operating system. This is probably the most popular client solution currently in use.
- *NT:* Microsoft's alternative to OS/2. The objections are similar to those of OS/2. The overhead required to run this on a client machine means that the client machine must be a robust 486.
- *other alternative workstation platforms:*
    SunOS
    Macintosh
    NCR 3000

3.4.3   Network Hardware and Software

We have covered some of this material in the first two chapters. It is important to reiterate that a major part of the client/server environment you are about to construct is based on all this LAN technology that is being presented. Its success in terms of alternatives, flexibility, and response time hinge upon some of the following decisions:

- *cabling:* twisted pair, coax, or fiber optics.
- *topology:* ring, star, bus, or mixed.
- *network interface cards:* they connect the servers and workstations to the LAN wiring. They differ based on the network platform chosen.
- *network software:* Novell's Netware, IBM and Microsoft LAN management products, Banyan VINES, or SUN NFS.
- *GUI (graphic user interface):* one of the important reasons to use PC technologies for client/server applications is the technology itself. The advent in recent years of windowing

technologies for user applications is one of the most important. These windowing technologies provide a new look at
using terminals. They are based on a mouse-like device
that is used to quickly traverse an entire screen of windows
upon windows and select another window or close one, or to
have a window fill the screen or move it and make it
smaller. The mouse technology also aids in the selection of
an item from a list, browse items, or block out sections on a
screen. Typing is done normally through the keyboard.

Another concern for the developer is whether the new mouse-
based window technology will actually be a help or a hinderance in
production environments. If the production requirement is high-
volume data collection, mouse technologies are a hinderance, but
windows may still be useful. The same is true of a high-volume
data entry situation.

Application tools to assist in developing within this windowing
environment aid the programmer in what would otherwise be a
difficult and non-cost-effective means of developing. When you
decide on a windowing direction, you must therefore consider both
what applications and tools already exist in the environment and
how popular this direction will be for future development.

IBM Presentation Manager, Microsoft's Windows, or other
GUIs, such as those that run on Unix-based systems, represent
some of the choices. You need to review the current trends and
vendor commitment. You can still choose GUI at this time and
replace what you have chosen later, but there may not be a simple
conversion tool available; conversion would then be expensive.

3.4.4   Homogeneous Configurations

A homogeneous platform refers to an operating system, network
operating system, database facility, GUI, and so forth that are a
compatible family of products, possibly available from the same
vendor. See Figure 3.8. An example is OS/2 (operating system),
IBM's LAN Server (network operating system), IBM's Presentation Manager (GUI), and IBM's DB2/2 (database). Another example is Microsoft's NT (operating system and NOS), Microsoft's
SQL Server and Microsoft's Windows (GUI). A third example
would be Novell Netware (operating system and NOS), a compat-

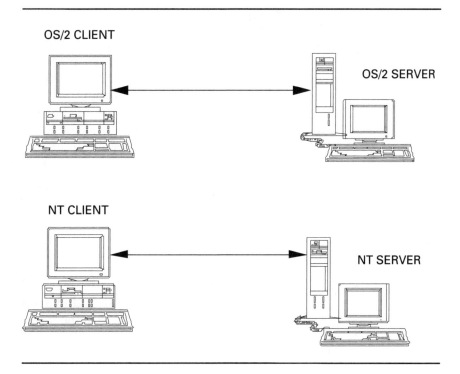

OS/2 CLIENT

OS/2 SERVER

NT CLIENT

NT SERVER

Figure 3.8   Homogenous Configuration

ible SQL server with DOS or Windows NT and Windows (GUI) on client workstations.

The advantages include:

- *single-vendor set of software:* developers have to learn only one set of software. This is especially important since they will have to be conversant in many pieces of software just to do client/server development in a single environment.
- *administration:* administration of a single topology is much simpler, not just because there is one topology instead of 2 or more, but because combining more than one and making them talk to one another without a hitch is difficult.
- *problem resolution:* having a single-vendor based system means you can go to that vendor for problem-resolution assistance and not have to worry about "finger pointing," which often occurs in multi-vendor environments.

The disadvantages include:

- *vendor dependency:* if the software doesn't work or doesn't have the features you want, you are dependent upon that vendor for help. Since this is a relatively new field and companies are relatively young, there is also a high probability that the company will fail and that you will be left with their software and no vendor assistance.
- *incompatible H/S:* existing hardware and/or software may not be compatible and therefore is unusable.
- *fewer alternatives:* having a single topology, especially one that is not very popular, means there are fewer choices of compatible "shrink-wrapped" software available.

3.4.5   Mixed Configurations

A mixed platform, as the name implies, refers to operating systems, network operating systems, and GUIs that are a mix of products from different vendors, or to multiple homogeneous platforms that have to talk to one another. See Figure 3.9.

The advantages include:

- *compatible H/S:* existing hardware and/or software is much more likely to be compatible.
- *more alternatives:* many more choices of "shrink-wrapped" software are available.

The disadvantages include:

- *testing:* a mixed environment implies that there are many more components that must be tested. Since you are interfacing multiple technologies, you will not only have to test the applications on all sides of the technology, but also test thoroughly the technology interface itself.
- *integration:* you are left with building user-written bridges or, if you are lucky, one or more vendors will supply a bridge. However, whenever one vendor changes their architecture your bridge may have to be changed.
- *administration:* administration of multiple topologies is much more complex. They were not designed to be compatible and have inherent differences in their architecture.

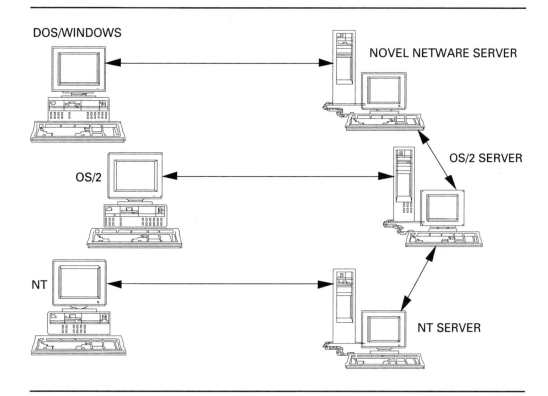

Figure 3.9   Mixed Configuration

- *problem resolution:* you may have to contend with "finger pointing," which often occurs in multi-vendor environments when problems arise.

The following are guidelines for choosing the right platform:

- *homogenous platform:* if possible, choose a single topology as a base for client/server. If you already have different topologies at your sites, install separate independent applications on the different topologies that have been carefully selected so that they do not have to be interfaced. Note that this refers to uniquely different topologies. Using a combination of Windows and OS/2 with the same platform family can be successful and manageable. Problems arise as you increase the number of variables and also whenever the topologies differ significantly, for example: station operating systems such as SunOS, Macs, OS/2, Windows, or NOSs such as Banyan, Apple, LanManager, Netware.

- *choose platform carefully:* choose the platform by reviewing your current hardware and software environment, and by reviewing your short- and long-range plans and requirements. Then inspect the alternative topologies and choose the one that most closely meets your needs.

4

Database Servers

Perhaps the single most important component of a client/server environment is the database server. Most client/server applications are centered around data/information that is to be accessed locally and stored locally but may also be accessed and/or stored remotely. A database server properly chosen will provide both a mainframe-compatible development environment and the building block for all client/server applications that run on LANs.

The database server maintains the data, manages its physical storage and retrieval, and also performs validation. The database server usually standardizes, automates, and centralizes such operations on the data as security validations, special transactions and routines, and so forth. In the client/server environment, data-related logic in a mainframe environment that would ordinarily be common to every program in an application is now shifted to the server.

Appropriately, the programming related to client data is simpler than programming on the mainframe, but the design and implementation of the database on the server is an additional complexity because many clients share the given server, requesting and updating the data in potentially many different ways. The concern is to gather and evaluate enough information to design the server so that it meets all known and unknown needs and to make this database available for a dynamic development schedule. The Relational Database Management System (RDBMS) software chosen must satisfy these needs.

4.1   GENERAL INFORMATION

The following topics have been provided to give the reader some background information concerning Relational Database Management Systems (RDBMS) as they apply to the client/server environment. The information overlaps with mainframe concepts and facilities but is also pertinent to client/server solutions.

4.1.1   Database Administration

A database administrator has similar responsibilities whether the database resides on a mainframe or a server. The responsibilities that apply to the client/server environment have been listed below. They overlap with those of a mainframe database administrator but have been listed to give the reader a perspective with which to evaluate the database administration component of the database server software. The DBA's responsibilities include:

- Creating the database
- Installing server programs and support files
- Diagnosing and resolving system problems
- Keeping the database server and associated programs running on a daily basis
- Backing up and recovering the database as required
- Controlling security and access to the database and its objects
- Monitoring and tuning the performance of the database
- Managing server space and estimating storage requirements based on design and growth
- Overseeing the installation of client programs that access the database
- Advising developers about table, index and view design; multi-user considerations; networking and loading; converting and unloading data
- Improving performance of applications through changes to the database server, to the database, or in the application itself

- Insuring data availability, accuracy, completeness, integrity, and consistency
- Auditing use of the database
- Administering the system catalog
- Assisting the user of database applications

4.1.2   SQL

Structured Query Language (SQL) is a set of commands that is used to access a relational database. It is the universal accepted interface to RDBMS and should be the basis for evaluating the RDBMS. SQL (sometimes referred to as "sequel") evolved from work done by E. F. Codd, D. D. Chamberlin, and R. R. Boyce in the early and mid-1970s at IBM's Research Laboratory in San Jose, California. They developed a language called Structure English Query Language (SEQUEL). The initial working language and system, called System R, from IBM implemented that language and its features.

The following are characteristics of SQL:

- SQL is set theory oriented and operates on row(s) defined by subset selection.
- SQL has a simple command structure for data definition, access, and manipulation.
- SQL is the accepted standard interface for many RDBM systems.
- SQL is not a programming language and does not have a screen dialog. It does have a simple reporting mechanism. It is used in conjunction with programming languages to provide database access.
- SQL is a non-procedural language, which means that you specify what you want but not how to do it. For example, you can access multiple rows in a database without specifying their location, storage format, or access methodology.
- SQL is built with layers of complexity and capability in such a way that a user with little experience can access the RDBMS.

SQL is the most widely used language for RDBMS and should be the focal point of the RDBMS chosen, for the following reasons:

- It is a widely accepted RDBMS access language. The American National Standards Institute (ANSI), the International Standards Organization (ISO), and the U.S. Department of Defense all support SQL. A version of SQL is available on most computer platforms.
- SQL is a complete database language and supports data definition, data control, and transaction management. The SQL commands can support complex operations.
- The SQL commands are simple to use in their basic form. The user can access and manipulate the data without being concerned about the physical organization and storage complexities of the data.

SQL is not a programming language, but it can be invoked by using one of two types of interfaces:

- Embed SQL commands in your program and then use the RDBMS software to interpret that code into the appropriate actions to access the database on the server. This usually includes intelligence to select the best method to access the data as well as the communications necessary to talk to the server.
- An interactive SQL facility that provides the user with the ability to construct an SQL statement and then dynamically execute it. Not all RDBMS software products provide this facility.

SQL can be used by end users if the RDBMS software provides an interactive interface. If the interactive SQL implementation is full function, the end user can retrieve, insert, update, or delete data. Similarly, DBAs use the SQL commands to define and maintain the database. The preference is that the RDBMS software will provide this interface interactively. Lastly, the applications developers write SQL commands and embed them within the programming language. The RDBMS software provides different interfaces for each language. One of the considerations prior to purchasing an RDBMS product is which languages and vendor compilers have interface support.

SQL commands can be grouped into the following categories:

- *data definition commands:* these create, change, or delete objects such as tables and views (for example, CREATE, ALTER, DROP).
- *data manipulation commands:* these commands add, update, or delete data (for example, INSERT, UPDATE, or DELETE) as applied to a row(s) of data.
- *data query commands:* these retrieve data. They can be built as simple or highly complex commands. They can also traverse more than one table through the JOIN command.
- *transaction control statements:* these provide data integrity during simultaneous transaction updates (for example, COMMIT, ROLLBACK, REVOKE).
- *data control statements:* these provide security and control data access (for example, GRANT, REVOKE, ALTER PASSWORD).

RDBMS implemented using SQL standards implies that the data is organized as follows:

- *database:* a collection of tables and associated indexes.
- *table:* essentially a two-dimensional array consisting of columns of data, each of which has a data element identifier, data type, and rows. In the tradition of flat files, the table equates to a file, the row equates to a record, and the column is a data element within the record.
- *index:* is an ordered set of pointers to the data in the table. Each index is based on the values contained in one or more columns in the table and the index is stored separately from the table.
- *view:* is an alternate mapping of the columns contained in one or more tables. To the user (programmer or end user) the view looks just like a table. However, the data may be contained in various tables but their definition may preclude the user from performing all actions that can be performed on a single existing table.

The actual processing that takes place to complete an SQL command can be described as follows. It has been included to provide the reader with a sense of the responsibilities of an RDBMS, particularly from a performance point of view.

- *parse the command:* check the command for syntax, prepare it for the optimizer, verify the names of objects in the command (tables and columns).
- *optimize the command:* review view references with actual table and column names, retrieve related statistical information from the system catalog, identify alternate paths to get to data requested, identify the cost of each path and choose the best one.
- *generate the code:* create an executable to accomplish the application request. This should be done during the compile stage rather than as an interpretive action during the execution for performance reasons.
- *execute:* run the requested code. This code may be run as a request from the client to the server or may be a routine that is placed on the server (for example, remote procedure call).

4.2   COMPARISONS AND FEATURES

The selection of an RDBMS involves many factors. The following questions should be addressed before the selection process is started:

- What type of user will be accessing the data? Do the possible users include professional programmers, system administrators, end users, executives, and so forth?
- What type of access will be required? There will be a significant difference in the RDBMS required if the data is read only versus highly active updating. Also, will the data be accessed through batch processes only or will it be accessed interactively?
- What level of programming is acceptable in order to define and maintain the RDBMS environment and writing application code?
- What tools will be required? Will decision support, third- and fourth-generation programming languages be required?
- What type of platform will the data be stored on? What types of networks will need access to this data? What types of client platforms are in place that will require access to this data?
- What level of transparency may be required? Do the appli-

cations need to access data from many different sources? Should the RDBMS provide a single API to access all data?

- What range of response time will be acceptable to the end user in various applications (including decision support systems)?

Each database server software product that runs on a LAN is designed to provide basic data services. The following list of considerations can be used as a starting point to begin the evaluation and selection process.

- Does the vendor have a worldwide presence?
- Does the vendor provide worldwide support?
- Does the vendor provide a 24-hour hotline?
- What share of the market does the vendor represent?
- What training does the vendor provide?
- Does the vendor provide consulting services?
- What are the vendor's future directions?
- Does the vendor have any alliances with other companies for tools, gateways, and so forth?
- What is the vendor's history regarding new releases (integrity and timeliness)?
- What is the software licensing arrangement and cost?
- What are the maintenance terms and cost?
- How adequate is the documentation?
- What server operating systems does the product operate on?
- What client operating systems does the product operate on?
- What networks does the product operate on?
- What vendor or third-party database administration tools are available?
- Which CASE tools will interface with the product?
- What fully developed applications interface with the product?
- What vendor or third-party database design, application development, and end-user tools that interface with the product are available?
- Does the vendor product provide transparent interface for distributed data?
- What data locking mechanisms are provided?
- What deadlock detection and resolution mechanisms are provided?

- What are the catastrophic failure facilities and procedures?
- Is the data access ANSI SQL compliant?
- Does the product provide SQL access support?
- Does the product optimize SQL code and queries?
- Does the product provide language interfaces for C? for COBOL? for what other languages?
- Does the product support BLOBs (binary large objects)—for example, images?
- Does the product support currency, date, and measure conversions?
- Does the product support user-defined data types?
- Does the product support stored procedures?
- What type of logon security is built in?
- What levels of data security are provided? Table, column?
- What backup and recovery facilities are provided? Full and incremental backups? Backups while database is in use?
- Is database maintenance supported while the database is active (in use)?
- What type of referential integrity is supported?
- What audit trails and facilities are provided?
- Does the vendor or third party provide RDBMS performance analysis tools?
- What migration paths (gateways) exist or are planned?
- Does the RDBMS provide a two-phased commit facility?

The following areas have been included in more detail to give the reader background on some of the features that should be reviewed in depth.

4.2.1   Response Time

Response time is often an overlooked factor. The focus is usually on functionality and mainframe compatibility when an RDBMS is being evaluated. However, if it doesn't run fast enough, no client/server application is worth developing. This is especially true in a high-transaction-volume-based environment.

As part of the SQL command processing, the RDBMS should optimize the request as described earlier. The best path (least amount of processing needed to retrieve the data requested) should be chosen by reviewing the available indices (alternate paths), catalog information (for example, number of rows in a table), and the overall SQL request (for example, number of columns, tables, and complexity of request).

Generally, there are three basic methods of accessing the data:

- *use the index to access the data:* in this situation a lookup of the command request is performed against the index and only the matching rows in the table are read.
- *table scan:* this is used if no index exists for this table or the indices that do exist cannot isolate the requested rows. All rows will be read.
- *index only access:* if all the needed information is contained in one or more indices, this can be the most effective access.

These are the most basic accesses. The actual SQL request may be serviced by some combination of these methods as well as with calculations, storing intermediate results and sorting operations. As a result the efficient processing capability of the RDBMS is a major influence on SQL request response time.

4.2.2 Software Compatibility

The following questions should be asked:

- Does the server operate on all major operating systems: DOS, OS/2, Windows NT, UNIX, and NetWare?
- Does the 4GL and EIS software you wish to use readily interface with this server?
- Does the windowing development software you have chosen, or are considering, interface to this RDBMS?
- If not, when will the vendors supply this interface?
- What programming languages does the SQL server provide interfaces for? COBOL, C, other languages?

4.2.3 Mainframe Compatibility

The following questions should be asked:

- Does the RDBMS have mainframe database compatibility? Oracle, for example, intends to run transparent on all platforms (mainframe, mini, micro). Some RDBMS vendors provide an SQL solution that is intended to be compatible with IBM's DB2. Can source code be developed and run on the LAN with the database server and then be migrated to the mainframe with no changes necessary?

- Does the RDBMS vendor (or a third-party vendor) provide an interface or gateway software to other relational databases on LANs or to mainframe databases? Is this interface transparent to the application programmer? Can the application programmer write the same SQL command and have it retrieve data from another RDBMS without having to change their program? Some of these vendors provide an API that is transparent across numerous different RDBMS and mainframe file organizations. This can be important if gradual migration of applications from mainframe to client/server is desired.

4.2.4   Backup

Generally there are two methods of backing up a database:

- *online:* copy the database and the associated log files while the server program is running and users are connected to the database. Transactions may be in progress during this operation.
- *offline:* after the database server has successfully been brought down, use a utility to copy both the database and the associated log files. No users are connected to the database and therefore no transactions can be in progress during this operation.

The RDBMS software vendors all provide offline backup facilities. Online backup, however, is a more complex situation. Ideally, backup of databases should be able to take place while the server is operational. It should be complete enough to provide input for a database recovery. But the key question is how the RDBMS vendor implements this online backup. Some of the approaches include:

- *inquiry only:* during the backup, only inquiries to the database are permitted. All update requests are terminated.

- *return code:* a special return code is provided to the application, indicating that a backup is in progress. The application must decide whether to wait, abort, or retry.
- *table based locks:* the backup locks one table at a time, backs up that table, and then frees it for update.
- *backup disallowed:* some RDBMS vendors do not have an online backup solution.

Another feature that should be available is automated backup based on time. This could be used to back up the server during off hours. It may include an automated procedure to shut down the server and then run an offline backup.

The other questions to be answered about backups are concerned with what type of media the backup will reside on and does that media necessitate manual intervention. If the database and associated logs can be backed up to a single tape cartridge, there is no problem. But most databases will be large enough to require more than one tape. In that case, the backup could be:

- *disk:* copy to disk, perhaps using a compression routine to reduce space requirements.
- *removable disk:* same as above, but using removable disk media also provides a means to keep multiple copies.
- *mainframe:* provide an upload backup capability to the mainframe. Use the existing mainframe tape backup facilities to provide multiple generations, offsite and disaster recovery versions.

4.2.5 Recovery and Rollback

A database can be damaged several ways, for example, by a power failure or an operator error. The top priority should be to prevent this damage by all possible means. To reduce the potential damage from a power failure, use a UPS on all critical database servers (see Chapter 9). To minimize operator error, keep the database server in a locked room and password protected in such a way that only a qualified DBA will be able to access the database server.

If the database crashes, however, three different recovery techniques can be used. They are applied by using the existing data, which consists of the most current database copy, the most recent database backup, and the database log, which contains transaction images applied to the database since the last backup copy. The images on the transaction log can be both before and after database images; the norm is to write the images to the log prior to the actual database update.

If the current database is recoverable, two techniques are used to establish the database integrity:

- *forward recovery:* complete any transactions which have been committed but were in flight during the database outage.
- *rollback:* back out any transactions which were in flight during the database outage but were uncommitted at that time.

If the current database is not recoverable, then the most recent backup must be restored and all completed transactions from the transaction log must be reapplied.

Although all of the above apply to any mainframe database, the questions to be answered are: What recovery facilities does the RDBMS provide, and how are they implemented? The latter question is important. For example, if the current database is recoverable after an outage, can the database server be restarted automatically and does the database then recover all in-flight transactions using forward recovery and rollback *automatically*? This is important if the server is to provide mainframe-like availability, especially for applications that require uptime beyond the normal workday.

4.2.6   Fault Tolerance

Database fault tolerance implies an automated means of continuing online services even if a copy of the database is corrupted. The following questions apply:

- Does the RDBMS software support mirror updates to a primary and image copy of the database?
- Does the RDBMS software support mirror updates of the database log files? This is important for recovery.
- Does it provide for automated cutover from one database to

another or from one transaction log to another if the primary database or transaction log is corrupted?
- Can these copies be on different servers?

4.2.7   Referential Integrity

Generally, referential integrity is a method of keeping all database references from one table to another valid. Referential integrity prevents problems that occur when one table that points to another is deleted or changed.

DB2 was implemented with three types of referential integrity:

- *cascade:* when a primary table row (parent) is deleted, all dependent rows that have a matching key are deleted.
- *restrict:* when a primary table row is to be deleted and a dependent row with a matching key exists, the delete request is disallowed.
- *set to nulls:* when a primary table row is deleted, all dependent rows with a matching key are modified, setting the corresponding key to nulls.

The RDBMS should be reviewed prior to purchase to determine whether referential integrity has been implemented and what types of methodology are available. Additionally, the RDBMS should provide a utility that will scan the database and identify referential integrity problems and then be capable of correcting them.

4.2.8   Server Requirements

Generally, the faster the machine the better the server. Although some of the products claim they will operate on a 286 under DOS, this is not desirable. A high-speed 486 should always be considered the machine of choice for an RDBMS SQL server. Also, when choosing hardware for the SQL server, consider the speed of the hard disk. Hard disks are now available in gigabyte sizes; the question is not only how much data can be stored on the server but also what the retrieval speed is. Overall, you are trying to minimize the duration of any server request from individual clients and from multiple clients simultaneously. The only other consideration focuses on the client machine itself: Does the RDBMS require a software component (driver, TSR, etc.) resident on the client in order to access the SQL server and how big is this component?

4.2.9   Remote Procedure Calls

Remote procedure calls is the capability of running database requests initiated by the client application on the RDBMS server. The executable objects or routines are stored in the server and are executed when the client calls them. These may be implemented within the RDBMS at different levels:

- *SQL statement:* only SQL statements can be stored and executed.
- *scripts:* SQL statements can be embedded in an RDBMS scripting language.
- *programs:* full programs (for example, C or C++) with embedded SQL can be stored and invoked.

The remote procedure calls provide for common application access design that isolates certain application database functions on the server. This can be more efficient and easier to maintain as well. Additionally, background transactions that do significant work (inquiry or update) can be offloaded from the client and run exclusively on the server so that client response time can be kept consistent. The client would initiate a background request and then continue to process the client requirements. The client can then either check on the results of the background task at a later time or have the server notify the client upon completion of the background task.

4.2.10   Locking

Database locking facilities provide the means to preserve data integrity and provide for common design in application transaction processing. OLTP (Online Transaction Processing) systems focus on sharing data for as many users as possible while minimizing inconvenience. Therefore, OLTP systems characteristically are concerned about speed of access, concurrent volume capabilities, accuracy of data, and isolation of problems. Locking schemes within the RDBMS focus on:

- *locking levels:* row, table, database, etc.
- *scopes of lock:* read, write, update, etc.
- *mechanisms:* lockout, rollback, etc.
- *establishing lock:* implicit, explicit.

The more locking functionality provided by the RDBMS, the easier it is for the DBA to customize a solution for that application and the easier it is to write application code.

4.2.11 Database Administration

Review the RDBMS data administration functions provided, including the following:

- *remote database administration:* if your databases are for mission critical operational systems (not decision support systems), a DBA should be able to administer them from a centralized location. All administrative functions, including system startup and shutdown, performance monitoring, space management, security and routing operational control, should be capable of being managed remotely.
- *active data dictionary:* a data dictionary that can be integrated with the development process is desirable. This dictionary could then be used to define default data element editing, display characteristics (both on reports and GUI screens), copy books for row and view definitions, and so forth. This dictionary should also provide a master cross-reference of all objects that reference specific columns and rows.
- *performance tools:* does the RDBMS provide performance tools? If the application response time is not acceptable, does the server provide the menus to monitor the SQL responses? Can it make performance improvement recommendations?
- *diagnostic tools:* does the RDBMS provide diagnostic tools? For example, if the application locks during server access,

is there a tool available on the server to identify why and where the lock has occurred?

- *API interface:* an API interface to the administration functions provides a means of automating database administration functions such as database startup and shutdown, generating administrative reports and backup.
- *security:* the type of data security that has been implemented within the RDBMS. DB2-like implementation of SQL GRANT and REVOKE commands are desirable. The security should address system level access by providing the authority to create the system itself, including new databases. It should address database level access, including the authority needed to control objects within the database, such as tables and columns, and also the type of access, such as read, write, update, and so forth.

4.2.12   Development Tools Available

The type of tools available and the number of vendors providing them are a good indication of the popularity of the server. Some of the questions that may be asked are:

- What development tools does the vendor supply?
- Which of the popular development toolsets interface with this server?
- What other tools are available on the market?

4.2.13   Access to Other Databases and Files

The target database access environment is one in which the database API is such that a request for data is coded the same no matter where the data resides or what type of database it resides on. If the data being referenced today is a mainframe DB2 database but tomorrow the data resides on a LAN-based SQL server, the application interface should be such that no program changes are necessary. Instead the database server data administration function is modified to indicate where the data is resident.

This transparent data access can be implemented through various means and combinations thereof:

- *gateways:* specific software solutions that provide access to non-transparent RDBMS software. A database gateway can be likened to an automated language translator whereby two people speaking different languages can have a telephone conversation with each other in their native language while a "black box" automatically translates the language in both directions.
- *drivers:* database software on the client or the server that provides direct access to other SQL RDBMS that are similar in access.
- *distributed component software:* software resident at data access locations. For example, to access mainframe VSAM and sequential files, a RDBMS software component may be installed within an IBM CICS region on the mainframe; this component interfaces directly with a corresponding component on the LAN database server.

4.2.14   Two Phase Commit

Two phase commit is a method used to coordinate updates in a RDBMS. After a database "commit" is requested by an application, the actual database update is done in two phases:

- *phase 1:* makes sure that all records written to the database log have actually been written to the media (for example, all buffers have been flushed). During phase 1 the two phase commit routine determines that all database resource managers (for example, if multiple databases) are ready. If any problem exists, the commit can be aborted at this point.
- *phase 2:* does all of the actual database updates, checks with the resource managers of multiple database for successful completion, and then responds with an "OK" to the application.

At the end of each phase, a record is written to the database log, indicating the status of that phase. These status records and the logged images on the database log are used for rollback and forward recovery processing.

Does the RDBMS software provide this two phase commit technology? is a question that has great relevance to the client/server environment.

4.3   DATA MANAGEMENT IN THE CLIENT/SERVER ENVIRONMENT

The following topics address some of the concerns that are relevant to implementation of client/server applications.

4.3.1   Remote Database Access

Applications written on the mainframe generally access data that resides on that mainframe. This is especially applicable to large databases. Frequently, the initial client/server applications that are developed use the mainframe as the data repository. Even mature client/server applications may choose the mainframe or mini-computer as the data repository because of its ability to house large amounts of data and provide the data administration facilities associated with mature environments (backup, restore, recovery, disaster recovery, and so forth). These mainframe applications also have a mature development path which includes review of SQL code generated and limiting adhoc SQL queries in such a way that database response time can be maximized for enterprise-wide applications.

Consider the client/server environment with the generic desktop tools that can construct sophisticated SQL statements as a simple by-product. These SQL requests can be constructed as highly complex statements but hidden from the developer or user. The desktop tool assumes that a local powerful database server is available to service these requests. However, if the database is actually a remote RDBMS used by hundreds of other people, such as a mainframe database (see Figure 4.1), then remote access should be guided by the following:

- *smart tools:* use tools that can generate smart SQL or SQL that minimizes the overhead necessary to retrieve the data.
- *adequate network:* the network must be able to deliver the data in our target response time of under 1 second. This in-

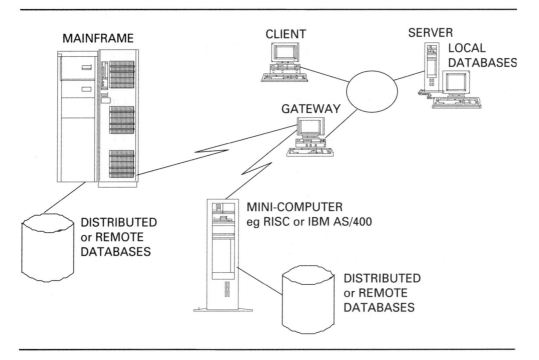

Figure 4.1   Remote and Distributed Database Access

cludes the LAN network and gateway connectivity through a network to the remote computer.

- *small table:* if the remote database consists of many small tables, the impact of complex SQL statements may be minimized.
- *decision support use:* if the client/server application will be using the remote database for decision support applications, then the number of requests will be minimized.

If the above situation is not the case, then consider *not* allowing direct access to the remote database. Instead, consider one of the following:

- *stored procedures only:* one approach is to limit access to the remote databases via stored remote procedures. Rather than allowing all users, developers, and so forth to access the remote databases via DML (for example, SELECT, INSERT, UPDATE, and DELETE), permissible and acceptable database access can be predefined through remote procedures stored on a local server or at the remote database site.

- *distributed local data:* copy required data from the remote database to the local server. The local database will be much more tolerant of complex SQL statements and can be tuned more effectively in this more-isolated environment. If the local database is the system of record for the data, this can be a more complex issue (see system of record section in chapter on design).

4.3.2   Distributed Database Access

Distributed or partitioned databases in the client/server environment are most frequently implemented on multiple nodes within the same LAN. The RDBMS software should provide a transparent interface to the application program such that the application need not code for any partitioning. Distributed or partitioned databases can also be across multiple LANs, WANs, LAN and mainframe, and so forth. Updates which traverse more than LAN become more complex because of the connectivity and availability issues. The following summarizes the pros of distributed database management:

- *tune based on need:* each database server can be tuned independently, based on processing requirements and data size.
- *common interface:* using the right RDBMS vendor will mean that the application code is transparent from the data location and access.
- *scalable databases:* based on production growth (increase or decrease) the dataserver can be scaled up or down without application changes. For example, if the company is a new company or a subsidiary in growth mode, the database can grow without having to change the application; for example, data can grow from one server, to multiple servers, to a mini or to a mainframe database.

The following summarizes the cons of distributed database management:

- *complex transaction control:* if a transaction must update more than one database on multiple servers, coordinating the update may be a concern.
- *data recovery:* how do you rebuild a database that traverses multiple servers? The RDBMS software should address this issue, but the DBA may need special procedures in place to rebuild these databases.
- *multi-vendor solutions:* if the databases in question are from multiple vendors (for example, mainframe, mini, and multiple LAN RDBMS vendors), coordinating updates may be very difficult. Each vendor has its own scheme for distributed database update and recovery; the schemes may not be compatible.

4.3.3   Microsoft's Open Database Connectivity (ODBC)

As you can imagine, so many different types of data in existence in mainframe applications and established client/server applications can present a development concern. It would be preferable to have a standard application interface to all database types and then have some type of gateway component (software in the form of a simple driver for each DBMS or more sophisticated software with components both on the server and the mainframe) that would provide the necessary access.

Microsoft has addressed this concern with their Open Database Connectivity (ODBC) direction. Microsoft has a system-level interface between Windows-based PCs and enterprise computing services called Windows Open Services Architecture (WOSA). ODBC is the database component of WOSA. Microsoft indicates that ODBC is based on a call-level interface developed by an industry consortium of over 40 vendors, including the SQL Access Group. ODBC defines an application programmer interface (API) for access to multiple DBMSs such that an application can access, view, and modify the data. Apple has announced that they will support ODBC to interface with their System 7.

Through the ODBC API, products such as Microsoft Access and Microsoft Foxpro can do the following:

- connect to and disconnect from remote databases
- provide a standard logon interface for users

- identify the tables, views, columns, and indicies available on the remote databases
- issue commands to the interface and receive resulting data
- create scrollable cursors for single-record processing
- use standard ANSI SQL error message formats

To access each new DBMS, you would install the driver corresponding to it. The application software should not require any modification. These drivers process the ODBC function calls. They translate the standard SQL grammar used by ODBC into the specific SQL grammar required by the DBMS being accessed. They manage all data and message exchanges between the application and the specific DBMS.

Vendors have announced ODBC drivers that will provide access to IBM DB2, Microsoft SQL Server, Borland, Paradox, Oracle, Xbase, Excel XLA, and other DBMS.

Additionally, ODBC is not a competitor of IBM's Distributed Relational Database Architecture (DRDA). Instead, it accesses DRDA-compliant databases through ODBC drivers and gateways the same way it accesses other DBMS.

4.3.4   IBM's Distributed Relational Database Architecture (DRDA)

Distributed Relational Database Architecture (DRDA) is IBM's protocol for connecting databases in the IBM Information Warehouse over Systems Network Architecture (SNA) networks. Ideally, the user should be concerned about the location of data. The ideal interface parses the requests, locates the database, points to the requested data [for example, open cursor(s)], executes joins, sorts and returns the data, and handles any error conditions. The user would never have to be concerned with the commands necessary to interface with the different DBMS, nor would the user have to be cognizant of the form the data is stored in. DRDA is a set of rules by which IBM has defined the ideal implementation among its products and platforms. This set of rules or protocols describes all of the information that is passed between all participants in the distributed database environment. This includes:

- valid response formats
- handling communication failures and interrupts
- data formats and conversions
- naming conventions for tables, views, etc.
- basic format for data requests

The following is a list of some of the vendors that are participating in DRDA:

- Computer Associates International, Inc.
- Gupta Technologies, Inc.
- Novell, Inc.
- Borland International, Inc.
- Informix Software, Inc.
- Oracle Corp.
- Sybase, Inc.

4.4   RELATIONAL DATABASE PRODUCTS

On the next few pages, we will briefly cover some of the popular relational database servers. What follows is not intended to be a comprehensive introduction to the SQL servers available in the client/server market place but rather enough of an introduction to give you a starting point for research. Based on the information covered earlier in this chapter, the RDBMS software candidates should be researched thoroughly prior to making a choice. The information listed is time sensitive; it may have changed since the writing of this book.

Four of these database vendors are major players in the Unix market place: Oracle, Informix, Sybase, and Ingres. The reader should note that they are not necessarily limited to the Unix market place (see information which follows).

Each of the database server products listed has a relational engine and supports SQL. Each is a major player in the market place and can support enterprise-wide applications. The products have been compared in terms of the following five points:

- the operating systems on which the product will run
- provision of a data dictionary
- inclusion of a query language

- inclusion of a report writer
- provision of application development tools or a fourth generation language

Oracle RDBMS

- operating systems: DOS, OS/2, Macintosh, UNIX, VAX/VMS, MVS, VM
- data dictionary: optional
- query language: optional
- report writer: optional
- application development tools/4GL: optional

The vendor indicates that SQL Server is both upward- and downward-compatible with the family of Oracle database products on multiple platforms. This means that the database can be ported up or down from micro to mini to mainframe. Oracle optionally provides a complete development toolset; however, few other vendors provide development tools for this environment.

Oracle Corporation
500 Oracle Parkway
Redwood Shores, CA 94065
(415) 506-7000

Ingres DBMS Server

- operating systems: DOS, OS/2, Macintosh, UNIX, VAX/VMS, OS/400, MVS, VM
- data dictionary: yes
- query language: yes
- report writer: optional
- application development tools/4GL: optional

This RDBMS operates on all major server platforms except NetWare, including DOS, OS/2, and UNIX. The Ingres DBMS Server product family includes a gateway product that provides access to DB2 on a mainframe.

The ASK Group
2880 Scott Blvd.
Santa Clara, CA 95052
(415) 969-4442

Informix-OnLine or Informix-SE
- operating systems: DOS, Novell NetWare, UNIX
- data dictionary: N/A
- query language: N/A
- report writer: N/A
- application development tools/4GL: N/A

Informix has three separate products that service DOS, Novell, and UNIX users. Their primary product base is the UNIX customer.

Informix Software, Inc.
4100 Bohannon Drive
Menlo Park, CA 94025
(415) 926-6300

Sybase SQL Server

- operating systems: DOS, OS/2, Macintosh, UNIX, VAX/VMS, MVS, ULTRIX, NeXT, Stratus
- data dictionary: yes
- query language: yes
- report writer: yes
- application development tools/4GL: yes

Sybase has provided an RDBMS solution for over ten years. They have extensive experience providing support for mission critical applications, including a 24-hour-per-day and 7-day-per-week hot-line.

Sybase Inc.
6475 Christie Avenue
Emeryville, CA 94608
(510) 596-3500

Microsoft SQL Server

- operating systems: OS/2
- data dictionary: yes
- query language: yes
- report writer: optional
- application development tools/4GL: optional

Microsoft's database engine is provided by Sybase; differences between the two database server products should be addressed to Microsoft. Microsoft's SQL Bridge extends Microsoft SQL Server to support UNIX, VMS, and Macintosh clients using applications based on the SYBASE Open Client interface. Additionally, gateways exist that connect to IBM'S DB2 and SQL/400 to Oracle and Ingres databases.

Microsoft Corporation
One Microsoft Way
Redmond, WA 98052-6309
(206) 882-8080

IBM Database 2 OS/2 (DB2/2)

- operating systems: OS/2, DOS
- data dictionary: no
- query language: yes
- report writer: optional (other vendors)
- application development tools/4GL: optional (other vendors)

This product is part of IBM's family of DB2 products which can be ported to multiple platforms. The services available are equivalent to those on mainframe DB2. Additionally, a gateway is available called Distributed Database Connection Services (DDCS/2) which provides access to DB2 on the mainframe.

IBM Corp.
Old Orchard Road
Armonk, NY 10504
(914) 765-1900

Gupta SQLBase

- operating systems: DOS, OS/2, Sun, UNIX, Netware
- data dictionary: yes
- query language: yes
- report writer: optional
- application development tools/4GL: optional

Using the Gupta SQLNetwork connectivity products, you can access other SQL database management systems transparently, including Oracle, Sybase, SQL Server, and OS/2 Database Manager. Gupta's SQLWindows product provides the report writer and application development tools/4GL facilities not packaged with the database server.

Gupta Technologies, Inc.
1040 Marsh Road
Menlo Park, CA 94025
(415) 321-9500

Netware SQL

- operating systems: DOS, OS/2, Macintosh, NetWare
- data dictionary: yes
- query language: optional
- report writer: optional
- application development tools/4GL: optional

Novell focused their early product emphasis on Network Operating Systems. They probably have a larger client base than any other NOS. However, database server software is a relatively new business for them. Their server product should be reviewed carefully and compared to the product of a well-established database server vendor. As an alternative, some of the SQL vendors listed here provide products that can operate on NetWare.

Novell Inc.
5918 W. Courtyard Dr.
Austin, TX 78730
(512) 346-8380

5

Client/Server Solutions Using Shrink-Wrapped Software

5.1 INTRODUCTION

Traditional mainframe development has been done using mainframe system hardware, software, and tools that have remained fundamentally the same for twenty years. An alternative approach is the use of the client/server solution, especially those that are sold as complete solutions. To better understand these client/server solutions, let's compare them to the mainframe solutions.

5.1.1 Traditional Mainframe Solutions

Traditional mainframe solutions can be viewed as stable, mature systems (often referred to as legacy systems) that have certain basic features and facilities (see Figure 5.1). The user has been provided with online screens that are basically two color (background and foreground—green or amber on black), with character representation only. Forms and reports (paper, microfiche, microfilm, etc.) have been the input and output medium.

Online transaction processing and batch job streams are the means to get the job done. Programs are written in second generation languages such as COBOL for each screen, report, process, and so forth required.

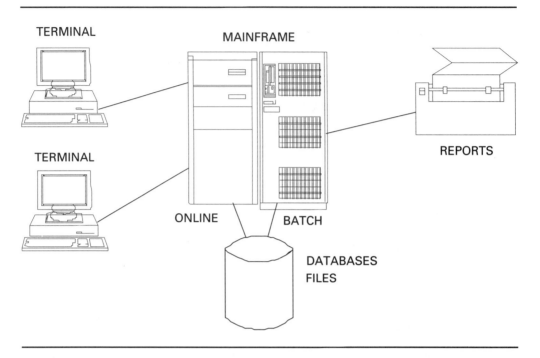

Figure 5.1

Most development is done by writing programs in a second generation language such as COBOL. Some of the coding is done by using third generation report writers that still require detailed descriptions of inputs, outputs, and processing to create the desired results. Tools to support this environment exist and are helpful, but these tools do not increase programmer productivity as dramatically as do the tools available in the client/server environment.

If you want a report in COBOL you must describe the files and records in detail for both input and output. Each different line of the report must be described in detail. All processing is done by describing each manipulation necessary for each specific field.

5.1.2   Shrink-wrapped Solutions

The term "shrink wrapped" is associated with software sold for the PC environment; this software is usually sealed with shrink-wrapped plastic to avoid tampering with the software, which is contained on diskettes.

System solutions and development environments are now available on a wide range of platforms that use existing software that can be integrated with existing databases and systems (see Figure 5.2). In addition to all the traditional means of presentation to the user, the client/server environment offers shrink-wrapped software that brings graphics, images, windows, and so forth to the solution. These are multi-color based, may use mouse technology, and provide a new approach to solutions.

The software can be used for word processing, spreadsheet, database, electronic mail, text retrieval, imaging, and so forth, running in DOS in character form, simulating windows, or running in a fully integrated GUI windowing environment.

These solutions may use cooperative processing, in which transactions have a front end (presentation and processing) on the LAN

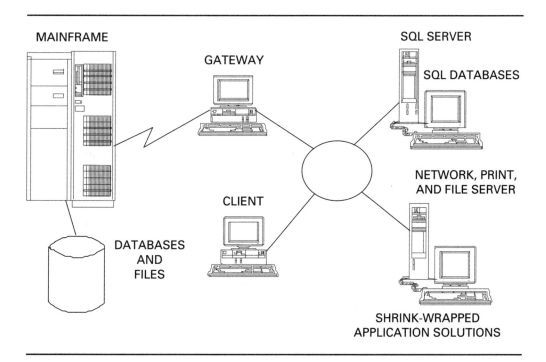

Figure 5.2

and back end data retrieval and updating on the mainframe. They may also run as offloaded mainframe distributed applications, with infrequent upload and download to the mainframe.

Batch files within the operating system are the equivalent of mainframe JCL. You can construct a job stream that runs various steps and invoke the job based on a time of day, much as you do on the mainframe. This type of facility can be used to automatically back up data overnight, route reports, upload and download files, collect data, and so forth.

Scripts provide the ability to run a sequence of events, including operator dialogue. This can be used to sign on to facilities such as the mainframe during off hours, which would otherwise require the presence of an operator.

These shrink-wrapped solutions provide development facilities of their own (for example, word processors and spreadsheets provide macro writing capabilities to create automated activities). These solutions are in some cases capable of interfacing with both mainframe and LAN databases and files.

Some of the mainframe languages are supported on the client/server platform in such a way that development on the PC or mainframe can be transparent. The client/server shrink-wrapped environment supports third and fourth generation language development.

5.2   WORD PROCESSING

Word processing may not come to mind as a classic client/server application, but it is! It replaces many mini-computer and mainframe computer systems with features, flexibility, and cost-effective hardware. The workstations can be used for many applications other than word processing, but let's focus on word processing on the LAN.

5.2.1   Word Processing as a Client/Server Application

Based on the needs of the office, the following may be contained on a single server or on several servers on the network (see Figure 5.3):

- *word processing programs:* the actual word processing software (off-the-shelf shrink-wrapped software) is housed on the

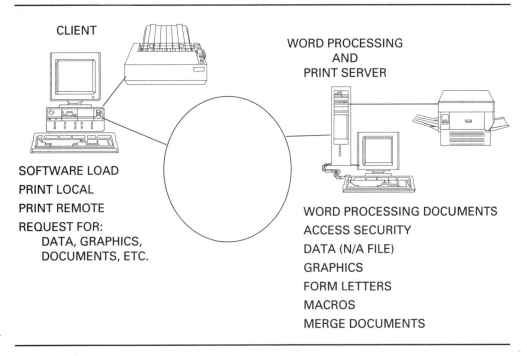

Figure 5.3   Word Processing Client/Server Applications

server. Whenever the user starts the word processing program, the program is retrieved from the server and loaded onto the user's client machine. This is the same technique for all the routines and functions that the word processing program supports (for example, online help, graphics, printing functions, etc.). Therefore, the LAN response time of both the server and the network is important to serve a large word processor client base.

- *shared documents directory:* all documents common to clients should be stored in a set of directories that can be shared by all users. The typical application is forms or form letters.
- *individual client directories:* these directories are the property of the individual client. LAN security can be used to prevent one user from looking into or changing a document in another user's directory.

- *LAN backup:* since LAN backup procedures encompass all servers, all clients will have their data automatically backed up at the frequency that the procedures call for.
- *shared printing:* since the clients are on the LAN, they share the LAN print facilities. This means that specialized printers (for example, envelope feed, printers with font capabilities, and the like) can be shared by all clients.

Based on the needs of the office, any combination of the following may be contained and processed on a particular client workstation:

- *sensitive documents on client workstation:* even though the LAN has security facilities to limit the access of clients to their own directory on the LAN, the LAN administrator has access to the data. There may be extremely sensitive personnel information, payroll information, and so forth that the user feels must be better protected. This can be done by placing that information on the individual client workstation. The workstation can be in an office that can be locked; the workstation itself can also be locked using the keyboard lock; and security software can also be placed on that single machine.
- *high-speed processing:* since each client workstation is a complete computer, the processing speed for any activity depends little upon the server itself. Therefore, it will operate much more quickly than a traditional dedicated word processing mini-computer that has dumb terminals attached and has only one CPU.
- *exclusive printing:* to meet special requirements, a printer can be attached directly to the client workstation for its exclusive use. Examples of these requirements include high-volume output, special forms output, and sensitive information that should not be printed at a public LAN printer.
- *user responsible for client backup:* if documents are housed on the client machine, the LAN backup will not include them. Therefore the user is responsible for the backup of these documents.

5.2.2   **Word Processing as a Cooperative Processing Application**

By gathering data from various sources, a word processing client/server environment can be extended to do heavy-duty mainframe processing. For example, customized legal contracts, insurance forms, and the like can be written through the inclusion of individual paragraphs of information and personal data that is merged into a boiler-plate document. The word processor takes care of rearranging the entire document so that all the pieces fit as though they were typed as one whole document. By contrast, on the mainframe the same activity would require extensive programming to merge in this variable information and then reformat the document. The programming necessary just to move text from one page to another and then reformat multiple pages in the document so that they are continuous would be prohibitive.

Another example is form completion, in which information from a database is extracted (see Figure 5.4) and placed on a form in specific locations. Again, this could be a mainframe application, but the creation of the form and the merging in of the data is done much easier within the client/server word processing environment.

The traditional mail merge is another application that is done most simply and easily on a word processing C/S application. The information for a mailing (letters) or labels is extracted from the database, sorted, formatted for the merge, and presented to the word processor. This type of application could function as follows:

- *data extract and format:* first identify the data to be processed. For example, a set of names and addresses for labels, specific information to complete a form turnaround document (for example, an inquiry addressed to a doctor, information to feed late payment letters or dunning notices). If you are extracting from the mainframe, use existing tools (utilities, 4GLs, and so forth) to extract the data and then transmit the data to the LAN gateway server. If you are extracting data from LAN server databases, use the built-in tools to extract the data (or one of many database software packages that can easily extract data). Then store it on the word processing server or the client workstation.

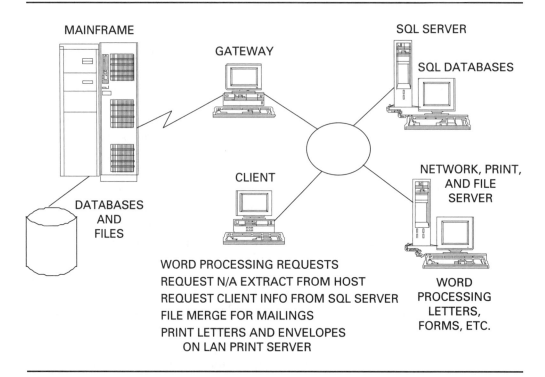

Figure 5.4   Word Processing Cooperative Processing Applications

- *format the data:* wherever the data came from it must be formatted for input to the word processing merge process. This usually means the data is presented in a certain sequence, with each field delimited and each record (next document or next label) delimited. Sometimes the database extract utility will format the data for direct input.
- *macro processing:* this can be a powerful tool that will let the developer automate a series of activities. For example, you can start the word processor in a batch file, passing it parameters about what you wish to do, and then merge all fields into a set of documents and repeat this operation for any number of records. Begin printing concurrently as soon as a document is ready. The user simply keys in the name of the macro and the rest is done automatically. Macros can

also be written to pause and request user input when decisions have to be made or the data was unavailable from the merge source.

For example, take 100 pieces of information pertinent to creating a series of legal documents and forms that are necessary for establishing a pension account. Automate the process to create customized contracts, letters of notification, forms to be filed and so forth, with appropriate numbers of copies of each. Write an application that provides entry capability and editing for the 100 data items, and then simply send one command to the word processor to merge and create all the documents.

5.2.3   Features

What is special about LAN-based word processors that is not true for dedicated word processing facilities? Somehow we have come a long way from the upgraded typewriter that was the dedicated word processor of the not-so-long-ago past. Here is what word processors can do today, and vendors continue to add and improve functionality every year.

- *basic editing:* in addition to basic editing of text, you can use redline or strikeouts, justify left, right or center, search and replace text, footers, headers, table of contents, index, bold, underline, subscript, superscript.
- *proofing tools:* you can spell check your documents and utilize an online thesaurus. You can add dictionaries that are specialized by profession. Grammar checking programs are available.
- *layout:* Margins of varying sizes, customizable tabs, options for word and character spacing. Columns of different widths, tables, calculation by rows and columns. View the document as it will be printed; this is useful for small-font print and graphics because most word processors do not display in WYSIWYG form while you are editing.
- *mail merge:* merge a number of data elements into a document for any number of records. For example, take 500 pieces of information and merge them into a 50-page document. Sort routines for label processing are also provided.

- *style sheets:* style sheets contain information about fonts, margins, indentations, borders, and other appearance characteristics. This information, along with boiler-plate text, can provide forms processing that is driven by macro and operator interrogation or be used as a mail merge.
- *printer and font support:* The software provides support for many different printers. As new printers are marketed, the word processing companies provide drivers to support them. These drivers include interfaces to software fonts, hardware font cartridges, and printers with built-in fonts.
- *document import and export:* import from and export to other word processors, database packages, ASCII files, and so forth. These tools are only as good as the vendor cares to make them. Since each word processing and database vendor is constantly changing their software and the way they store data, it is almost impossible to provide a complete import/export program. The programs do, however, handle most simple text very well. They can always be used to convert word processing documents to an ASCII file that will be acceptable input to any word processor.
- *macros:* some languages are so sophisticated that you can perform conditionals, arrays, do-loops, while-when, if-then-else, and so forth. They provide the means by which you can automate the generation of sophisticated copy (inclusion or exclusion of text or run a series of activities with no hands on).
- *labels:* sort names and addresses, and print the labels 1, 2, 3 or more up on continuous forms or single-page labels.
- *charts and graphics:* charts and graphics that have been developed in other software packages can easily be included in the word processing document. Many word processors are also capable of producing simple charts and have built-in graphic images. Overhead foils for presentations can be prepared by using the large-font capabilities. The charts and graphics can be included to provide complete and sophisticated written presentations.

5.2.4   Types of Software Available

There are many word processing products on the market. The list that follows covers those that run under Microsoft's Windows and are also available in DOS versions.

MICROSOFT WORD FOR WINDOWS
Microsoft Corp.
Redmond, WA 98052
(800) 426-9400

AMI PRO
Lotus Development Corp.
Atlanta, GA 30342
(404) 394-8718

WORD PERFECT FOR WINDOWS
WordPerfect Corp.
Orem, UT 84057
(800) 451-5151

DESCRIBE
Describe Inc.
Sacramento, CA 95834
(916) 646-1111

WORDSTAR FOR WINDOWS
Wordstar International Inc.
Novato, CA 94949
(800) 227-5609

The April 15, 1994 issue of *Datamation* has a "Monthly Roster of Best-Selling Software," which rates the word processors as follows:

1. WordPerfect
2. Word
3. Professional Write
4. Ami Pro
5. WordPerfect LetterPerfect

5.3 SPREADSHEET

The reader is probably familiar with spreadsheet software. This software is usually run on a single PC, with files shared between users by passing the spreadsheets and data via diskette. This software can be used directly as a client/server application and can also be used in a client/server environment.

5.3.1   Spreadsheet as a Client/Server Application

In the client/server environment (see Figure 5.5) the server responsibilities can be the following:

- *defined spreadsheets:* predefined spreadsheets may be stored on the server and made available for common use. Additionally, the spreadsheet software and macro facilities are powerful enough to create small user applications that can be housed on the server.
- *spreadsheet software:* licensing discounts are based on multiple concurrent users on the LAN. The software is stored on the server and concurrent usage restrictions are implemented on the server.
- *security:* some of the data may be sensitive. This requires security, which is provided by the server.
- data input for the spreadsheet can be provided from mainframe hosts (see next section) as well as data housed on the server.

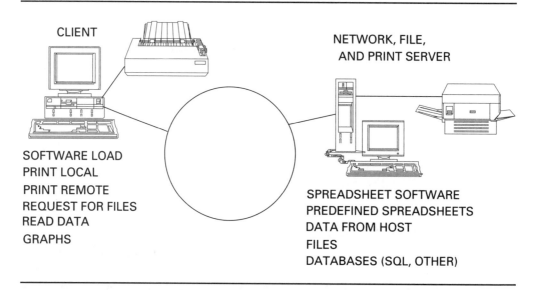

Figure 5.5   Spreadsheet Client/Server

The client responsibilities include:

- *high-speed processing:* since each client workstation is a complete computer, the processing speed for any activity depends little upon the server itself. This is important because many spreadsheet activities require heavy number crunching and therefore a client machine should be properly configured.
- *exclusive printing:* to meet special requirements, a printer can be attached directly to the client workstation for its exclusive use. Examples of these requirements include high-volume output, special forms output, and sensitive information that should not be printed at a public LAN printer.
- *user responsible for client backup:* if spreadsheets are housed on the client machine, the LAN backup will not include them. Therefore, the user is responsible for the backup of these documents.

5.3.2   Spreadsheet as a Cooperative Processing Application

By gathering the data from various sources, spreadsheet analysis can be a serious client/server application as well as a cooperative processing application (see Figure 5.6).

A cooperative processing spreadsheet application could function as follows:

- *data extract and format:* identify the data to be processed from any file or database. The data can be from operational data or archival data; the source can be host, mini's, SQL servers, and so forth.
- *data from host:* use tools available (database utilities, 4 GLs) to extract and transmit the data to the LAN gateway server and then on to client workstation.
- *data from server databases:* extract by using tools available (SQL database tools or spreadsheet interface itself) and send data to client workstation.
- *format:* wherever the data came from, it must be formatted for input to the spreadsheet. As indicated, some spreadsheets accept data from certain databases. However, assume

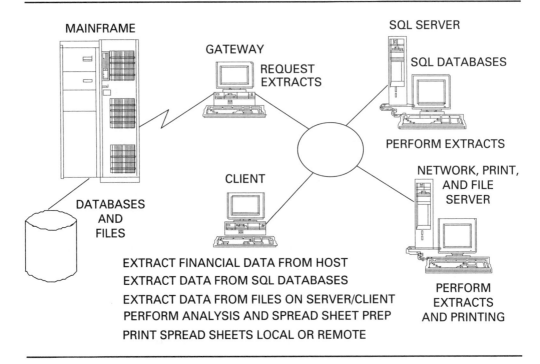

MAINFRAME

GATEWAY

REQUEST
EXTRACTS

SQL SERVER

SQL DATABASES

PERFORM EXTRACTS

CLIENT

NETWORK, PRINT,
AND FILE
SERVER

DATABASES
AND
FILES

EXTRACT FINANCIAL DATA FROM HOST
EXTRACT DATA FROM SQL DATABASES
EXTRACT DATA FROM FILES ON SERVER/CLIENT
PERFORM ANALYSIS AND SPREAD SHEET PREP
PRINT SPREAD SHEETS LOCAL OR REMOTE

PERFORM
EXTRACTS
AND PRINTING

Figure 5.6   Cooperative Processing Spreadsheet Applications

that the data must be converted into a flat file with a comma delimiting fields. This is done by many utilities. You can also write a simple COBOL or "C" program, as required.

- *automating the process:* by using a combination of basic DOS batch processing and the spreadsheet-provided macro facilities, this entire activity can be automated. As an example, once a week you can extract all the pertinent information to produce a set(s) of spreadsheets that detail sales analysis for the company. This activity can be further automated by scheduling the job on the server and distributing the output to predefined destinations.

5.3.3   Features

Generally, spreadsheet software can be used to support any business function that requires calculation or graphing. For example:

balance sheet analysis, product profitability, department profitability, auditing, new business proposals, sales analysis, what if's (planning new product pricing).

Spreadsheet solutions as a client/server application should be present on most LANs. Users have an opportunity to access number crunching software with management-level presentation results. Number crunching is one of the shrink-wrapped software programs that has serious machine requirements. The minimum CPU should be a 386 with more than 1 meg of memory—at least 2–4 meg. The speed of the CPU is a factor in getting the job done, whereas the extra memory is used for larger spreadsheets and handling more than one spreadsheet at a time.

These software products provide the following facilities:

- *formulas and analysis:* all of the products include the basic analytical tools to satisfy the needs of the majority of users. They all offer a full range of built-in functions. Tools include regression analysis, matrix functions, and dynamic what if tables. A library of macros with simultaneous equation solving, goal seeking, and other features is usually supplied.
- *compatibility:* data can be imported from Lotus 1-2-3, Lotus Symphony, Dbase, and comma or tab separated text files. Using the latter two formats, data can be extracted from any mainframe database and provided as input to the spreadsheet software.
- *database interface:* these products can import selected records from a Dbase file. The new version of Excel includes Q+E which allows you to work with relational database files such as Dbase, SQL Server, and Oracle. Quattro Pro, sold by Borland, will interface with their database product Paradox.
- *graphics capability:* the features include mixed graph types (bar and line), high, low, close graphs, dual y-axis graphs, logarithmic scaling, area charts, and horizontal orientation. You can create on-screen slide shows and customize colors and fonts. The software produces quality graphics but not as well as presentation graphics software.
- *macros:* the macro language lets you set up user menus and develop sophisticated models that are easy for the end user to use.

- *spreadsheet consolidation:* you can reference cells or ranges in other worksheets that are in memory or on disk. Some software provides the ability to work with multiple spreadsheets simultaneously.

5.3.4   Types of Software Available

The most popular spreadsheet software currently available runs either under DOS or Microsoft's Windows. The list below is available in either version.

MICROSOFT EXCEL
>   Microsoft Corp.
>   Redmond, WA 98052
>   (800) 426-9400

LOTUS 1-2-3
>   Lotus Development Corp.
>   Atlanta, GA 30342
>   (404) 394-8718

QUATTRO PRO
>   Borland International
>   Scotts Valley, CA 95066
>   (800) 841-8180

SUPERCALC 5
>   Computer Associates Inc.
>   Islandia, NY 11788-7000
>   (516) 342-5224

INFORMIX WINGZ
>   Informix Software Inc.
>   Lenexa, KS 66219
>   (913) 492-9922

The April 15, 1994 issue of *Datamation* has a "Monthly Roster of Best-Selling Software," which rates the spread sheet software as follows:

1. 1-2-3
2. Excel
3. Quattro Pro
4. Improv (Lotus)
5. SuperCalc 5

5.4 ELECTRONIC IMAGING

Image Management Systems provide the technology to present copies of documents, reports, charts, graphics, pictures, and the like to the user. These images are stored in a central location and accessed electronically via flexible indexing software. Images can be captured by using scanning devices or directly from computer output. Imaging systems typically run on PC workstations, with servers providing the storage and management of the images.

5.4.1 Electronic Imaging as a Client/Server Application

In Figure 5.7 you can see the function of each component in the imaging system, including client and server responsibilities.

In addition to these basic facilities, electronic imaging systems usually provide workflow facilities that can automatically route documents through their normal processing cycle. You can alter this routing in accordance with decisions made by users and the actions they take. This routing can include approvals, review, and other actions. The processing may contain word processing files, images, notes on the documents, and so forth, simulating activities that would take place on real paper files. Documents appear in your in basket and you process them much the same as you would using outbaskets, file cabinets, and faxes. You can annotate the document, pass variations of the same document to different departments, determine who is authorized to change the documents, and so forth. The software provides indexing capability, allowing you to attach keywords to each document so that it may be located by searching by keyword, author, subject, date, and the like.

5.4.2 Components

An image management system consists of the following components:

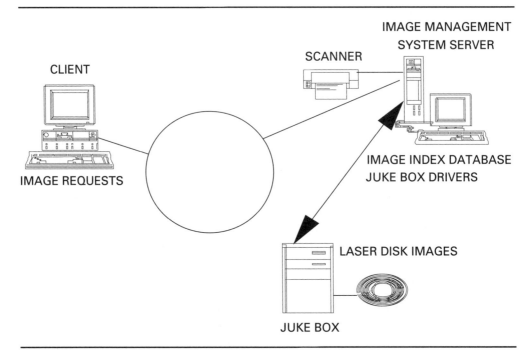

Figure 5.7   Electronic Imaging Systems

- *input scanning:* volumes of documents (for example, claims, applications, correspondence, etc.) are scanned into the system as an image (picture) made up of thousands of points on a graphic (black and white or color) representation of the image. Expensive scanners have a 50 or more page input tray stacking capability and high resolution. Top-end scanners create both microfilm and image copies, at high resolution, and are capable of scanning thousands of documents an hour. Additionally, input may consist of electronic output (bills, customer computer-generated letters, reports, etc.) stored as digital data (not as an image) in compressed form (without spaces). Input may also be from cameras that can feed directly into computer image storage.
- *image storage:* images are stored on a special medium called laser disk, which is similar to a CD. When these are stored in sets and can be loaded by selecting a desired laser disk, the technology is referred to as a "juke box." The images

must have a "key" for retrieval purposes. During the scan process or when the images are stored from electronic output, they are assigned a unique reference identifier.

- *image server:* imaging systems are driven by their ability to group images and reference them by index. These indices are built at scan or electronic input time. For example, in a claims application, each claim might be given a header sheet that references pertinent index information such as the policy number. When the associated claims documents are captured (scanned), an index of that policy and the claim laser disk documents is created.

- *image management software:* Imaging Management Systems have a potentially wide business usage as C/S applications. The application could be administrative based and all correspondence (fax, mail, E-mail, inter-department, etc.) would be captured in image form on a LAN. A server application then reviews all the administrative clerks' mail boxes and distributes the mail based on individual work loads. The client workstation user reviews his or her mail box of work and either completes the transaction or passes the transaction to a supervisor, another department, and so forth. This is all done electronically by using images of the customer's request.

- *image output devices:* imaging systems require a high-resolution client workstation monitor for documents and images (for example, signatures, pictures). If documents are going to be printed (for instance, customer correspondence) and they include images (perhaps a copy of bills or receipts) a laser-jet printer is a must.

Note that the greatest drawback of imaging client/server applications at the present time is the cost of storing and transferring images. Because these images are stored as graphic representations, they are individually the size of a large file (for example, 40,000 bytes). This means that they require both significant storage space and they are a potential access and traffic problem on the LAN. Consider the storage demand of a small claims operation of 2,000 claims per day at 5 documents per claim:

$$2,000 \text{ (claims per day)} \times 5 \text{ (documents per claim)} \times 40,000 \text{ (bytes)}$$
$$= 100,000,000 \text{ bytes}$$

That enormous amount of data would need to be stored and transferred on the LAN each day. Paging through a 100-page document on a client machine means the transfer of 100 40K files and then having storage space on the client machine to accommodate the document.

5.4.3   Alternatives—Vendor and Other

Imaging software alternatives can be placed in two categories: (1) build-it-yourself and (2) turnkey. The build-it-yourself alternatives usually offer you the software to build a full imaging solution, including scanning the documents, filing, retrieving, and routing them based on workflow requirements. Additionally, these vendors usually are resellers for a variety of hardware components to complete the system. These vendors provide consulting services to help you customize your system or they are associated with third parties that provide these consulting services. You can do it all yourself, including hardware selection and installation, or take advantage of any of the services offered. The cost of these solutions starts at under $10,000 and increases according to the number of stations and the hardware chosen. A typical complete solution runs between $30,000 and $50,000. A limited list of these vendors follows. Some of these vendors allow you to modify the images viewed, whereas others provide view-only facilities. Some of these products run under DOS; the others run under Microsoft's Windows.

KEYFILE
  Keyfile Corp.
  Nashua, NH 03063
  (603) 883-3800

SOFTSOLUTIONS
  SoftSolutions Technology Corp.
  Orem, UT 84057
  (801) 226-6000

PAPERCLIP
  PaperClip Imaging Software Inc.
  Hackensack, NJ 07601
  (201) 487-3503

DOCUMENT ADMINISTRATOR
Interpreter Software Products Inc Technology Corp.
Wheat Ridge, CO 80229
(800) 232-4687

PC DOCS
PC Docs Inc.
Tallahassee, FL 32301
(904) 942-3627

QMS 2001 Knowledge System
QMS
Mobile, AL 36618
(205) 639-4474

METAFILE
Metafile Information System Inc.
Rochester, MN 55902
(507) 286-9232

IMAGE BASIC
Diamond Head Software Inc.
Honolulu, HI 96813
(808) 545-2377

PAGEKEEPER
Caere Corp.
Los Gatos, CA 95030
(408) 395-5148

FIREPOWER
Optika Imaging Systems Inc.
Colorado Springs, CO 80919
(719) 548-9800

The turnkey solutions are usually much more expensive, start-ing at $100,000 and exceeding $1,000,000. The vendors survey your needs, develop a list of requirements for you to sign off on, and then custom build a solution using existing hardware and software. They install the solution and train your staff. There are many of these vendors, including the following:

FILENET
Filenet Corp.
Costa Mesa, CA 92626
(714) 966-3400

IMAGEPLUS
IBM Corp.
Armonk, NY 10504
(914) 765-1900

5.5 SINGLE IMAGE

Single image applications take multiple host screens from disparate host applications and provide a consistent user interface. This is often used to create a graphic user interface for legacy applications without modifying the legacy application. It is sometimes referred to as the technology of distributed presentation or renovating host-based systems.

Frequently, host-based systems have applications written that do not follow the same conventions, for example, different directional keys used for screen flow. They are also not compatible with the new GUI designs being implemented on PCs. If the user will be working with client/server applications developed on a LAN and will still have to interface with mainframe applications, changing the face of the mainframe applications to work much closer to the look and feel of the client/server application is desirable.

Another application of single image may simply be that the user needs several pieces of information that are on several different mainframe screens and traversing them requires too much time and knowledge of the applications.

5.5.1 Single Image as a Client/Server Application

The single image is achieved by traversing a series of screens on the mainframe behind the scenes without the user's knowledge and presenting the data gathered in a manner more consistent with the GUI standards of other applications. This is all done without changing the mainframe applications (see Figure 5.8).

The server responsibilities include:

- *gateway:* the LAN to host interface is via a gateway server equipped with the hardware and software necessary to emu-

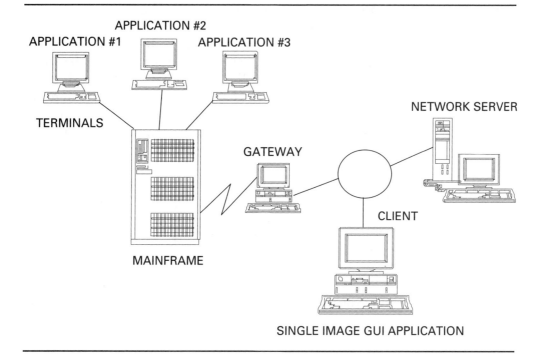

APPLICATION #2
APPLICATION #1   APPLICATION #3
TERMINALS
NETWORK SERVER
GATEWAY
CLIENT
MAINFRAME
SINGLE IMAGE GUI APPLICATION

Figure 5.8

late host controller communications. The gateway server, in conjunction with the gateway interface software resident on the client machine, places the screen buffer on the client and provides access to it.

* *image application solutions:* these application solutions (scripts, programs, etc.) can be stored on the network server and invoked by the client as required.

5.5.2   Components

Single image applications have several components:

* *screen scraping:* this is the component that reads mainframe screen images in the communications buffer. The developer searches for specific information in the buffer either by the coordinate on the screen (specific location in the buffer) or by searching for keywords such as field titles to locate associated data.

- *scripts:* often a series of screens need to be traversed to get to the specific screen(s) that contains the data in question. An example of a typical sequence might be a sign-on screen, main menu, sub menu, entering an account number, and then the fifth screen in the sequence contains the data required. A script language facility is required to simulate operator entry, including data and PF keys. The script then runs with an appropriate mainframe gateway interface that sends and receives the data.

There are several special concerns with applications of this type. The first has to do with security. Since the application may require retrieving data from several existing legacy systems, each of which requires a special sign on, there are several alternatives. You can embed the ids and passwords in the script. However, this may violate auditing policies because the ids and passwords can be viewed by someone interrogating the script. An alternative is to interrupt the screen-scraping process and dynamically request operator entry of the password. Another alternative is to encrypt the password in the script.

A second consideration is response time. Since a single operator activity may generate multiple mainframe activities, the response will be dependent upon the mainframe response time for several host transactions.

5.5.3   Alternatives—Vendor and Other

Solutions exist at two levels: (1) for a low-level product that requires writing a combination of scripts and application code and (2) for a high-level product for which application programming may not be required.

The low-level solutions utilize IBM's HLLAPI (High Level Language Application Programmer Interface) for host to PC communications in 3270 emulation (LU2) to access the mainframe buffer on your PC. You can write your own screen-scraping applications in any PC compatible language (for example, COBOL) and interface to HLLAPI to access the screen buffer in the mainframe session. At least three vendors provide the low-level buffer access and scripting capability necessary to support this activity.

IBM 3270 EMULATION and PWM
IBM Corp.
Armonk, NY 10504
(914) 765-1900

RABBIT
Rabbit Software
Malvern, PA 19355
(215) 647-0440

ATTACHMATE EXTRA
Attachmate Corp.
Bellevue WA 98006
(206) 644-4010

More sophisticated tools attempt to provide the implementation discussed previously with a high-level interface using scripts and routines. Infront is one of these tools, as is Easel. Easel Corp. of Massachusetts got its start by specializing in the technology of renovating existing applications and has the tools to do the job but has recently changed its emphasis to C/S tools support.

5.6   TEXT RETRIEVAL

Text retrieval software processes large amounts of data, creates an index of all but common words in the documents, and then provides instant reference for the viewer. For example, all of your word processing documents contained in a directory (or multiple directories) can be searched for by name, phrase, and so forth. A second usage is as a research tool. Volumes of information can be purchased, scanned into a directory, or entered. They could be legal based (laws or contracts), medical based (dictionaries of information), or manuals of information. The text retrieval tool can then be used to search this large database of information.

5.6.1   Text Retrieval as a Client/Server Application

The data to be searched and the indicies necessary to support the search are handled best on a large text server on the LAN (see Figure 5.9). The server would provide the following:

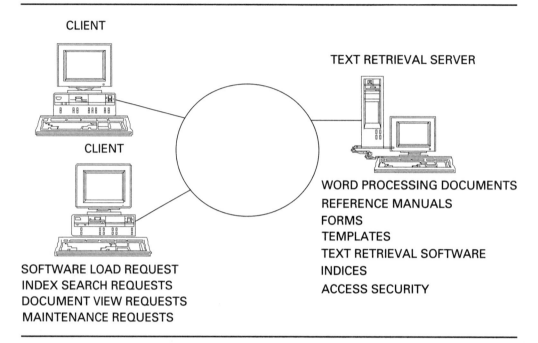

CLIENT

TEXT RETRIEVAL SERVER

CLIENT

WORD PROCESSING DOCUMENTS
REFERENCE MANUALS
FORMS
TEMPLATES
TEXT RETRIEVAL SOFTWARE
INDICES
ACCESS SECURITY

SOFTWARE LOAD REQUEST
INDEX SEARCH REQUESTS
DOCUMENT VIEW REQUESTS
MAINTENANCE REQUESTS

Figure 5.9

- *disk space:* since the documents or text to be searched are usually large in size and access will be required by multiple users, this data should be stored on the server.
- *text retrieval software:* licensing discounts are based on multiple concurrent users on the LAN. The software is stored on the server and concurrent usage restrictions are implemented on the server.
- *security:* the information stored on the server will need to be restricted to be read only for many users and updatable by a few users. This security access is implemented at the server.
- *data and index:* all of the text is stored on the server. Additionally, the indices that the software builds are also stored on the server. These indices are built as part of a batch process, which can be time consuming if many new documents have been added or changed. A common approach is to update these documents, files, and so forth during the day and then re-index them overnight. A scheduled activ-

ity can be started on the server during the night to re-index the new information.

The client is responsible for the following:

- *start and run the process:* load the software from the LAN. Request index searches by reading the index on the server. The software will return a list of documents which contain the word, set of words, or phrase requested. At this point the user (client) can view specific documents and point instantly to the selected word or phrase within the document. If that word exists more than once in the document, the software can skip to each occurrence.

5.6.2   Features

These software products generally provide the following:

- *indexing:* most of the products index every individual word in a file except words kept in a stop or noise word list such as "and" or "the." In addition to indexing, the programs also keep track of where each word goes. When you search for a text string, the program refers to the index and displays an exact image of the file and highlights the search terms it has found. Some programs place no limits on the size or number of indicies they can create or the number of files one index can hold. Most programs create indicies the same size or smaller than the files being indexed. The more files the program puts in one index, the more efficiently it can index and the less space indicies will occupy on your hard disk. Although searches are done in seconds, it may take hours to build indicies. Therefore, index building is best left to an overnight process to minimize impact on client usage.
- *search capability:* the products are able to execute compound Boolean (AND, OR, NOT, etc.) searches. Some can handle directional searches in which you specify that a term must precede or follow another term by a certain number of words. Also, proximity searches by lines, sentences, paragraphs, and pages can be carried out.
- *building text:* all products will take standard ASCII files as input. Certain products will also interface directly with

word processor files (WordPerfect, Microsoft's Word, etc.), spreadsheets, and databases. Some products have entry capability and separate out special pieces of the text for retrieval purposes. This means, for example, that you can search a directory containing 2,000 form letters, find the letter you wish to use, and then by simply pressing a single key invoke your word processor, load the form letter, and begin completing the letter. The entire process from start to finish can be a matter of seconds.

5.6.3 Types of Software Available

The following list represents some of the products available. They do not all have the same features and therefore should be reviewed carefully before the product is purchased. Most of these products are available in DOS and Microsoft Windows versions.

ZYINDEX FOR WINDOWS
  ZyLab
  Buffalo Grove, IL 22664
  (703) 459-8000

ISYS FOR WINDOWS
  Odyssey Development Inc.
  Denver, CO 80111
  (303) 394-0091

PERSONAL LIBRARIAN
  Personal Library Software
  Inc.
  Rockville, MD 20850
  (301) 990-1155

SONAR PROFESSIONAL
  Virginia Systems Software
  Services Inc.
  Richmond, VA 23112
  (804) 739-3200

DTSEARCH
  DT Software Inc.
  Arlington, VA 22202
  (703) 521-9427

ASK SAM
  AskSam Systems
  Perry, FL 32347
  (904) 584-6590

5.7 DATABASE SOFTWARE

Database shrink-wrapped software packages can create full-function client/server applications up to a point. They can provide all the services and react just like a fully functional client/server application. They differ simply in that many functions are performed at the client machine and not the server. Since some of the database software packages can interface with an SQL server, the full database responsibilities are offloaded to the SQL server and the database software package becomes similar to a GUI report-writing interface; in this case the software could be categorized as a RAD tool. This software may not, however, be able to handle databases with large record volumes and still provide adequate response time.

5.7.1   Database Software as a Client/Server Application

In the client/server environment (see Figure 5.10) the server responsibilities can be the following:

- *database application:* pre-defined application software may be stored on the server and made available for common use.
- *database:* the database itself is housed on the server. The server is responsible for update integrity and servicing inquiry requests.
- *database development software:* licensing discounts are based on multiple concurrent users on the LAN. The software is stored on the server and concurrent usage restrictions are implemented on the server.

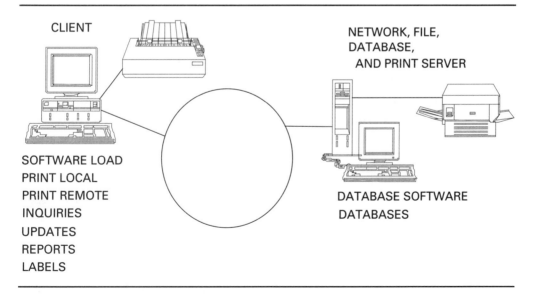

Figure 5.10   Client/Server Database

- *database run time software:* the preferable method of running the individual clients is as an executable application with no runtime license required. If a runtime license is required, licensing discounts are based on multiple concurrent users on the LAN. The software is stored on the server and concurrent usage restrictions are implemented on the server.
- *security:* individual databases can be secured by using the server security facilities. Specific records or data within records must be secured via the application software.
- *data input:* input to the database can be provided from mainframe hosts (see next section) as well as data housed on the server.

The client responsibilities are similar to those of the spreadsheet client, which were presented earlier. They include:

- *high-speed processing:* constructing reports and queries will be done on the client machine.
- *exclusive printing:* to meet special requirements, a printer can be attached directly to the client workstation for its exclusive use. Examples of these requirements include high-volume output, special forms output, and sensitive information that should not be printed at a public LAN printer.

5.7.2   Database Software as a Cooperative Processing Application

By gathering the data from various sources, the database application can be a serious client/server application as well as a cooperative processing application (see Figure 5.11). A cooperative processing database application could function similar to the spreadsheet application in the prior section, as follows:

- *data extract and format:* identify the data to be processed from any file or database. The data can be from operational data or archival data; the source can be host, mini's, SQL servers, and so forth.
- *data from host:* use tools available (database utilities, 4 GLs) to extract and transmit the data to the LAN gateway server and then on to the client workstation.

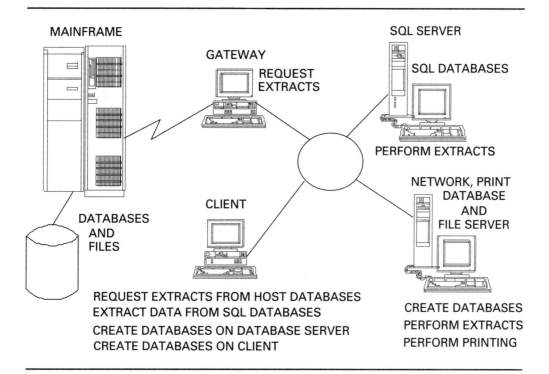

MAINFRAME

GATEWAY

REQUEST
EXTRACTS

SQL SERVER

SQL DATABASES

PERFORM EXTRACTS

NETWORK, PRINT
DATABASE
AND
FILE SERVER

CLIENT

DATABASES
AND
FILES

REQUEST EXTRACTS FROM HOST DATABASES
EXTRACT DATA FROM SQL DATABASES
CREATE DATABASES ON DATABASE SERVER
CREATE DATABASES ON CLIENT

CREATE DATABASES
PERFORM EXTRACTS
PERFORM PRINTING

Figure 5.11   Cooperative Processing Database Applications

- *data from server databases:* extract by using tools available (SQL database tools or spreadsheet interface itself) and send data to the client workstation.
- *format:* wherever the data came from, it must be formatted for input to the database import function. A common input format is a flat file with a comma delimiting fields. This can be created by utilities or you can also write a simple COBOL or "C" program, as required.
- *automating the process:* by using a combination of basic DOS batch processing and the database-provided facilities, this entire activity can be automated. As an example, you can extract data daily from a mainframe and update your server-based database. This activity can be further automated by scheduling the job on the server and distributing the output to predefined destinations.

5.7.3 Features

These products are excellent as basic tools in the RAD (Rapid Application Development) arena. They can be used to develop full client/server applications within the limitations of the tools themselves. The following features and concerns should be reviewed prior to developing a client/server solution:

- *application definition:* with this feature, you can group together all of the files, programs, screens, reports, and so forth that make up an application. Then when you want to check and make sure the project is current, you tell the software and it will refresh only those files that have been changed. When your application is ready to be made into a live production version, the software produces the final runtime version.
- *automated documentation:* since the screens, files, programs, and the like all funnel through the same software, it is possible for the software to produce cross-referenced modules, data items, screens, and so forth, as well as an application flow. This provides some basic documentation and also assists during maintenance of an existing application.
- *object oriented:* the screen building in these products lets you draw data entry and query screens and generate the appropriate code. You can use mouse technology to locate fields, text lines, and boxes by assigning special attributes to fields and finally attaching specialized codes to create an object of the screen or screen window.
- *data entry:* a data entry screen is built by simply filling in a screen by typing text, drawing boxes, making menu choices for display attributes, and defining fields by pressing function keys and filling in a field definition form. You can specify entry fields, derived fields, and calculated fields. You can define help text for each field and for the entire screen.
- *query facilities:* some of the database software packages do not do well when asked to query multiple files simultaneously on a single screen (form). Generally you can specify any combination of fields and conditions to be satisfied to select records. Records from a primary database that satisfy the primary criteria can be selected along with any related records that also satisfy the secondary criteria. After specifying the record selection criteria, define fields that will be

listed in the result and any fields that will be used for sorting, grouping or statistics such as count, sum, mean, max, min, variance, standard deviation, and so forth.

- *reporting facilities:* when creating a report format you can choose from predefined report layouts, including columnar field per line, record entry, and mailing labels, or you can define your own reports. You can place fields, system variables, and calculated variables anywhere on the report. You can specify any number of group breaks on fields or variables. Calculated fields are used to perform lookups, compute totals, and combine columns.

- *multiuser features:* these generally include record locking, table locking, and screen refresh of data when another user has updated the data. In some cases you can specify the duration of the lock and the timeout.

- *data integrity:* some of these products offer security, transaction processing and logging, a data dictionary, and file recover utilities.

- *programming:* debugging tools, code generation, SQL support, and low-level I/O are all part of the environment in some combination. A few of these products may offer code generation only.

- *speed:* the developer must be cautioned that user response time will probably make or break the resulting application. Even the simplest request, query, or a print can take a long time (that is, tens of seconds to minutes) when the database has many records. The speed of the server, the type of inquiry made (for example, Is this a summary report that requires all records to be read?), and the search algorithm of the vendor software influence the resulting response. If you will be using databases with medium to large record counts, consider an SQL server instead. At the very least, review the vendor software carefully to determine whether it can provide the response time you require.

5.7.4 Types of Software Available

There are many types of database software on the market. The first list covers those based in DOS. They may or may not have a Microsoft Windows version.

PARADOX
Borland International
Scotts Valley, CA 95066
(408) 438-5300

ADVANCED REVELATION
Revelation Technologies
Stamford, CT 06902
(203) 973-1000

DATAEASE
DataEase International Inc.
Trumbull, CT 06611
(203) 374-8000

DBASE IV
Ashton Tate
Torrence, CA 90509-9972
(310) 323-1403

FOXPRO
Microsoft Corp.
Redmond, WA 98052
(206) 882-8080

CA-CLIPPER
Computer Associates Inc.
Islandia, NY 11788-7000
(516) 342-5224

RBASE
Microrim
Bellevue, WA 98007
(206) 649-9500

Q&A
Symantic Corp.
Cupertino, CA 95014
(408) 253-9600

The following list of products are Microsoft's Windows based and are geared toward the end-user. They can be used by non-data-processing professionals to define and construct database applications and reports.

ACEFILE FOR WINDOWS
Ace Software Corp.
San Jose, CA 95035
(408) 232-0300

FILEMAKER PRO
FOR WINDOWS
Claris
Santa Clara, CA 95052
(408) 987-7227

APPROACH FOR WINDOWS
Approach Software Corp.
Redwood City, CA 94063
(415) 306-7890

MICROSOFT ACCESS
Microsoft Corp.
Redmond, WA 98052-6309
(206) 882-8080

DATAEASE EXPRESS FOR
WINDOWS
DataEase International Inc.
Trumbull, CT 06611
(203) 374-8000

WINDOWBASE
Software Products
International
San Diego, CA 92121
(619) 450-1526

The April 15, 1994 issue of *Datamation* has a "Monthly Roster of Best-Selling Software," which rates the database software as follows:

1. Microsoft's Access
2. Borland's Paradox
3. Microsoft's Foxpro
4. Claris's FileMaker
5. Symantic's Q&A

5.8 ELECTRONIC MAIL

Electronic mail is simply the sending of messages from one client to another. A mail box is set up for each client and the messages are placed in the mail box as they arrive. You are alerted when the mail arrives, you open the mail, keep it, discard it, forward it, attach comments, or take some other action.

5.8.1 Electronic Mail as a Client/Server Application

The mail must be kept at some common location (post office) to be sent, stored, or otherwise handled. This is best done on a server (see Figure 5.12). Mail may be forwarded or received from other LANs and mainframe hosts. However, the mail for a set of clients is best kept on the server for that LAN or group of LANs. The server would provide the following:

- *disk space:* the amount of mail stored could be significant. Therefore, a server with sufficient disk space is recommended. Depending upon the amount of mail to be processed, a dedicated server may required.
- *E-mail:* licensing discounts are based on multiple concurrent users on the LAN. The software is stored on the server and concurrent usage restrictions are implemented on the server.
- *security:* the mail may be sensitive. This requires security, which is provided by the E-mail software in combination with server security access facilities.
- *E-mail gateway:* software and hardware that interface with other E-mail systems on mainframe hosts or distant LANs

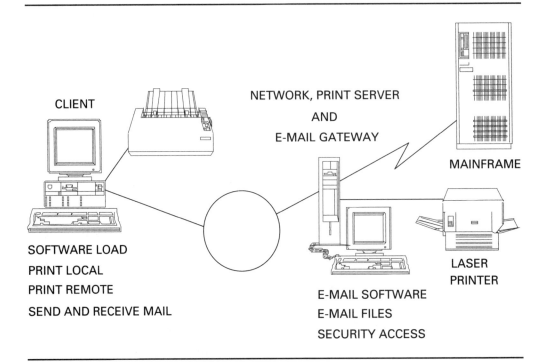

CLIENT

NETWORK, PRINT SERVER
AND
E-MAIL GATEWAY

MAINFRAME

SOFTWARE LOAD

PRINT LOCAL

PRINT REMOTE

SEND AND RECEIVE MAIL

E-MAIL SOFTWARE

E-MAIL FILES

SECURITY ACCESS

LASER
PRINTER

Figure 5.12

would be placed on a server, with access provided to all clients.

- *route the mail:* the mail destined for a specific client can be routed to that client or the client can be alerted that mail has arrived.

The client is provides the following:

- *start and run the process:* load the software from the LAN. Send and receive mail; print the mail as desired.

5.8.2   Features

Electronic mail software products generally provide the following:

- *messaging:* they can do message composition by using pre-defined forms, including a meeting, memo, phone message, request form, transmittal memo, and customer support form. They can send mail to others by selecting names from public lists or construct a mailing list. You can attach files. The products provide notification via TSR (Terminate and Stay Resident) programs that will alert the client that mail has arrived. They also provide pop-up windows so that you can view the mail without interrupting your current activity. Routing can be automated through scripts.

- *archiving:* the software will save composed or received messages as drafts for future composition. They can be saved in folders; you can then search individual folders or all folders.
- *printing and word processing:* they provide a little bit of word processing, cut, copy and paste, and find option to locate words. Other features are search and replace, and spell checker. Printing choices include header information, margin, spacing, number of copies, page breaks. Printing can be directed to a text printer. If something more is required, you can feed the message to a word processor and take it from there. Also messages, texts, and documents can be created on a word processor and then attached to a mail message.
- *security:* the software provides user log-in passwords and message encryption when stored on the mail system. Some software has intruder lockout features that lock out log-in attempts after a number of failed log-in attempts. Administration privileges are controlled, limiting deletion capability and access to user files.
- *inter-LAN linking:* by using vendor-supplied software you can have a gateway that will support connectivity to IBM's Profs (a mainframe E-mail facility), X.400, and other mail systems. Novell's Message Handling Service (MHS), for example, can provide this gateway connectivity.
- *installation and maintenance:* mail platforms come with an administration learning guide and reference manual. There are user's guides for each client. Users maintain their own mail box. LAN backup procedures prevent potential data loss. Administrator maintenance adds and removes mail boxes.

5.8.3   Types of Software Available

The following is a list of popular E-mail software products that operate under Microsoft's Windows. The unfortunate situation is that although E-mail within a client/server environment can easily be handled by these products, a complete corporate E-mail system that handles exclusive users of the mainframe, mini's, and LANs, has all of the features, and is easy to use does not appear on the horizon at the present time.

An additional concern is that these products do not interface with each other across the board. Some interface better than others but not successfully with all other products. A small corporation may have only one E-mail system, but in large corporations with somewhat autonomous divisions, especially those acquired during mergers, multiple E-mail systems may already be installed and interfacing them is a concern.

BEYONDMAIL FOR WINDOWS
Banyan Systems Inc.
Westborough, MA 01581
(508) 836-4832

CC:MAIL FOR WINDOWS PLATFORM PACK VERSION
Lotus Development Corp.
Mountain View, CA 94040
(415) 335-6400

DA VINCI EMAIL FOR WINDOWS
Da Vinci Systems Corp.
Raleigh, NC 27609
(919) 881-4320

FUTURUS TEAM DOS/WINDOWS COMBO
Futurus Corp.
Atlanta, GA 30346
(404) 392-7979

MICROSOFT MAIL FOR PC NETWORKS
MICROSOFT MAIL FOR APPLETALK NETWORKS
Microsoft Corp.
Redmond, WA 98052-6309
(206) 882-8080

QUICKMAIL
CE Software Inc.
West De Moines, IO 50265
(515) 224-1995

SOLARIS MAIL TOOL
SunSoft Inc.
Mountain View, CA 94043
(415) 960-3200

WORDPERFECT MAIL FOR WINDOWS
WordPerfect Corp.
Orem, UT 30342
(800) 451-5151

5.9 PRESENTATION GRAPHICS

Graphics in general and presentation graphics in particular can be produced on a single workstation and do not necessarily fall into the category of a client/server application. However, the hardware required and the need for more than one individual to have access to the facilities tend to make graphics a real client/server application. The printers used are generally expensive and hard to justify when they are used for a single workstation presentation graphics platform. Also graphs are often a very useful tool in documents and the graphic software products can take input from spreadsheet programs and product graphs easily.

5.9.1 Presentation Graphics as a Client/Server Application

The server (see Figure 5.13) is responsible for providing shared usage of expensive peripherals: color printers, 35mm slide producers, scanners for input graphics and so forth. Additionally, the server can provide the input data (for example, on an SQL server) for graphs, documents for inclusion in the presentation, and clip art to be shared by the presentation developers. The client machine runs the presentation development software and utilizes the server facilities for input and output.

5.9.2 Features

Presentations in the form of foils or slides have come a long way. The presentation software today takes advantage of the features present on PCs either as a small presentation to be viewed on a PC or projected on a screen. Most importantly, the presentations no longer have to be sent out to make them professional looking.

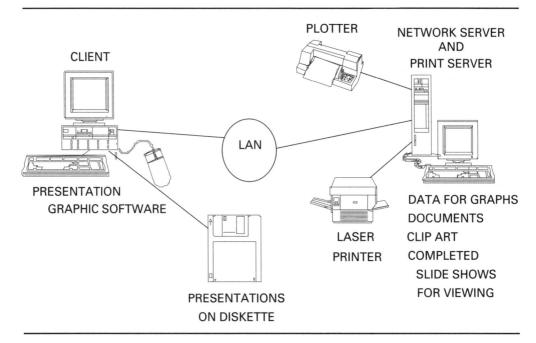

Figure 5.13

You can produce foils, slides, PC screens, and handouts from the same original material.

As the market has matured and new technology has evolved, vendors have changed their focus from charting and graphing to full-fledged presentation packages. These packages incorporate clip-art, drawing tools, special effects, and—by using the Windows graphical interface—are easy to use.

These products provide the following facilities:

- *presentation organization:* charts are created by using a master slide page that can contain a custom frame, logo, color scheme, and so forth, which is then sized for the output device you select, including 35mm slides or laser printer. All parts of your presentation text, charts, chart order, and speaker's notes are organized. You view them, reorder them, and re-edit them until the presentation is done. Clip art can include thousands of images.

- *text facilities:* some of the programs include dictionaries, search and replace facilities for text and special characters, import from word processors, and also include scalable font sets.
- *numeric charting:* chart types include area, bar, stacked bar, column, stacked column, line, pie and exploded pies, scatter, data table, and organizational charts are provided. 3-D perspective is available for charts.
- *graphic editing:* you can add lines, rectangles, circles, arcs, polygons, and freehand drawings. You can shadow objects with a variety of patterns or shades, and paint areas with colors.
- *presentation tools:* output can go to dot matrix, laser jet and color printers, plotters and film recorders. You can assemble the screens into a screen show with special effects such as scrolls, wipes and fades, and then place the resulting slide show on a diskette for presentation on any VGA PC. This same slide show could be used for mass distribution as information to staff on a LAN or as a diskette used as a marketing tool.

5.9.3 Types of Software Available

The following presentation graphic software runs under Microsoft's Windows:

ALDUS PERSUASION FOR WINDOWS
Aldus Corp.
Seattle, WA 98104
(800) 628-2320

HOLLYWOOD
Claris Corp.
Santa Clara, CA 95052
(408) 987-7000

HARVARD GRAPHICS FOR WINDOWS
Software Publishing Corp.
Santa Clara, CA 95056
(408) 986-8000

FREELANCE GRAPHICS FOR WINDOWS
Lotus Development Corp.
Atlanta, GA 30342
(404) 394-8718

STANFORD GRAPHICS FOR WINDOWS
3-D Visions Corp.
Houston, TX 77042-4598
(800) 222-4675

The April 15, 1994 issue of *Datamation* has a "Monthly Roster of Best-Selling Software," which rates the graphic software as follows:

1. Harvard Graphics from Software Publishing
2. Freelance Graphics from Lotus
3. PowerPoint from Microsoft
4. ABC Flowcharter from Micrografx
5. Visio from Shapeware

5.10   PERSONAL INFORMATION MANAGERS

Generally, personal information managers provide a daily scheduler with alarms for appointments, a dialer and phone log, and an address book. Often this software runs only on the client machine. Since it is personal, there is no need to run it on the server. It has been included here because the client machines for both development and production will probably have additional capacity available. Additionally, since one of the facilities of personal information managers is calendaring, a client/server application could be a common calendar for a business unit.

5.10.1   Personal Information Managers as a Client/Server Application

The office calendar is a valuable client/server application. Scheduling for conference rooms can be handled through this application, with all personnel having access and booking capability. If all personnel use the calendar to book their business day, arranging meetings can be simplified; just check each attendee's availability and book a common available time.

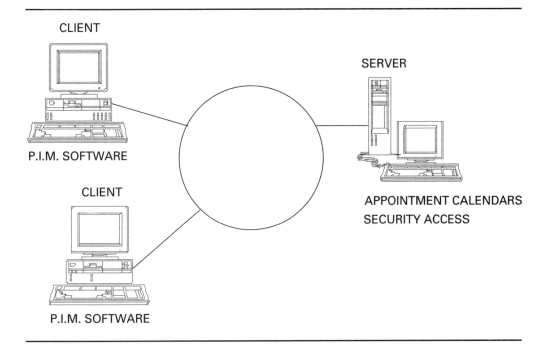

CLIENT

SERVER

P.I.M. SOFTWARE

CLIENT

APPOINTMENT CALENDARS
SECURITY ACCESS

P.I.M. SOFTWARE

Figure 5.14

In this application, the server holds the appointment calendars and is responsible for access security. The client runs the personal information management software (see Figure 5.14).

5.10.2   Features

Personal information managers software products have the following facilities:

- *information management:* they provide the tools to manage appointments, letters, notes, people, phone calls, tasks, and travel expenses.
- *calendar/scheduling:* the software provides an alarm to alert you when it is time for a specific scheduled event. The calendar information is stored by the day and by time of day. Some software supports flexible, cyclical scheduling; recurring events can be entered on a weekly, biweekly, monthly, quarterly, and yearly basis.

- *reporting:* you can create customized headers and footers, adjust margins, and print using different fonts to provide a printed copy of these calendars. This could be useful in a practice where events are scheduled for the professional, for example, in a large medical or legal practice.
- *other features:* by using scripts, you can automatically log on to electronic mail at an outside source and check your in-box. The software provides various calculators, such as simple business, scientific, and programmer calculators.

5.10.3   Types of Software Available

The following is a list of some of the personal information managers that run under Microsoft's Windows.

ASCEND
   Franklin Quest
   Salt Lake City, UT 84119
   (801) 975-9992

COMMENCE
   Jensen-Jones
   Red Bank, NJ 07701
   (908) 530-4666

DESKTOP SET
   Okna
   Paramus, NJ 07652
   (201) 909-8600

ECCO PROFESSIONAL
   Arabesque Software
   Bellevue, WA 98005-1754
   (206) 869-9600

INSTANT RECALL
   Cronologic
   Tucson, AR 85704
   (602) 293-3100

LOTUS ORGANIZER
   Lotus
   Cambridge, MA 02142
   (617) 577-8500

PACKRAT
   Polaris Software
   San Diego, CA 92128-3401
   (619) 592-7400

5.11   MULTIMEDIA

Multimedia adds video, animation, and sound capabilities to existing text and graphics products to make applications come alive. Multimedia aims to bridge the best technologies of computers and consumer electronics to provide users with powerful but easy-to-

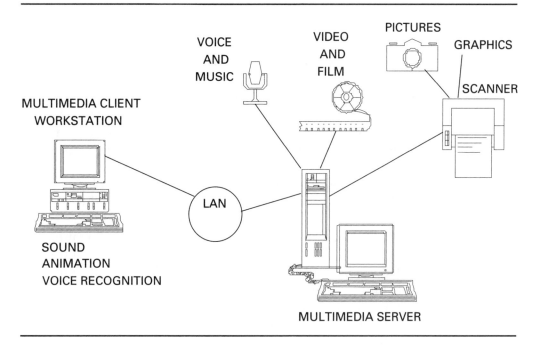

Figure 5.15

use information presentation applications (see Figure 5.15). The best examples of the by-products of this technology are the CD-ROMs that have been released containing education and information from a to z, anatomy to zodiac. Since multimedia makes use of audio, video, film, graphics, animation, and so forth as part of the application, any PC that will run this application must have some basic components in place: a sound board and speakers, a high-quality monitor, high-speed disk access (to retrieve frames or images at the rate of 30 per second to support video or animation) or CD/ROM and a high-speed CPU.

5.11.1   Multimedia Applications

Multimedia can be applied to many different application requirements. Because the cost to both produce and run multimedia is still on the high side, cost-justifiable solutions are harder to identify. Some of the solutions already in use include:

- *school education:* multimedia is an excellent tool for education. The limitations are probably cost based, depending upon budget constraints.
- *corporate education:* multimedia is well suited for training with routine or repetitive types of tasks.
- *police department:* the police are using multimedia technology to access and view mug shots. With CD-ROM as a portable file for mug shots, these could be shared between many police departments throughout the county, state, and other jurisdictions.
- *audio-visual production:* the multimedia development facilities are sophisticated enough to create productions for marketing, sales support, and advertising.
- *information kiosks:* another application is public information kiosks that educate people about various state and federal institutions and procedures. The state of California is planning to install 20,000 to 30,000 PC-based kiosks. As part of the state's Info California project, the kiosks are intended to help agencies and citizens more quickly expedite processes such as paying traffic fines, renewing licenses, and finding out how to get welfare services.
- *video conference:* the concept is to provide a full-motion video conference in a dial-up mode. The additional piece of equipment required in this situation is a video camera or video capture facilities at all conference locations.

5.11.2   Networking Multimedia

Networking multimedia as a client/server application is another matter. The multimedia presentation itself consists of many individual graphic images to support video and animation and even non-motion graphics; each of these images is a 40–100,000-byte file. Moving these images across the network at high speed and high volume presents a traffic problem. It would be difficult to have the network provide all the images necessary for a real-time execution of the application on a client. Running many clients simultaneously would degrade response time to an unacceptable level.

One improvement is to use compression software and hardware in such a way that the images can be stored in a compressed state while being transported through the LAN and then decompressed at the client workstation. Compression software alone usually will not provide the necessary response time to support 15 or 30 frames per second for video or animation. Therefore, both the server and all multimedia clients must have compression/decompression boards. A second improvement would be to store the application on the server, load it onto the client prior to run time, and then use the client's individual hardware resources to provide the needed response time. Each client in the client/server multimedia environment must have a minimum hardware configuration including adequate sound, VGA monitor, CPU and hard disk speeds.

The server in this environment can take on other responsibilities. For example, in applications such as training, the server would gather information about the students, such as answers, scores, time to take the course, and so forth. If the application was to train students in mechanical repair, the server could store information such as the number of attempts and the time required to complete the task. At this point the information could be retrieved and analyzed to determine what users are learning, problem areas within the course material, and so forth.

5.11.3   Multimedia Development

Development of a multimedia application starts with a well-thought-out script that organizes the production. You then collect all the appropriate media for the production, including scanned documents, bit maps, video stills, full-motion video, and audio segments. Note that the visual clarity of scanned documents and pictures may not be satisfactory.

The following tools assist in creating multimedia application solutions. The functions that they provide, whether they run on Windows and/or the Macintosh and their price vary.

AUTHORWARE, ACTION,
& DIRECTOR
   Macromedia
   San Francisco, CA 94103
   (415) 252-2000

ICON AUTHOR
AimTech
Nashua, NH 03063
(603) 883-0220

COMPEL
    Asymetrix
    Bellevue, WA 98004
    (800) 448-6543

ASTOUND
    Gold Disk
    Santa Clara, CA 95054
    (800) 982-9888

Q/MEDIA
    Q/Media
    Vancouver, B.C., Canada
    V5TIH4
    (604) 879-1190

SPECIAL DELIVERY
    Interactive Media Corp.
    Los Altos, CA 94023-0089
    (415) 948-0745

MOVIEWORKS
    Interactive Solutions
    San Mateo, CA 94402
    (415) 377-0136

CINEMATION
    Vividus
    Palo Alto, CA 94306
    (415) 321-2221

They provide the following facilities:

- *programming:* the first requirement is that the software integrates the many different media elements into a presentation. It should have editing, variables, flowchart, printing, and real-time debugging capabilities.
- *media and data tools:* the software needs to create and manipulate data, import ASCII text and audio, create backgrounds, buttons and text objects. It should provide tools that enhance images, edit video, and manipulate graphic files.
- *animation:* the software should be able to display and control the smoothness of the action and the speed and direction of objects. The editing and transition capability should include effects such as fade, wipe, zoom, transparency, and object rotation.
- *linking to applications:* the software should provide hooks to leave the authoring package and perform other functions and return. This assists during the development process to prepare additional input for the presentation.
- *platform portability:* the software should be able to create a presentation that can run on DOS, Microsoft's Windows, Macintosh, and Unix platforms.

The final product is delivered on disk or CD-ROM. Since the amount of data displayed in a multimedia application is usually very large because it includes graphics and motion, disk capacity requirements may be significant. CD-ROM can deliver high-speed access without imposing on disk space, but creating a CD-ROM can be expensive. Using a service bureau to create your CD-ROM costs $1,000–$2,000 for the master and then $1–$1.50 per CD copy. The alternative is to purchase a CD-ROM writer; a high-quality CD-ROM writer is priced in the range of $10,000–$15,000.

One final note: input video is also a concern. It requires a special interface that is best accomplished by using a video capture board in the development PC. The following vendor provides a video capture board with software that runs under Microsoft's Windows:

VIDEOSPIGOT FOR WINDOWS
Creative Labs
Milpitas, CA 95035
(408) 428-6600

5.12   PROJECT MANAGEMENT SOFTWARE

There are many project management PC-based software products on the market. Those that are PC-based tend to be used at a single client workstation. Other, more powerful software exists that will adequately handle every need for large-scale project management.

In the client/server environment (see Figure 5.16), the server performs the following:

- *maintains the project management database:* this database may suffice for all corporate planning or may simply be one of many. It may be for a single department which is then interfaced to a centralized project management database.
- *printing:* shared printing can be done at the network printer. High-quality printing is required for most project management output, especially for graphs and charts, and is best done on a laserjet printer, which is usually shared on the LAN.
- *software licensing:* licensing discounts are based on multiple concurrent users on the LAN. The software is stored on the server and concurrent usage restrictions are implemented on the server.

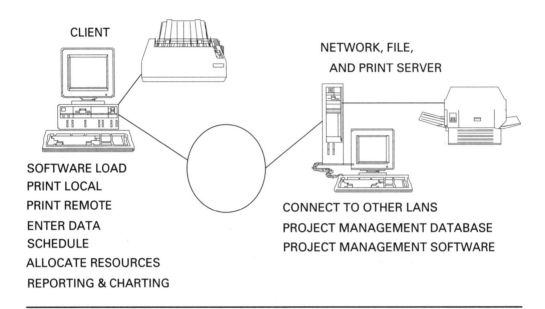

CLIENT

NETWORK, FILE,
AND PRINT SERVER

SOFTWARE LOAD
PRINT LOCAL
PRINT REMOTE
ENTER DATA
SCHEDULE
ALLOCATE RESOURCES
REPORTING & CHARTING

CONNECT TO OTHER LANS
PROJECT MANAGEMENT DATABASE
PROJECT MANAGEMENT SOFTWARE

Figure 5.16   Project Management Software

5.12.1   What They Offer

High-end project management software products provide the following:

- *large capacity for project plans:* if you are going to plan very large projects or run a small corporation with automated project plans, these software tools are useful.
- *consolidate many projects:* data can be collected from department managers, team leaders, and others throughout the organization. These software packages have the ability to consolidate many projects and access these projects via LANs or enterprise networks.
- *planning, scheduling, and tracking:* the software provides basic project management facilities. Additionally, these products let you control various scheduling options, such as project calendars and imposed dates. Also, multi-project scheduling is integrated into the software facilities.
- *reporting and charts:* the software packages provide what

you would expect of any project management software tool in text and graphic form including Gantt charts. Customized reporting facilities are available so that whatever your needs may be, they can be satisfied.

- *import and export:* you can export and import data to and from hosts, LAN databases, and project management subsidiary databases distributed throughout a network. Most of these applications are built on an industry-standard database such as SQLBase or Oracle. Therefore, you can write your own interface as required to import and to automatically update the database, based on project status information or export data for specialized reporting requirements.
- *cost management:* the products provide entry of billing rates and then calculate costs based on resource usage. During the project and upon completion, performance can be measured by comparing baseline estimates to actual costs.
- *resource control:* you can put resources in different categories, each with a unique calendar. Resources can be allocated in different ways so that modelling or what ifs can be done.

5.12.2   Products Available

There are a few products available in the market place. They have different features and therefore need to be reviewed thoroughly before a purchase is made. The following products are for large-scale project management.

ARTEMIS PRESTIGE
　　Lucas Management Systems
　　Fairfax, VA 22033
　　(703) 222-1111

OPEN PLAN
　　Welcom Software Technology
　　Houston, TX 77079
　　(713) 558-0514

PARISS ENTERPRISE
　　Computer Aided Management
　　Petaluma, CA 94954
　　(707) 795-4100

PRIMAVERA PROJECT PLANNER
Primavera Systems Inc.
Bala Cynwyd, PA
(215) 667-8600 19004

PROJECT WORKBENCH
Applied Business Technology Corp.
New York, NY 10013
(212) 219-8945

The following products will handle small to medium-range projects. They are also capable of handling more than one simultaneously.

MICROSOFT'S PROJECT
Microsoft Corp.
Redmond, WA 98052
(800) 426-9400

CA SUPER PROJECT
Computer Associates Inc.
Islandia, NY 11788-7000
(516) 342-5224

5.13   COMMUNICATIONS SOFTWARE

Communications software allows the user to upload and download almost any type of information from a variety of sources, such as remote PCs, mainframes, bulletin boards, information services, and so forth. The typical client/server setup would have a server(s) that contained the modem and telephone line that would access the outside services. The greatest inconvenience is usually that each of these services requires special "hand shaking" to gain access, including a specialized sign-on sequence. This process can be stored as a predefined script with all of the hand shaking taking place without user intervention. These scripts would be stored on the communications server and be shared by all users.

Figure 5.17 outlines the basic client/server responsibilities in this software solution.

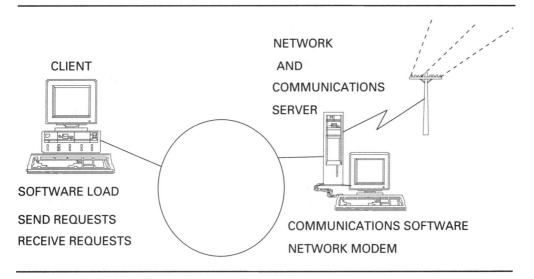

Figure 5.17   Communications Applications

5.13.1   What They Offer

Communications software products offer the following:

- *scripting:* a scripting language is available that will allow you to write complete conversations with automated key-strokes to access mainframes, bulletin boards, information services, and so forth. These languages are often powerful enough to run an entire activity without operator intervention; you can upload or download a file automatically based on a time of day. You can sign on to a facility, do an inquiry, extract information, and store that information on your PC. This can be done without operator intervention.
- *terminal emulation:* these software products provide a wide selection of terminals that they emulate, such as VT52, VT100, CompuServe, and TTY. These are necessary if you will be accessing a variety of outside services, such as CompuServe and MCI Mail.
- *file transfer:* these products support ASCII file transfer. These protocols include Xmodem, Ymodem, Kermit, Zmodem, and CompuServe B. Some of them even provide

for host-initiated download capability, which would provide for overnight distribution of software, data, reports, and so forth to LANs throughout the country.

- *modem support:* these products support most modems on the market through drivers that interface with their unique hand-shaking requirements. Since you can purchase a modem already supported by the software product, why should this be a concern? Because the real concern is the modem you are dialing into. Most of these vendors will work with you and provide a special driver if you have a unique requirement. The modems can be accessed on your COM1 through COM4 ports, IBM Gateways, via SDLC, NetBIOS, and so forth. This means you can share your modem on the LAN, which is important if this is going to be a real client/server solution. Note that some of the software products listed below run on the client only and cannot support a shared modem on the LAN.

5.13.2 Products Available

The products listed below all run under Microsoft's Windows. The Windows environment, even though it provides for multiple applications running simultaneously, is not a multi-threaded environment like OS/2. Therefore, running a communications activity (such as a download) and then starting several other applications that require heavy processor time may lead to unpredictable results, such as lost data. Other than this concern, these software packages integrate well with windows and can provide the connectivity needed to support activities such as files loads, access to remote databases of information, and so forth.

RELAY GOLD FOR WINDOWS
  Microcom Inc.
  Norwood, MA 02062
  (617) 551-1000

TERMINAL PLUS
  FutureSoft Engineering Inc.
  Houston, TX 77079
  (713) 496-9400

UNICOM
Data Graphics
Renton, WA 98058
(206) 432-1201

CROSSTALK FOR WINDOWS
Digital Communications Associates Inc.
Alpharetta, GA 30202
(404) 442-4000

MICROPHONE II FOR WINDOWS
Software Ventures Corp.
Berkeley, CA 94705
(510) 644-3232

PROCOMM FOR WINDOWS
Datastorm Technologies Inc.
Columbia, MO 65201
(314) 443-3282

5.14   CLIENT/SERVER FAX SOLUTIONS

Sending and receiving faxes from your desktop workstation increases productivity. It eliminates making trips to and from the fax machine, waiting for availability, and then making sure the fax has been sent successfully. Even if the fax facility is handled as a clerical function, additional staffing is required. The electronic fax turns your LAN into a WAN via the phone system. Additionally, adding optical character recognition (OCR) capabilities allows you to convert the fax (only an image) to text to be included in other documents without retyping.

The advantages include printing faxes on regular paper instead of thermal paper, automatically printing incoming faxes or routing them to the intended destination (specific workstation), and providing statistics on faxes sent and received.

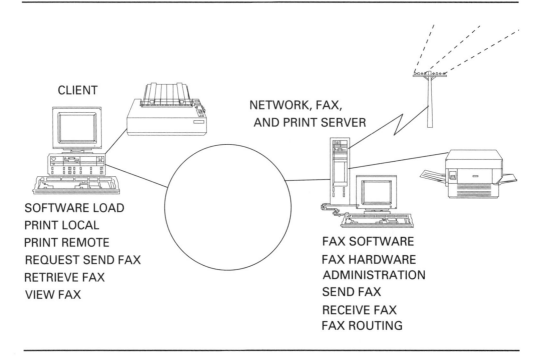

Figure 5.18   Fax Client/Server

Figure 5.18 outlines the individual client and server responsibilities in this shrink-wrapped solution. The fax software is usually held on the server, and any component required at the client is downloaded when the function is invoked. The client issues requests to send, receive, and print faxes; the server performs all other functions.

5.14.1   What They Offer

Generally, this type of software solution provides the following facilities:

- *administration:* they provide the ability to define user access. For example, there are three levels of user access: user, administrator, and supervisor. Users can send, hold, view, print, save, or discard their own messages (faxes). Administrators and supervisors have these privileges and more. They can view the first page of all incoming faxes, route faxes to other users, and delete faxes; they can add, delete, and manage users and groups of users; they can print and delete activity reports; they can set up the system to automatically print incoming faxes; they remotely manage the fax server. But the administrators and supervisors usually cannot print or route faxes to themselves for security reasons.

- *sending:* you can send a fax from within a word processor itself (for example, Microsoft's Word for Windows). The software usually accommodates sending tables, text and graphics, all integrated in a single fax. Additionally, these products provide a phone book facility for you to store all the numbers that you fax to.

- *viewing:* these software products can view a fax as a graphic image and then zoom in on the fax. This is important if the document contains a signature and you need to verify it, for example. The zoom will enable you to fill the screen with the signature. Additionally you can rotate the document 180 degrees, invert it (black background, white writing), and shrink it horizontally or vertically.

- *printing:* the fax can be printed on the LAN printer or a printer attached to the workstation. The printer should be a laser jet to reproduce the fax image. The exception would be if the fax was text only and had been run through an OCR to convert the entire fax to a text file from the original image. Some products allow you to print select pages from within a faxed document; they also provide the ability to print a group of faxes.

- *routing:* the software products provide automatic routing to individual workstations. Each user is assigned a routing code. Incoming faxes are routed to the individual user by the caller, who directs the fax to a specific routing id.

5.14.2   Products Available

The following software products provide some combination of the basic services listed above. Currently they run only under DOS or Microsoft's Windows. However, most of the vendors are working on a version that will run under OS/2.

CASTELLE FAXPRESS
    Castelle
    Santa Clara, CA 95054
    (408) 496-0474

OAZ NETFAX
    OAZ
    Fremont, CA 94539
    (510) 226-0171

INTEL NET SATISFAXTION
    Intel
    Beaverton, OR 97006
    (510) 226-0171

Additionally, there are products available that run in the background of the fax server. They can automatically convert the fax into text by using optical character recognition (OCR) software. When the software detects an incoming fax, it does the conversion and stores the fax in the format you requested (for example, as a word processing document). You can do this manually by first reviewing the fax and determining whether you want to translate it, and then running the OCR software as required. Some of the products available are listed below:

FAXGRABBER
    Calera Recognition Systems
       Inc.
    Sunnyvale, CA 94086
    (408) 720-0999

WINFAX PRO 3.0
    Delrina Technology Inc.
    San Jose, CA 95119
    (408) 363-2345

FAXIBILITY PLUS/OCR
    Intel Corp.
    Beaverton, OR 97006
    (503) 629-7402

ELIPSE
    Phoenix
    Chicago, IL 60602
    (312) 541-0260

FAXMASTER
    Caere Corp.
    Los Gatos, CA 95030
    (408) 395-5148

5.15 GUI SUITE/GROUPWARE SOLUTIONS

Up to this point we have covered shrink-wrapped application solutions or partial solutions in the client/server environment that require little or no applications development. These can be run as stand-alone applications on a PC, integrated into DOS-based menus much like a mainframe, or integrated in a GUI environment like Microsoft's Windows or IBM's OS/2 Presentation Manager. In the latter case, a variety of different "shrink-wrapped" solutions would be combined to run under this GUI interface. Since the GUI has a special look and feel, all of these applications will tend to be more similar than their DOS counterparts.

5.15.1   What They Offer

Vendors are beginning to package a variety of software applications, word processing, spreadsheet, graphics, mail, and so forth into a "suite" of software that is sold as one package running under Microsoft's Windows, for example. The pros and cons are as follows:
Pros:

- *many for the price of one:* these software suites are usually priced in such a way that the combination of software packages are sold at a combined price that is far less than the discounted price of the individual components.
- *simplified problem resolution:* since all of the software components are from a single vendor, if you have a problem only one phone call has to be made to get help. Secondly, if there are interface problems (for example, between a spreadsheet and word processor), there cannot be finger pointing, as there might be if two different vendors were involved.
- *simplified license tracking:* corporations have always had difficulty tracking software with individual PCs on which it is licensed. The more software, the more difficult the tracking. If four or five software packages are rolled into one license instead of four or five, license tracking is simpler and easier.
- *common user interface:* when you choose a variety of applications from different vendors, even though they may all run under windows, they tend not to work the same way. The user must be acclimated to multiple, different interfaces. Multiple software packages from the same vendor will tend to have the same user interface.
- *one-stop shopping:* sometimes product comparison is difficult if there is a large variety of excellent choices. The pur-

chase process can also be time consuming if the corporation attempts to find the best price for each software component that is purchased individually or in small quantities.

Cons:

- *locked into one vendor:* whatever combination of software the vendor offers is the only choice you have. Also, if the vendor is not easily accessible or responsive when problems arise, this lack of service applies to all products instead of only the one purchased from a specific vendor.
- *pricing may not be favorable:* if you are paying for various components in the suite that you will not be using, the suite price may no longer be attractive.
- *settling for second best:* since these suites are a family of products from one vendor, the "best" software in a particular application (for example, word processing or spreadsheet) may not be in that vendor's product line.
- *may not be complete:* The suite may not offer a complete solution for your workstations. If you purchase additional components separately, you still have all the problems of integrating and tracking various pieces of software.
- *one-stop shopping:* this may not be difficult if it is done at the corporate level with an eye toward simplicity.

Additionally, a workgroup synergy is emerging within these product sets to include common scheduling (via common calendars) and document routing (sequentially or broadcast style) to provide some basic form of workflow.

5.15.2 Alternative Vendors

At this time there are several vendors which supply suite or groupware solutions as follows:

MICROSOFT OFFICE
Microsoft Corp.
Redmond, WA 98052
(800) 426-9400

SMARTSUITE
Lotus Development Corp.
Atlanta, GA 30342
(404) 394-8718

OFFICE for WINDOWS
    Borland International
    Scotts Valley, CA 95066
    (800) 841-8180

LINKWORKS
    Digital Equipment Corp.
    Maynard, MA 01754
    (508) 493-5111

WORDPERFECT OFFICE
    WordPerfect Corp.
    Orem, UT 84057
    (800) 451-5151

Additionally, Lotus Notes is currently the best example groupware. Lotus Notes focuses on the sharing, organization, access and tracking of information (documents). It supports electronic group discussions, report distribution, tracking activities, managing projects and so forth. It can be used to support customer service, product development, account management and so forth. It does not itself contain the popular word processing, spread sheet, and E-mail software packages but can be customized to interface with them. Suites generally do not however provide document management capabilities to keep track of document flow throughout the organization; Lotus Notes does.

Some of the concerns with the product include:

- It uses a proprietary messaging backbone while other suite packages interface with common messaging protocols.
- It is built around a proprietary database model.
- It is a unique environment which requires user training.

LOTUS NOTES
    Lotus Development Corp.
    Atlanta, GA 30342
    (404) 394-8718

Designing Applications in the Client/Server Environment

Designing applications in the client/server environment is an issue complex enough to warrant a text by itself. This book introduces the reader to some of the concerns and alternatives.

Generally, the concern in the client/server environment is that developers are challenged with tasks that are new and different from those of the mainframe. In the mainframe environment, designers and developers are less concerned with the complexity of the hardware and software. In the PC/LAN environment, they need to be concerned about how the hardware and software components will interact with the application and their impact on user response time. Also, in the client/server environment the process is controlled by the user; this is a very different approach than in the mainframe, where the processes are controlled by the application. Client and server machine configurations will tend to differ; even though this should not influence the overall design and implementation, it may. This new environment requires a new way of thinking on the part of designers and developers:

- They can no longer isolate application issues from platform issues.
- They need to be flexible in design. Platform changes and user exposure to this new environment will cause more design changes than in a traditional environment.

- They need to make data-distribution decisions that are based on response time, amount of data, and user access requirements.
- Utilities need to be developed (for example, data transfer between mainframe and LAN to satisfy cooperative processing applications as well as distributed data needs).
- User security in this environment for the client, LAN access, data access, and so forth will require custom solutions.
- Coordination with LAN administrators is needed on issues of application requirements on the client and server machines.
- Coordination with data administrators is needed on issues of data security, distribution, access requirements, and so forth.

6.1   GENERAL DESIGN CONSIDERATIONS

The following is a general set of considerations for the design of the client/server application. The idea is to keep the client small and simple so that the machine and software cost is minimized and the complexity is limited to the server not the client:

- *client primary responsibility—user interface:* the front end client machine should simply provide the user interface. The less applications code on the machine, except as it affects response time, the better.
- *server responsibility—back end processor:* this is where the bulk of the application services are performed. Servers should provide the following: database services, gateway services, shared file access, print services, and so forth.
- *fully loaded server machines:* purchase top-end servers if you can afford to do so; these servers will be able to do the processing for many low-end client machines. The server should be the fastest machine possible, with extra memory for caching, extra disk for expansion and backup, the best and fastest gateway access, quality print facilities, and so forth.
- *use transaction-driven database services:* these transactions should be an all-or-nothing set of operations. If all operations complete successfully, the transaction is marked completed. If a single operation fails, the entire transaction is backed out and marked as not completed.

- *access the server logically, not physically:* the server's inner workings should be transparent to the client. The less the client knows about them, the better the programming and resulting application. The SQL servers discussed in a prior chapter are a prime example of logical access software.
- *partition for multi-tasking:* wherever possible, take advantage of multi-tasking features that are available to speed up services. The RDBMS servers covered in a prior chapter, for example, will take advantage of the multi-tasking facilities of your servers. It is up to you to design your applications to take advantage of the RDBMS software. For example, design your applications in such a way that bulk database work is done on the server as remote procedure calls rather than done on the client.
- *use LAN technology:* LANs, when configured properly, are high-speed and low-cost connections between clients and servers.
- *use maintenance and configuration tools:* client/server applications are by nature complex to install and maintain. Wherever possible, consider the tools necessary to support the environment as part of the basic design.
- *use off-the-shelf "shrink-wrapped" solutions:* don't "reinvent the wheel." As we stated in a prior chapter, many excellent solutions already exist. Integrate them with your application during the design stage. Spreadsheet, word processing, electronic mail, text search, fax, and communication software can all be integrated into your client/server application solution.

6.1.1   Security Issues

Generally, the PC is more vulnerable than mainframe terminals. It is an intelligent device and therefore it is in jeopardy itself. It also has access to all servers on the LAN, the mainframe, and so forth (see Figure 6.1). Chapter 9 covers the issue of security more thoroughly. This chapter discusses some basic issues, especially those that should be considered during the design phase, as follows:

- *physical security:* physical security may be necessary, especially for highly sensitive decision support system applications that house cooperate data on specific clients for

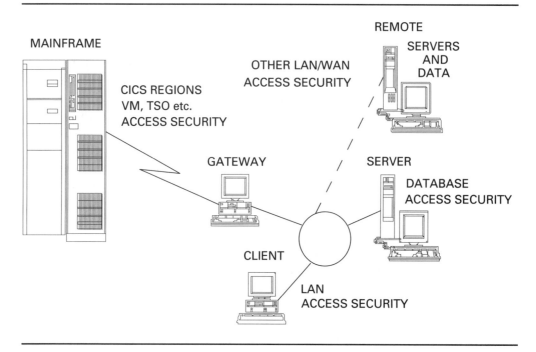

Figure 6.1

analysis. Check corporate data security policies as they pertain to data resident on PCs in general. If necessary, use locked rooms and locked keyboards as a means to secure client machines. Servers, as a matter of course, should be in a secure room.

- *PC security:* the PC/workstation itself presents a unique problem. Although you can install a piece of software in the workstation to check for a sign on (for example, AUTOEXEC.BAT points to LAN logon requiring an ID and password), a "boot" diskette" can be used to bypass that security. Software does exist to secure a PC from a "boot diskette."
- *LAN security:* all LAN Network Operating Systems have built-in security facilities that limit access to LANs, servers, directories, files, and so forth. This should probably be used as a basis for implementing security for the client/ server applications. If the same LAN ID and password can

be used for mainframe access as well, you can limit the user confusion.

- *RDBMS SQL servers:* the RDBMS software you will use provides various levels of data security. Review carefully to determine how they can effectively be integrated with the LAN security and your applications.
- *single system sign on:* in the client/server application you will need authorization to access the LAN, the data on the database server (authorization by database, table, row, and so forth), the mainframe and each application on it (as well as security within the application for example, by function). If many of these components require individual security or sign ons, their combined complexity will tend to encourage the user to write down the sign ons and passwords and have them handy, thereby defeating the entire security idea.
- *available security software:* currently, a universal security software solution is not available on the market. However, some of the generally accepted mainframe security facilities are addressing all of the WAN, LAN, and PC concerns. Research the available commercial alternatives before you develop your own security software.
- *virus checking:* perhaps the single most visible security concern in most organizations are viruses that are easily introduced on a single workstation and then begin to encroach upon the LAN, the workstations on it, and all the other CPUs the LAN accesses (for example, other LANs and mainframes). Since the workstations are intelligent, simply loading on or running an infected piece of software can start the problem. The client/server application should be designed to accommodate a built-in virus check. For example, use a shrink-wrapped virus check program boot process for the PC. This will check for a virus each time the client station is booted. Further processing should be halted if a virus is detected. Additionally, the LAN servers should be inspected daily, perhaps as an overnight job, with alerts issued when a virus has been detected.

Most of the time the developer has to custom program a solution in order to meet auditing requirements. So the best advice is to keep it simple, solve as many problems as possible by using existing software solutions, and limit the number of IDs and passwords a user requires. Remember, the more comprehensive the solution, the more difficult maintenance may become.

6.1.2 Operational Versus Decision Support System Issues

Operational systems and decision support systems (DSS) frequently share information on the mainframe. They also share the CPU. In the client/server environment this may be a concern because the shared resources can degrade the overall processing.

Operational systems (applications) work with current data that is constantly changing, whereas decision support systems (applications) operate on historical data that does not change.

Let's consider an example of an order processing system. The orders themselves throughout their life cycle—which includes entry, fulfillment, and payment—are all part of the operational database. Once the order has been fulfilled and paid for, the data can be viewed as historical; no more changes will be applied.

Consider Figure 6.2. The operational data is stored and maintained on the SQL server. All clients access that server, performing activities such as order entry (from phone, mail or fax requests), inventory control, order fulfillment, billing, customer services, and the like. Each of these functions and other services are performed by personnel who require immediate response (especially telephone-based services). The data is dynamic and accurate up until the most recent inquiry.

Now consider the same application data used in a decision support system. Consider Figure 6.3. The order processing data could reside on the mainframe, with the order processing system entirely mainframe based, or it could reside on an SQL server on a LAN. Let's consider a pricing DSS application that takes all of the fulfilled order information as well as customer information in order to derive new market potential and pricing for the following year. The data required is all historical, but it traverses much of the order processing database.

In a mainframe environment, multiple data extractions might be run until the right data population has been selected. The impact on the mainframe-based operational system is usually minimal.

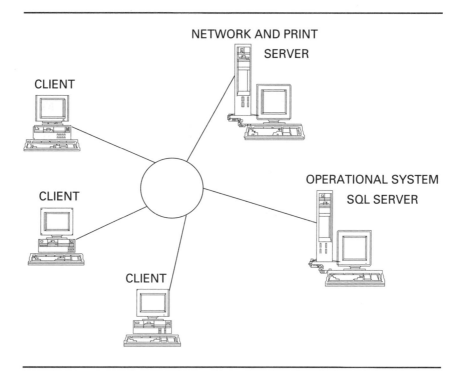

Figure 6.2   Operational System Data and Processing

Now let's consider the same DSS application operating on the SQL server. The client iteratively extracts data and operates on it. Since the data is substantive, there can be an impact on LAN traffic, SQL server access, and so forth.

Generally, the design guideline is logical and physical separation of operational and DSS data and processing. This includes physically separating the DSS data from the operating data. For example, place the DSS data on the client, not on the operational server. Also, as a simple approach to separating the processing as well, do all data extracts directly from the SQL server, but do them off hours when there is little impact on the LAN and SQL server.

One of the considerable advantages of the client/server environment is adhoc query capability. Many tools exist that provide easy access to the data. These tools can be easily understood and invoked by users as well as programmers. However, if they are

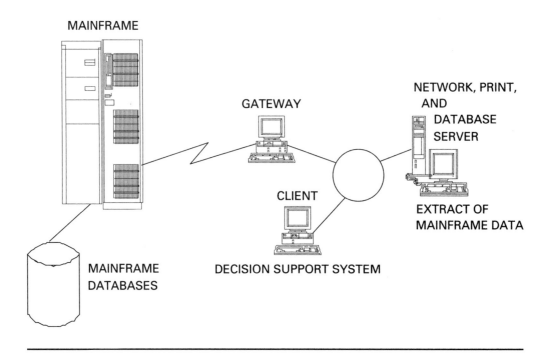

MAINFRAME

GATEWAY

NETWORK, PRINT, AND DATABASE SERVER

CLIENT

EXTRACT OF MAINFRAME DATA

MAINFRAME DATABASES

DECISION SUPPORT SYSTEM

Figure 6.3   Decision Support System Data and Processing

accessing operational system data, they should be considered DSS systems. They have the same potential impact.

Using data to serve both operational and decision support systems can lead to:

- data maintenance bottlenecks (DSS operating on operational data)
- performance bottlenecks
- unnecessary application complexity

6.1.3   System of Record Concerns

What is the system of record (SOR)? This is simply the concept that, at any one time, one and only one node is responsible for updating a piece of information. In a client/server environment the SOR should be defined during system design. The system of record may take various forms (see Figure 6.4):

- *client/server LAN system of record:* this is the simplest and most popular client/server application design. In this case data is stored exclusively on the LAN server.
- *mainframe system of record:* each transaction must go to the host in a cooperative mode to access data. Response time is a major issue. Using the mainframe as the system of record for a client/server application is problematic. Under the right design circumstances or for specialized applications it may be acceptable. The most important factor is response time. Since all data must pass through the communications network as well as the LAN and gateway, the response will be slower than on the client/server LAN by itself.

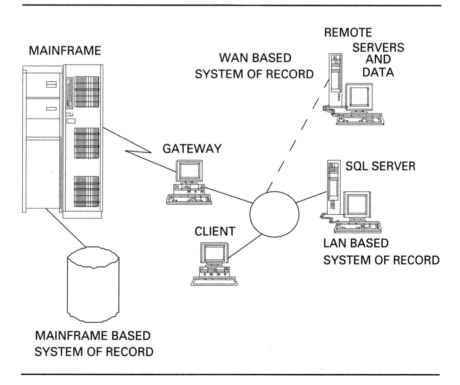

Figure 6.4   System of Record

If the application is data entry and many PC screens are traversed prior to a single mainframe update, this may be an acceptable configuration. If the application has been designed to minimize communications to the mainframe (for example, one mainframe transaction for every four PC transactions) and the data transfer is minimized to keep the response time good, this may be an acceptable configuration. An extremely large database may necessitate the use of the mainframe as the data repository, for example, a corporate-wide client/customer database.

* *multiple LANs and mainframe system of record:* A more complex version of SOR is one across multiple LANs and includes the mainframe. Requirements may be such that the majority of the data for an application is housed on the mainframe because of size and access requirements, but remote LANs exist and require data to reside on those LANs for performance reasons. In this case the data must be partitioned in such a way that each of these nodes is the SOR for a piece of the business, with no overlap. Each node can request information from the other and can request an update of that information, but the actual update takes place on the SOR itself.

The location of data should be transparent to the client/server application. This is usually made possible by the RDBMS software that we covered in an earlier chapter. However, the actual data requirements to meet performance objectives may require special utilities to satisfy the application. The requirements should be identified and satisfied during the design phase.

For example, let's consider a manufacturing application with two sales regions on either coast of the United States and an order processing facility in the Midwest. Each location has a LAN to service their individual operational needs. Where should the SOR be located? One implementation scheme that is geared to performance would separate the West Coast sales data from the East Coast sales data, with each location being the SOR for their respective section of the country. The order processing center in the Midwest could be the SOR for order processing data for the entire country. They can either take a daily or more frequent upload of sales and order data from each sales region for informational purposes (improved access and response time performance) but the individual sales regions still retain the SOR responsibility.

The best direction to take is to consider isolating data and processing per LAN, based on the following:

- *design based on organizational use:* the objective is to design the node(s) of residency along organizational lines, which may be corporate headquarters, subsidiary headquarters, and so forth.
- *design based on functional departments:* if an organization is based on functional responsibilities/departments, node residency might best be organized along departmental lines, focusing on the business responsibilities of that department, as in our example of the sales offices separate from the order processing location.
- *design based on geography:* if the organization is structured along geographical lines, as in our prior example, node residency should be split geographically (by region).

6.2   DATABASE DESIGN ISSUES

The following topics focus on database design issues in the client/ server development environment. Some of these issues are similar to issues that must be addressed in the mainframe development process but, where appropriate, the specific concerns within the client/server environment have been emphasized.

6.2.1   Data Partitioning

Data partitioning refers to breaking large databases up into distinct and separate physical units. Each "partition of data" has the same structural definition but contains a different range of the data than the other partitions. Data can then be spread across different nodes, servers, LANs, WANs, mini's, or mainframe (see Figure 6.5).

The data is defined the same way on each node but is joined together using a database vendor-supplied partitioning utility. For example, if all data is under an SQL server with one common shrink-wrapped software, the vendor (see section on database servers) often supplies a partitioning interface that is transpar-

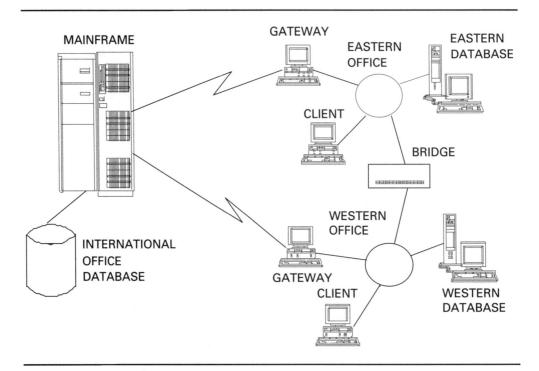

Figure 6.5   Data Partitioning

ent to the programmer. That is, the SQL request is made in a program without knowing where the data resides and the database interface determines where it will be serviced. The other alternative is that the developer writes an interface routine to access the data on various databases within the LAN and outside the LAN (another LAN or a mainframe). This second alternative is not desirable, because any change to the residency of the database means a change to application code to point to the new location.

The database designer should consider the need for partitioning during the design phase. Some of the reasons that data partitioning may be desirable include:

- *data size:* the production data may be too large to be contained on one server. For example, the server's hard disk is 300 meg to 500 meg but the data is one gigabyte in size.
- *efficiency:* the data may be highly volatile and require fre-

quent updates, the data may be accessed frequently due to a large client base, or the server may be required to service time-consuming access requests. In each case the solution, for performance reasons, may suggest partitioning the data. Estimates during the design stage may indicate that a single server is adequate, but live production experiences, with a large user base and frequency of access, may reduce response time to an unacceptable level. Partitioning the data will improve the response time.

- *data in the proximity of the user:* if the user base and operational needs are uniquely located in different locations, data partitioning may be appropriate. If, for example, there are four operating regions in the country and each has its own LAN and each operates mostly on its own data, it may be practical to design a partitioned database with each region holding its own data but still having access to the other regions' data via LAN bridges or routers. The local SQL server should make accessing the data at the other locations transparent.

Consider partitioning the data, if any of the above concerns are encountered during the design phase.

6.2.2   Encoding/Decoding Data

Encoding data is simply compressing and decompressing information that can be stored in tabular form. Simple examples of encoding information include the two-digit abbreviation for a state (decoded to the full state name), the two-digit representation of a month (decoded to the full name of the month), and M/F for male and female. The encoded and decoded arguments are stored in a table. Only encoded data is stored on the database. The encode/decode table is then used to interpret the data on the database (see Figure 6.6).

If this is to be a universal function within the application, a database should be built consisting of a series of tables. Each table would represent a data type and contain all of the encoded and corresponding decoded values for that data type. An example would be all 50 states and their two-character abbreviations. This is a much better approach than embedding these tables within the

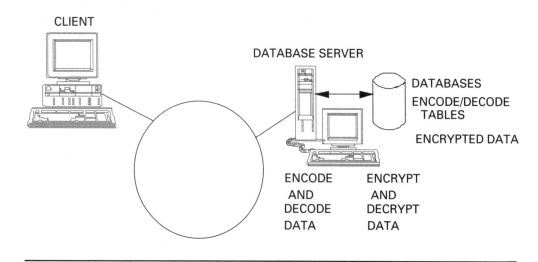

Figure 6.6   Encode/Decode and Encrypt/Decrypt

application or, worse yet, hardcoding them within the code itself. In these latter cases, if the table requires modification (add, delete, or change table entries), the table must then be modified in multiple places and also may require changing the application. The most typical mainframe solution is to store the encode and decode values in a copybook which is then included in every program that references the information: for example, edit and display programs. All programs using this copybook must then be recompiled whenever the copybook changes.

The following are some of the pros of encoded/decoded data:

- *reduced database size:* if all data on the database were carried as full information, the databases would out of necessity be much larger. Just think about carrying the full state name wherever it was used. Additionally, there is usually a large amount of application-related data that falls into the encode/decode scheme.
- *common values for disparate applications:* with one database of encode/decode values you eliminate variations on different applications and even within a single application.

The following are some of the cons of encoded/decoded data:

- *it can be complex and difficult to maintain:* this centralized encode/decode database must be designed, data gathered and entered, a maintenance function implemented, and so forth. Even if a "centralized" encode/decode database is planned, copies will need to exist on each database server and on the mainframe because this data will be accessed heavily. This means that updates must be done at the system of record and then distributed to all copies of the database.
- *it can have a negative effect on response time:* since this central database of encode/decode values must be referenced by any screen wishing to display or update an encoded value, the I/O to the database can be prohibitive.

6.2.3   Data Encryption/Decryption

Encryption algorithms store data in a non-readable form and then use decryption algorithms to reinterpret the data in readable form. This is done most frequently in such a way that a casual viewer of the data in its backup form or any other form cannot read the data. Examples include passwords and sometimes human resource and payroll information.

With this technology, data is made unreadable as it is being stored on the database or file (see Figure 6.6). The data is modified by using an algorithm that is not available to the general development staff in such a way that the data is no longer readable (encryption). The encrypted data is decrypted back to usable form by a separate routine. The source code for these routines is generally secured within the organization and the decryption module invoked only with the proper authorization (for example, on the SQL server only). The data can remain encrypted as it traverses a LAN, MAN, or WAN and then decrypted on the client workstation. This prevents "listeners" from viewing sensitive corporate data as it travels through public transmission lines.

The following are some of the pros of encrypting/decrypting data:

- *secure information from viewing:* any sensitive information can be encrypted. The encryption and decryption routines are stored on the server and the appropriate security authorization for access protects against invoking those routines on an unauthorized basis.

The following are some of the cons of encrypting/decrypting data:

- *negative effect on response time:* the server must run special routines to both store and retrieve the data items that are to be encrypted or decrypted. Depending upon the amount of data to be manipulated and the frequency of access, this can degrade server usage and therefore response time.

6.2.4   Variable Length Data

Within the mainframe environment, DASD space is usually not a design concern issue for an operational system. For example, you would not generally be concerned about making a text field, such as a name, variable in length to save space. Disk capacity on a LAN via gigabyte servers is approaching that of the mainframe but it is not there yet. Additionally, access speed for large servers and delivery of the data via LAN is slower than the equivalent mainframe disk access combined with channel speed. Savings in data storage through design can impact the amount of information stored and access speed on the LAN.

Variable length data may appear to be a standard mainframe consideration but let's consider the client/server implications. Two types of variable information should be recognized:

- *variable data:* a single field may be larger or smaller, depending upon its content. A person's name is generally used as an example, but in the client/server application a variable text field is a better example. You can argue justifiably that a name field should be a fixed length because the data space to be saved is small. But if there is a 500-character text field that varies in length from 0–500 characters, the savings is significant if it is stored as variable data.
- *arrays:* arrays or simply multiple occurrences of information based on a variable is the other common type of variable data. Again there is a significant savings in space if

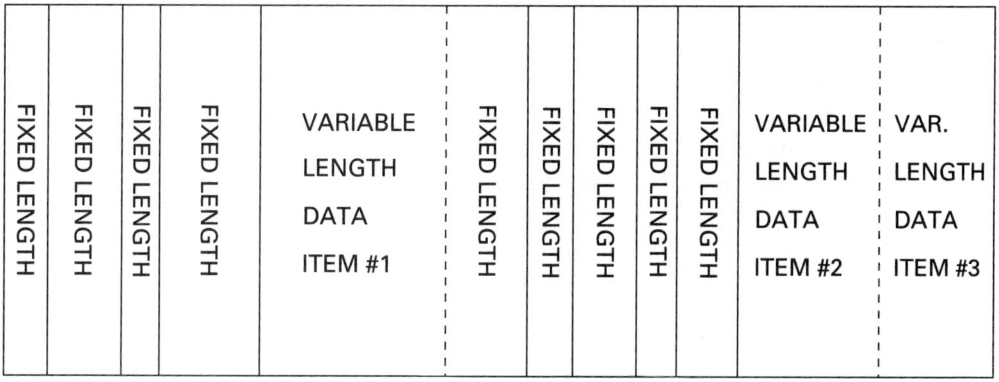

Figure 6.7 Variable Length Data

the number of occurrences varies greatly and the size of each occurrence is substantial.

As a general rule, variable data should always be placed at the end of the record or row. If there is only one variable field (data or array) at the end of the record, the variable piece can be programmed very much like a fixed field. Multiple variable fields in a record should be avoided because determining the starting position of each piece of data is made complex (see Figure 6.7).

An additional concern is that programming and development tools that make the client/server environment so desirable may not be able to handle the variable processing. The recommendation is that, before designing the database for the application, you should review the SQL server and tool set software to determine what will be supported and then design accordingly.

6.2.5   Meta Data

Meta data is information about data on the database. It describes the structure of data, attributes, physical characteristics, measurement, and so forth. Meta data includes the copybook of a record that describes each data item to some degree. It includes information such as editing criteria for the data element and information about how the data element should appear on a report or be displayed. Using the information in this data dictionary or repository, it is possible to build input screens, display windows, and create reports without writing specific code for each field. If development tools exist that interface with this data dictionary, the development process can be very efficient.

Ideally, a common facility to house this information, called a central repository or data dictionary, should be available on the LAN to establish and maintain this information for the entire client/server environment. This central repository should include the following:

- Table (file) and row (record) information, including keys, attributes, physical characteristics, structure of attributes, relationships between data structures, attribute units of measure, encoding/decoding information, compression/decompression information, default information, display or report presentation method, data element description, and so forth.

Some of the issues to consider are as follows:

- *highly accessible:* generally, meta data is necessary for all developers and also for designers and those doing documentation. It must therefore be readily available. This implies that if development is on the LAN the data dictionary should also be on the LAN.
- *restricted change capability:* once data structures are defined and are in use, change is complex and must be made carefully. Since the impact of a change potentially traverses existing screens, reports, programs, and so forth, changing the data dictionary needs to be restricted. Typically, a database administrator, perhaps at the corporate level, is charged with changing established definitions.
- *development tool compatibility:* if the dictionary is to be a major player in development, it should be integrated with the development environment and the development tool set.

6.2.6   Derived Data Considerations

Primitive data is accurate up to the second data that exists on the database as a single element; it is used to drive the day-today activities of a corporation. Each piece of primitive data is a single occurrence of a subject; for example, in a banking withdrawal transaction, date of withdrawal, amount of withdrawal, account number, and teller id are pieces of primitive data.

Derived data, on the other hand, is calculated or developed based on a number of primitive data elements and/or an algorithm applied to one or more primitive data elements. For example, interest on a bank account is calculated by using one or more interest rate(s), account balance(s), and the number of days in an interest period. Derived data must be calculated or developed each time it is referenced. Some of the client/server considerations are as follows:

- *store derived data:* if a calculated field requires a significant number of rows and/or columns and is accessed frequently, it may be better to store it on the database. Deriving the data each time may be too time consuming or costly (in terms of CPU cycles) on the server or workstation. The tradeoff, however, is that you must update the derived data element whenever a component of the calculation (derivation) changes.
- *derive on the server:* data derived by the SQL server is the ideal design situation. This limits potential errors that may take place if each client does its own calculation. However, there may be situations in which the server does not own all the elements to complete the derivation. Also, based on the efforts the server must expend to derive this data (number of times and complexity), the load may be too much.
- *derive on the client:* this can reduce the server load by placing the overhead on the client. Also, if the derivation process changes, it must be modified on all clients that reference that data.

6.2.7   Indexing Tables and Files

The pros and cons of indexing tables (see Figure 6.8) in your RDBMS client/server application can be stated simply as follows:

- *pros:* indicies provide the direct method of accessing data. In the absence of an index, data must be searched sequentially. If the data requested is, for example, in the row of that table,

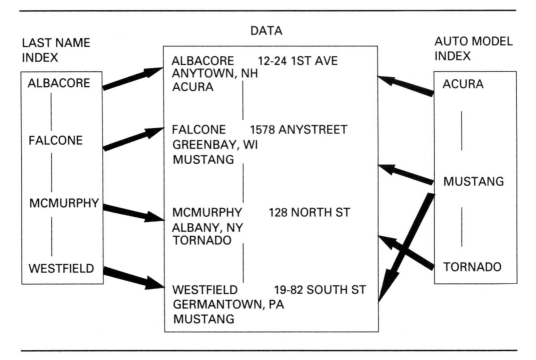

Figure 6.8   Indexed Table

all the data in the table must be read. This seems to imply that indicies should always be built and used.
- *cons:* for each update, deletion, or addition to data that is being indexed, the index itself must be updated. Because indicies require this overhead, additional time is spent maintaining them, thereby effecting response time. Moreover, additional space is required to house the indicies.

Since the client/server environment should target one second or less as the user response time, all server requests must be tuned to handle volume. The following indexing guidelines should be considered during the design phase:

- *many updates but limited access:* consider limiting the number of indicies to one or two. If the data is updated heavily (especially the data that is being indexed) and has limited access (especially the different ways it is accessed), the file (table) should have a limited number of indicies.

- *heavy access but limited updates:* consider creating more indices: for example, three or more. If data is accessed heavily (especially in varied ways) but has limited updates against it, the file (table) should have many indicies. This will speed access without incurring substantial overhead because the updates are light.
- *no indices:* lastly, some indices may not be effective. If, for example, the make of each car the customer owns is on the database, the number of makes may not warrant an index. A sequential search would be more effective.

6.3   PROGRAM DESIGN ISSUES

The following issues apply to program design. Similar to the database design issues, they are based on mainframe concepts but have been applied here to the client/server environment.

6.3.1   Multi-tasking

Multi-tasking is the running of more than one task/activity at the "same time." PCs cannot actually do more than one activity (task) at the same time (the same split second) but simply overlap activities so that while one activity waits on an event other activities are running. For example, let's consider a windows-based environment with many activities: printing, downloading, spreadsheet, word processing, data entry application, data inquiry. All of these can be "running" simultaneously.

A task can be writing to the printer. While it waits for the printer to complete a page, the file download requests another record from another LAN or mainframe and, while that record is being downloaded, passes control to the spreadsheet application that is processing a series of calculations and reading and writing to the financial files. During each of these reads or writes, the other three user applications are reviewed to see if any request has been made and then returns to printing the next page.

A client may not have to wait, especially if there are no long-running operations (for example, over 2 seconds) and only one activity takes place at a time. For example, if the operation is basically a data entry application, each activity is dependent upon the prior and there are no concurrent activities required. However, a server on a LAN operates best (maximizes use) when

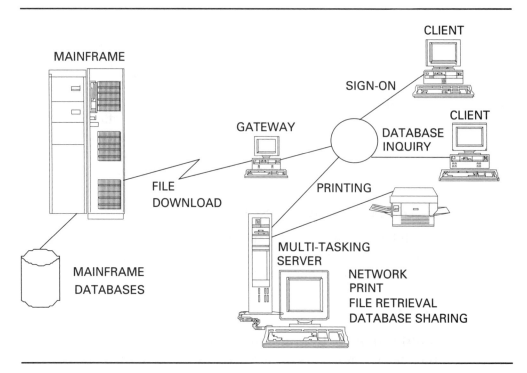

Figure 6.9   Multi-tasking

multi-tasking. The server can be printing to multiple printers simultaneously. Or, if it is an SQL server, it should be servicing more than one user at a time.

Client machines may also have a need to multi-task. An example would be if you are using a spreadsheet application requiring reading of the database, calculation, and printing without operator intervention. If this takes one-half to one hour, the client machine could not be used unless multi-tasking is available.

The following focuses on IBM's OS/2, which is a multi-tasking operating system. However, the concepts can be applied to any multi-tasking environment. In this environment there are two basic activities:

- *processes:* a process is a program loaded into memory and prepared for execution. A process consists of code, data, open files, open queues, and so forth. Creating a process requires a significant amount of overhead because the programs associated must be loaded into memory, files opened, and data read.

* *threads:* a thread is a runable/dispatchable piece of code which has enough resources to survive on its own (for example, it owns a stack, registers and priority). OS/2 multi-tasking is thread based and therefore every running piece of code has a thread; therefore, every process has at least one thread. OS/2 allocates CPU time to threads, and a piece of code associated with a thread executes when the system scheduler gives that thread control. Threads have little overhead associated with them, but debugging multiple threads within a process can be complex because multiple events are occurring simultaneously, with each affecting the other.

Choosing the method of multi-tasking is dependent upon the application requirements. It depends upon factors such as the time available for switching between tasks, how long it takes to create a task, and whether it is possible to share information between tasks. The debugging difficulty and memory protection are other factors.

Generally you should use a process if the application:

* *is a complete and independent module:* if the application can be packaged as a complete module to be called by others or "sold as software," it meets this criteria.
* *is very large:* if the application is very large and will not easily fit into memory with other applications, you can use the memory-swapping facilities of the operating system to manage your memory needs instead of writing your own.
* *needs memory protection:* at the process level, all memory information programs, data, and so forth is protected from other processes. If a problem occurs within the process, what you have done, and not another process, is the cause. This is not true of threads that operate within that process's memory protection space.
* *must be portable:* if this application is to be ported to another operating system, processes are supported but not necessarily threads.

Generally you should use a thread if the application:

- *handles many devices simultaneously:* each device should be handled by a separate thread. Since this is a relatively simple application and probably would not be ported to another operating system, it makes an ideal candidate.
- *requires time-based activities:* whenever you need to run something based on time (for example, a backup of the LAN at 2 am or a long-running job that interferes with LAN response time that should be run between 1 am and 5 am), a thread is the best way to activate that job.
- *has a high wait time:* if most of the process time in the application is wait time (wait on a system resource not a user), this wait time can be overlapped by using threads to reduce the overall process time.
- *does background processing:* if the application is an interactive user interface supporting a CPU-intensive or I/O-intensive background requirement (for example, spreadsheet application), threads can be used to separate the two activities and allow the application to be user-responsive during the background operations.

6.3.2   Mainframe Data Retrieval

Data retrieved via the mainframe by a client/server application on the LAN is significantly slower than data retrieved in a mainframe program for a mainframe application. The mainframe data is retrieved at the DASD access speed and then transmitted to the application at channel speed. In the client/server application, all of this mainframe overhead takes place and then the client/server data transmission process starts. Consider the following components in a client/server-based mainframe data retrieval:

- run a transaction to gather data on the host.
- invoke mainframe network software to transmit the data to LAN gateway.
- the transmission speed of the line connecting the host to the LAN.
- package and send data on the LAN. Consider the optimal LAN network speed and network use contention.
- store the data on the PC. The application may require saving the data between transactions.

There are two basic design philosophies for retrieving mainframe data:

- Get all of the data required in one mainframe retrieval and save this data on the client (or server). This eliminates multiple trips to the mainframe, but the user may suffer poor response time whenever this is done. Consider an application servicing a customer account. All of the data associated with this account could be 10,000 or more characters. If all of the data is retrieved and stored at one time, the effort can take five or more seconds. The user should not have to wait while this is taking place. Therefore the application should be designed to allow other processing while this data transfer takes place in the background.
- Get small amounts of data frequently from the host. This approach eliminates the single large retrieval, which takes many seconds. However, each trip to the mainframe has an inherent overhead of one-half or more seconds due to the list of components that make up a data transmission. Now we are incurring that overhead for many of the transactions on an as-required basis.

The recommendation is to understand the problem and consider both alternatives during the application design. Choose which method to use and then design in an open-ended manner so that a change in method can be implemented without having to rewrite the application. For example, if all information is requested through an I/O routine, this I/O routine could be modified to utilize one method or the other, or even a combination, without having to change the application code.

6.3.3   Single Site Sign-On

The user should not be required to have multiple ids and passwords. Consider designing a single interface with one id and password as the trigger for multiple ids and passwords to be used in the background. Since the user must sign-on to the LAN as a basic access requirement, this should be the only security required. LAN client/server technology requires authorization to each server on every LAN. If the application spans multiple LANs, consider writing a security administration transaction that will update all associated servers across all LANs. Maintaining security on a single LAN is difficult; doing so across multiple LANs or a WAN can be a major effort in production. Security access within the application, including data access, can be a further complication. Consider these concerns at design time to minimize application modification during or after development of the application and also to minimize potential user dissatisfaction which originates with multiple security checkpoints and ids.

6.3.4   Programming Standards

Standards should be developed and enforced for the client/server environment. We discuss this in a later chapter, but it is important to note that, because the client/server environment is new, the tendency is for the developer to try all the new facilities out of curiosity. If standards are not imposed, this may make maintenance more difficult.

6.4   PERFORMANCE ISSUES

Performance is a design concern in a client/server environment because poor performance means:

- Users' time is wasted.
- Hardware solutions mean more expense.
- The solution may be more difficult than simply upgrading the hardware or systems software. It may mean redesigning the application after it has been built. This is obviously a very expensive solution.

6.4.1   Hardware as a Solution

Performance can be viewed as a hardware problem: a faster processor can always be installed to boost performance if it is CPU bound. A faster disk or distributing the database can be the solution for I/O bottlenecks. In a worst-case scenario you can break up processing into multiple nodes. However, there is a limit to the size of machine that you would place on a LAN as a server. Using the mainframe as a server is another complex and potentially response time negative solution. Additionally, splitting the work load over more than one node will not always boost performance.

6.4.2 LAN Performance Design Issues

Performance problems within the LAN network can manifest themselves in various ways. In each case the application should be analyzed prior to development to determine whether there is a potential for the following and then design to minimize their impact:

- *too many messages on the network:* this is less likely to occur on the LAN, but a combination of high SQL server usage, image applications, and gateway traffic could cause this problem. Understand the application(s) that you are designing and the capacity of the network. In a multi-application LAN environment, you need to consider all of the applications that are running or will be running and their network traffic requirements.
- *too many large messages on the network:* this can be defined as large blocks of data being read from SQL server or gateway on a frequent basis.
- *large data transfers:* mainframe to node or SQL server to node transfers of large amounts of data should be run off hours as a regular practice to minimize impact on the network during the prime operational system hours.
- *error traffic:* an application may be designed well and may run well, but periodically it degrades in performance. As we discussed in the LAN introduction, this can be due to hardware failure (wire, connector, card, etc.) and until the error traffic stops being generated the LAN will degrade.

6.4.3 Server-Related Performance Design Issues

The actual traffic on the LAN may be minimal and yet the response time is poor. This can occur if there is congestion on the server, which can be caused by many factors. Two of the more-frequent occurrences are:

- *data update contention:* since updating requires row locking minimally and in some cases table locking (depending upon database software), there is the possibility of degraded performance resulting from many users attempting updates to the same row or table. Additionally, there is always a potential "deadly embrace," where two users wish to update row A and row B (or table A and B) but one user has row A for update and the other user has row B but cannot complete until the other user is done. The same is true of table locking.

- *user contention:* if an SQL server is used heavily due to the high volume of users on the LAN, even though the message traffic on the LAN is small, the response time could be poor because the server is over-used. Generally, the number of users of the application must be considered at design time. Can the project client base be serviced by a single LAN? Are multiple LANs or is a mini-computer or mainframe necessary as the server? Even if the current application requirements can be satisfied by a single server on a single LAN, consider the potential for growth, and design to accommodate that growth.

- *complex retrieval:* a complex retrieval that must traverse many rows and tables can impact the server ability to deliver to other users. Design the application carefully so that these complex retrievals are identified and tuned to minimize their impact.

6.4.4   Client-Related Performance Design Issues

The following are concerns that apply to the client and should be reviewed during the design:

- *limit I/Os:* I/O on a PC (server or client) is perhaps the slowest component of a transaction and therefore should be limited wherever possible.

- *minimize data transferred between client and server:* remember that the data transfer rate on the LAN is substantially slower than the channel speed on the mainframe. This leads to good response time because reduced data means less time spent on the server, less time spent in transmission on the LAN, and less data sent across the LAN means less LAN traffic.

- *common routines in memory:* programs and routines must be retrieved from disk. The time spent retrieving them and loading them into memory can exceed their actual execution time.
- *common data passed in memory:* avoid passing data between programs by storing it on disk and then having the next program retrieve it from disk. The reason is again based on I/O being the slowest component.
- *long-running programs:* these are typically not operational system programs or transactions but rather decision support system activities. If they are operational, they are not "online" but rather they are "batch"; an example is gathering data for a report once a day. The following suggestions may apply:

  run when network is least used: run these when the network is least used because they will run faster and have less impact on other users.

  use a checkpoint facility or break the job into series of shorter-running activities: the last situation you want is to have the program run for an hour and be 90 percent complete, only to have a problem on the server or client and need to rerun the program from scratch. The old mainframe rule was that if a program runs more than one-half hour, checkpoint the data so it can be restarted at that point.
- *monitor programs during early testing:* no matter how well the design work has been done, there may be problems when the program is run in the production environment. These may relate to factors outside the program itself, for example, database software running on the server that is very slow. Therefore, early testing results that indicate poor response time should be investigated because they may represent the "tip of the iceberg."

7

7

Graphic User Interface (GUI) Design Considerations

This chapter is not intended as a comprehensive discussion of GUI design considerations and guidelines. Instead, basic information on the subject is presented, along with recommendations for additional reading.

One of the questions the reader should consider is what makes GUI design difficult. The following points should be considered:

- Users know what they want and need, but only after they see it in action.
- Users get a better feel for what they want after they have seen what they asked for in action.
- The guidelines that govern GUI design are still being developed. They will change as the technology changes. With the exception of the texts referred to below, the existing guideline concepts have not been well documented.
- A good GUI changes users' needs. The GUI has so many features that a user is probably not familiar with that, after they are exposed to these features, the user's requirements change. This improves the user interface and its productivity but makes the design process more difficult.
- Many designers are confident of their skills and can readily produce a GUI design. However, they must be prepared during the design process to make many modifications to

this initial design in accordance with the users' reactions and needs. Sometimes the ego gets in the way.

7.1   INTRODUCTION

Multiple GUI platforms exist, each with a significant base in the market place: IBM's Presentation Manager (runs under IBM's OS/2), Microsoft's Windows (runs under DOS and Microsoft's NT), Motif and OPEN LOOK (use X-Windows under UNIX), and Macintosh (from Apple Corp.). Each of these environments provides mechanisms for creating and interacting with graphical images. Generally, they have features such as those that follow.

7.1.1   Primary Window

The primary or basic window is represented by Figure 7.1. As you review this figure you will find the follow components:

- *border:* this is the narrow strip around the outside window and around any windows defined inside.
- *window sizing buttons:* in the upper right-hand corner are arrows that indicate the window-sizing options.
- *information area:* the bottom line of the window is a single horizontal line which is used as an information area.
- *window title:* this appears as a single horizontal line at the top of the window.
- *menu bar:* this is a horizontal line immediately below the window title.
- *scroll bars:* Figure 7.1 has an example of both horizontal and vertical scroll bars to browse the directories listed (vertical) and the files within the directories (horizontal).
- *small icons:* these provide a visual re-inforcement for text. In Figure 7.1 the upper left side of the window has icons that represent various sources.

7.1.2   Push Buttons

Push buttons allow you to get information from the user that typically initiates an action or designates a routing action. The user chooses the desired button to perform an action described by the button's prompt. Each push button has a word or two that

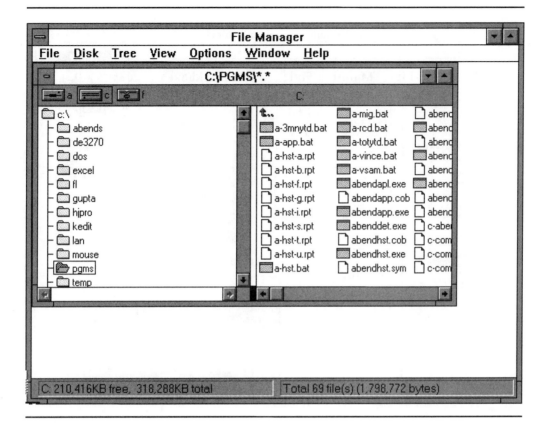

Figure 7.1   Primary Window

describes the choice. Push buttons are often used after you have completed the remaining screen activities. In Figure 7.2, there are two push buttons listed vertically. You use the cursor or tab key to traverse up and down the list to choose your action.

7.1.3   Check Boxes

Check boxes act like toggle switches. They are used to indicate a state that is one of two values, such as "on" or "off." Check boxes often appear in groups. Even though they appear as a group, each check box is defined individually. Unlike radio buttons, a combination of check boxes may be selected. In Figure 7.2, the first selection is marked with an "X" whereas the second is not.

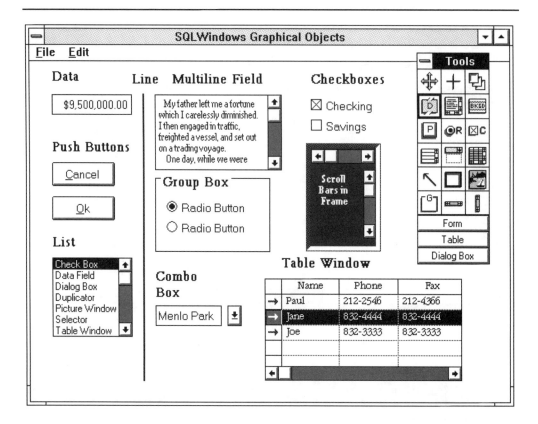

Figure 7.2   Check Box, List Box, Entry Field, Text Box

7.1.4   List Boxes

This facility supports a list of choices for the content of a field or a list of objects. You can browse the list and select only a single choice. This list appears at the entry field as a vertical box (see Figure 7.2). The list is often longer than can be displayed with the box. List boxes provide a facility to move up and down the list. If the list is a set of choices for a field content, once you have identified the selection you wish, you depress the enter key (or click the mouse) and that selection then appears in the entry box.

Several different methods are used to move up and down the list: (1) use the arrow keys to move up and down one entry at a time, (2) use the page up (PGUP) and page down (PGDN) keys to move up and down at one time as many entries as are in the list box, (3) Microsoft Windows has a button that slides up and down corresponding to the entire list in such a way that you can control the speed of movement up and down.

7.1.5 Entry Field and Editing

All GUI tools provide field entry capability (see Data Field in Figure 7.2). The windowing interface provides editing masks, color palette options, and choices of surrounding boxes. Entry fields for text allow scrolling if more information is available than is currently visible in the field box.

7.1.6 Text Box

This is variable-length input that may be a description, text destined for word processing and so forth. The entire variable data area is not displayed on the screen but rather a box is built consisting of one or more lines and then the text wraps around the box left to right and top to bottom. Additional text is entered or viewed by going to the last character in the box (bottom right) and entering more data or moving the cursor to the right (see Multi-Line Field in Figure 7.2). The GUI may provide a text box object which has a button which slides up and down the text or left and right.

7.1.7 Menu Bars and Pull-Down Menus

A Menu Bar (see top line on Figure 7.3) is an area near the top of a window, below the title bar and above the rest of the window. It contains routing choices that display pull-down menus and typically contains single word entry choices. It is analogous to a traditional mainframe menu, with the following differences:

- The menu selections are abbreviated in one or two words.
- The menu selections are not numbered.
- Selection is made by depressing the ENTER key at the selection desired.
- The menu is horizontal not vertical.

Pull-down menus are activated by selecting an item from a menu bar. The user moves the arrow key on the keyboard or a mouse pointer along the menu bar and selects (clicks) on the menu

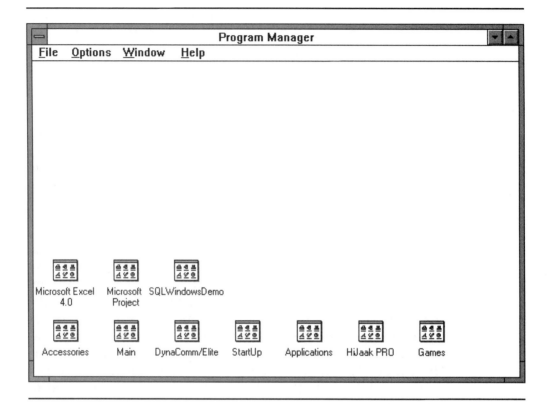

Figure 7.3   Pull-down Menus, Icons

item desired. At this point the pull-down menu appears (see box below Menu Bar in Figure 7.3). This pull-down menu is usually a vertical list of options that the user then selects from. After selecting an option, some action is taken; the selection may then require additional information. The pull-down menu resembles a sub menu within menu-driven mainframe applications, with the following differences:

- The menu selections are not numbered.
- Selection is made by depressing the ENTER key at the selection desired.
- The other sub menus associated with the menu bar (equivalent of mainframe main menu) can be viewed by simply moving the cursor left or right (or selecting from the menu bar using the mouse) along the menu bar.

This is one of many advantages of the GUI interface facilities over traditional mainframe screen design, because the main menu is always in sight while the sub menus are viewed. Additionally, the sub menus can be viewed much more quickly.

7.1.8   Radio Buttons

Radio buttons (see Figure 7.4) allow the user to choose from a list of mutually exclusive options. Choosing one button automatically unselects whichever button was already selected.

7.1.9   Icons

These are pictures of objects that can be activated. Upon activation, these objects normally become dialog boxes or applications

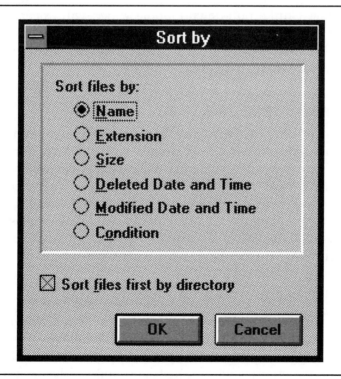

Figure 7.4   Radio Boxes

which provide a menu bar (horizontal menu) or dialog box which starts up the application. Ideally, the icon is a self-explanatory picture of the application. Most windows products are built with icons that do not explicitly define the application. Icons usually have a short title or phrase attached (listed under the icon), which further defines what the icon represents (see bottom of Figure 7.3).

Icons frequently represent minimized windows of running applications. When a user double-clicks or restores a minimized window's icon, the icon disappears from the desktop and is replaced by an open window.

7.1.10   Popup Windows

Popup windows are used to assist in completing a field or screen. Help windows are a good example of popup windows. These help windows provide information to assist the user in completing a specific field or action (see Figure 7.5).

Popup window features may also be used to support popup menus. Unlike pull-down menus, which will appear under the item selected on the menu bar at the top of the screen, popup windows can appear anywhere on the screen. They are normally activated when a push button is selected.

7.1.11   Message Boxes

Message boxes are windows that convey a message that an unexpected event has occurred, a warning that a situation may occur that is undesirable, or additional status information after a process has been completed. IBM's Common User Access (CUA) guidelines define three types of messages: information message, warning message, and an action message. These message boxes may warrant the use of highly visible display characteristics such as blinking the message on and off or very bright colors.

7.1.12   Dialog Boxes

A dialog box or window is one that supports a dialog or conversation with the user. There are two types of dialogues: serial (modal) and parallel (modeless). The serial dialog is a box which contains a group of activities which must be completed before the user can resume an activity in the primary window. The parallel dialog is

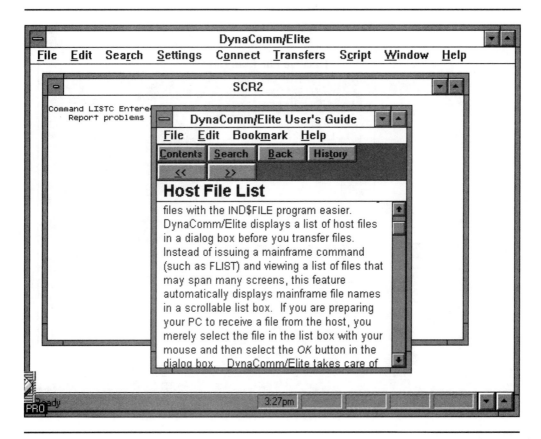

Figure 7.5   Popup Window

available concurrently with the primary screen and can be acted upon concurrently.

Minimally, a dialog box has two command buttons: OK and Cancel. The OK button accepts all changes and closes the dialog. The Cancel button aborts the dialog in process and closes the dialog window. A third choice, the Apply button, can be useful because its properties are such that all changes requested are completed the same way they would have been if the OK button had been used but the dialog remains open. For repetitive operations based in the same dialog window, this avoids re-opening the window for each entry.

The dialog box typically has the command push buttons described, check boxes, radio boxes, field entry, list boxes, and so forth (see Figure 7.6).

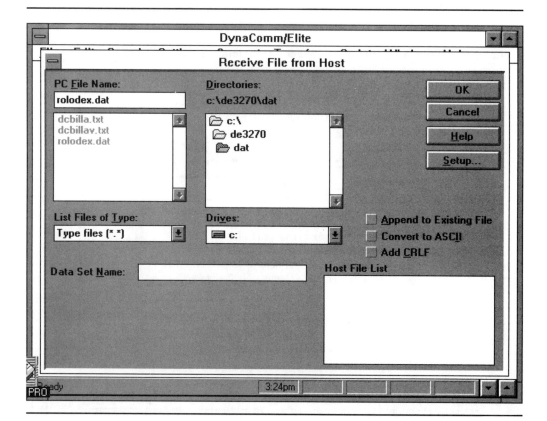

Figure 7.6   Dialog Box

7.2   THE HUMAN FACTORS

One of the important basic considerations in designing good GUI screens is the human factor. The human factors are based on how the human eye is attracted to specific locations/objects on the screen. Understanding how the eye is attracted can help during the design process to make the application more easily understood.

7.2.1   Motion

The human eye is most sensitive to motion. You can try an experiment yourself, such as changing the mouse arrow to a blinking arrow. When you first bring up the screen you will notice that you are attracted to the arrow immediately. If you have any application that does have motion (for example, a video on screen), notice that you have to concentrate to focus on any other section of the screen. Since the eye is most sensitive to motion:

- Use motion infrequently.
- Save motion for important anomalies.

7.2.2   Size

The next most powerful stimulus to the eye is size. Try a full color background for your base window: for example, plaid or the Fall leaves in Figure 7.7. You are attracted to the background instead of the objects or windows on the screen. The following considerations apply:

- Since the background of the screen is the largest screen component, a black or neutral background is suggested.

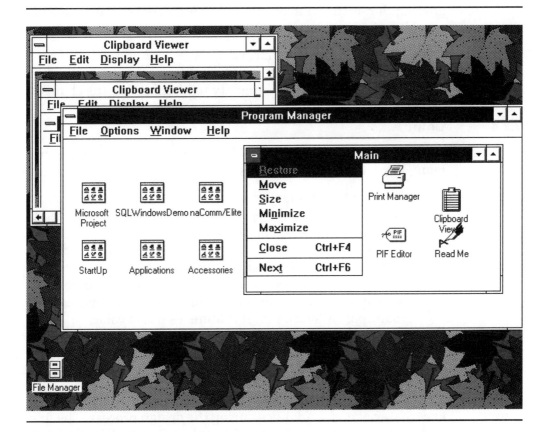

Figure 7.7   Example of Poor Background Choice

- Multiple boxes on the screen of equal size will equate to the same attraction provided that they have the same next level stimulus.

The same size stimulus applies to information on a screen; if all data is presented in the same size, a single data item presented in a larger size will attract the eye. Multiple large data items intermixed with smaller-sized data items on the same screen will be a distraction.

7.2.3   Intensity

Bright colors are attention getters. These can be used as the background in a window or a box, or as the background for an individual object. Think about a screen on which multiple windows of equal size appear but one window has a bright red background; that is the window you will be attracted to. The following considerations apply:

- Use high-intensity alarms.
- Use high intensity for critical values.
- Consider using high intensity to highlight status changes.

7.2.4   Color

Although color is at the lower end of the stimulus list, it has many important considerations:

- The number of colors on a single display should be few and consistent, or else the eye will be confused and attracted to too many locations simultaneously.
- Consider the color-blind user. The most basic approach is to make a color palette modification available to all users such that your application color set can be modified if necessary. Secondly, consider the basic color-blind needs and develop your application so that it minimizes use of color.
- Use color to highlight values and relationships between values.

7.3   IBM'S COMMON USER ACCESS (CUA) GUIDELINES

The author recommends two texts which provide excellent reference material and guidelines during the design process. The first of these is IBM's *Object-Oriented Interface Design, IBM Common*

User Access Guidelines, Que Corp. This text and the CUA principles and guidelines therein provide the basis for GUI design. The acceptance of these CUA guidelines has been widespread throughout the GUI world. Many applications that are available adhere to many of these guidelines; some of the applications adhere to all of the guidelines. By developing applications that follow these guidelines, the user will be able to utilize many applications, both the ones you build and those supplied as shrink-wrapped solutions from third-party vendors without requiring retraining in the application interface. Readers that have worked with numerous shrink-wrapped solutions which run under Microsoft's Windows will note that they operate very similar. If you are wondering what guidelines were used to develop these applications, they are based on IBM's CUA.

Considering all of the input (keyboard, mouse, etc.), palettes (16 or more color choices), and objects (windows, buttons, etc.) available, each application could be written to interface with the user in a substantially different way. Indeed, some popular shrink-wrapped applications do! This means that the user must first learn a whole new look and feel of how the application runs. This is time consuming and nonproductive; it can create a negative reaction to the application.

The primary goal of the CUA interface is to assist the user in transferring knowledge across applications, vendor-supplied software, client/server platforms, and so forth. If the user learns to use one product that was built using the CUA interface, learning another product can be done quickly. A CUA-compatible application means that the user is already proficient in the look and feel of the application. This gives the user the sense that he or she already knows about the application. The user can walk through it, concentrating on the substance instead of the packaging.

The other stated goals of CUA include:

- increase the user's productivity
- increase the user's satisfaction with a product
- reduce the user's error rate

Factors that are outside of the designer's control—such as development or run time costs, usability, and performance—may influence the application design. But during the design of a GUI client/server application you cannot always provide specific guidelines for all activities taking place. The following is a group of user-interface design principles that can be used when guidelines do not cover a specific issue:

- *user in control:* the user should be in control of the application whenever possible. Mainframe online-systems user interfaces tend to be program driven. The example used is that of riding a train; the user has few choices. In GUI design, on the other hand, the application interface should be user driven. The example used is that of driving a car; the user is in control.
- *limit use of entry modes:* an entry mode is a state in which the application uses the input facilities (keyboard, mouse, etc.). An example of two modes would be line draw and text entry. The line draw mode might make use of the keyboard cursor and the mouse to draw lines; as you move the cursor a line is drawn or the line follows the mouse arrow. Text entry would use the cursor and move completely differently: the mouse arrow simply moves while the arrows control the location of the cursor.

  Switching frequently between modes should be avoided. Also, while in a mode, make it apparent which mode you are in. For example, if one is switching between draw and text, change the cursor and/or the mouse pointer so that the mode is different.

  Modes can be useful in some situations; for example, they can extend the capabilities of input devices by providing alternative means of accomplishing the same action by using multiple keys, a button, or multiple mouse clicks. Modes can help an expert user perform a series of actions very quickly.
- *provide different skill levels:* an application should be built in such a way that a novice or casual user can successfully and comfortably traverse it. Less frequently used advanced features should be provided for the expert user but not made readily available to the novice. For example, provide two levels of menus based on the user's degree of expertise. The novice user can choose the simplified menus while the expert user can select the comprehensive version of the menus.

  Users at any level of knowledge and experience can

benefit from help information that describes a product's choices, interaction techniques, objects, and so forth, and generally offers the user assistance in completing the task. A novice user might require extensive help information about each component of an application interface while an expert or highly experienced user might require only a brief description.

For the expert or highly experienced user, a designer can provide hidden mechanisms, such as short-cut keys that condense sequences of steps. Some of the visual cues can be eliminated; for example, an expert user should be able to turn off the display of certain kinds of information that he or she does not require.

Generally, the interface should be flexible enough to satisfy a full range of users, but the designer should first make sure that it serves the needs of the primary users.

- *descriptive and helpful messages:* the situation in which a message is displayed is often one in which the user needs the most help. The response for an abnormal occurrence or an invalid entry or action should be supportive, clear, and concise. It also should provide an opportunity for the user to resolve the issue. Methods of responding include text in the form of a message, audible cues, and graphic ques. For an example of the suggested approach, let's consider a user who attempts to save a file on diskette. If the diskette is unformatted, the user should receive a message during the save process, be provided an opportunity to format the diskette, and then continue to save the file.

- *provide immediate feedback:* feedback to a user's action should be immediate so that he or she can react and continue the activity. If you consider mainframe applications, the target response time is too often as high as 3 or 5 seconds. In the client/server environment the target should be instant response, within a maximum time of 1 second. This is not as difficult to achieve as it may seem because the GUI applications are really responding with an element or object at a time. For example, a data entry field responds to the user upon successful entry or a pull-down menu appears after a selection is made on the menu bar; these are instant responses.

When responses cannot be immediate (for example, when there is a mainframe access which may take several seconds), the application should provide some interim feedback, such as a message that the request is being processed.

- *provide reversible actions:* by providing reversible actions, the interface will be more forgiving to the novice or the person exploring the application. Ideally, the action can be done again after reversal. If the action cannot be reversed, the design should provide for an alternative. For example, if the user is about to reformat a disk with some data on it, provide an alternative to abort or replace the diskette with another before proceeding.

   A designer is responsible for determining which actions can be undone and which cannot. The designer should always keep users' needs in mind and therefore overdo reversible actions rather than short cut them. A designer also determines how many actions in a series of actions can be undone. Apply the same tendency to help the user.

- *transparent interface:* the interface is simply the tool with which the user accomplishes his or her tasks. Therefore, the interface should focus on the task, not on itself. The interface should require little thought on the part of the user. Users want to write letters, calculate profits, prepare presentations, process an order—they are not interested in sliding scroll boxes, pull-down menus, and navigating through dialog boxes. A designer should make sure that the tools provided by a user interface do not get in the users' way. A good user interface requires little conscious thought on the users' part.

- *allow user interface customization:* because user's abilities and preferences vary, they should be able to customize some aspects of the interface. A user should be able to vary the intensity and hue of colors, arrange menu choices, customize the volume and duration of sounds, modify the sequence of steps in a process, and so forth. Try not to underestimate a user's creativity or desire to personalize the application.

   A user may have a need to increase the volume on audible cues to compensate for a hearing impairment or a noisy environment. A user may need to modify colors to compensate for a visual impairment (for example, color blindness) or poor lighting in the environment. However, designers should provide good defaults and should not depend on the user to customize these settings.

- *reduce a user's memory load:* the user should not have to remember something that the interface can tell them. Users perform better when they are using recognition rather than recall. Therefore, use lists of choices as a means of traversing a product instead of forcing users to memorize a list of commands.

  The application should also provide reminders to help a user keep track of the current task; for example, the application can provide visual cues such as highlighting or progress indicators. This highlighting can remind a user that a specific object has been selected.

  Another way to reduce a user's memory requirement is to provide default settings and to save previously selected settings. The window in which the settings are saved should also remind a user about which settings are in effect. Additionally, allow the user to reset settings to the original default.

- *define meaningful and recognizable objects:* objects and their associated properties should be designed so that a user can understand the class of objects and what distinguishes one class of objects from another. For example, consider the differences between a chart object and a parts catalog object. Interfacing with each will be different simply because of the nature of that object. Additionally, the objects should build on the user's real-world experience. Using our examples, the parts catalog interface should be intuitively the same as a real parts catalog; the chart interface should be similar to other computer chart program interfaces.

  When an object represents a more abstract concept that does not have a real-world counterpart, the representation of the object should still help a user visualize and remember relationships. Perhaps, for example, the designer can draw upon a real-world analogy for the abstract and provide this analogy in the interface design.

- *consistent interface:* each application should be conceptually, visually, and functionally consistent with itself and with other applications that will be in the user's work place. Consistency helps a user transfer knowledge from one product to another, thereby reducing the training required and creating a sense of understanding without prior experience. For example, the user should be able to use the same technique to edit text no matter where the text entry is implemented.

- *sustaining the context of user's task:* a product should maintain points of reference while the user works on a task. For example, when a user adds objects to a folder, the folder appearance should remain the same but the contents should change.

    The user should be able to complete a set of steps without having to alternate between input devices. For example, a user should not have to use a mouse to scroll text while editing that text from the keyboard. The text should scroll automatically when the cursor reaches the boundary of the area the user is in. Provide instead a keyboard scrolling mechanism such as cursor keys and page up and down keys that move up or down in the window either a line at a time or a screen at a time, respectively.

    The user should be able to predict the result of an action. Provide consistent response to actions and provide actions appropriate to a user's tasks. Label actions with appropriate terms in such a way that a user can develop expectations about the outcome of the action.

- *maintain product continuity:* the designer should not disregard the user's prior experience with either products on the market or prior versions of the application in question. The new product or version should build upon the user's experience.

- *aesthetics:* the appearance of a product's interface can affect a user's acceptance of that product. The designer should focus on basic graphic design concerning spatial grouping, contrast, and multi-dimensional representation. Attention to aesthetic appeal and visual clarity can make an interface more efficient, effective, and appealing to the user.

7.3.1   GUI Components

Object-Oriented Interface Design, IBM Common User Access Guidelines which focuses on defining guidelines for components of a CUA interface. Over 130 of these components are identified. The following components have been selected from the text to provide the reader with a sense of the depth and complexity of these components and the special consideration which must be given to them during the design phase.

- *Action Choice:* a choice which immediately begins to perform an action. For example, the choices CUT and PASTE in a pull-down menu.
- *Action Message:* a message that indicates that a condition has occurred that requires a response from the user. For example, the printer is out of paper; do you wish to retry after adding paper or cancel the print request?
- *Action Window:* a secondary window that is used to allow a user to further specify settings that are needed to complete the user's initial request.
- *Cascaded Menu:* a menu that appears when a cascading choice (for example, a choice on a pull-down menu) has been selected. This sub menu appears if the initial selection requires further clarification; the purpose is to reduce the initial menu entries. This cascaded menu appears to the right and on top of the choice selected.
- *Check Box:* see prior description in Section 7.1.3.
- *Column Heading:* label above a column of information that serves to identify the contents of the column.
- *Combination Box:* this combines the functions of an entry field and a list box. A user can either select an entry from the list or type in the actual contents of the field whether or not the entry exists in the list.
- *Contextual Help:* help information that applies specifically to the current object or group of objects.
- *Cursor:* guidelines that apply cursor usage and movement.
- *Field Prompt:* text that identifies a field and acts as a prompt for that field.
- *General Help:* an action choice on a menu bar which, when activated, provides a help window with an overview of the window on which the choice was made.
- *Help Index:* a series of alphabetically listed help topics which appear when the General Help is selected on the menu bar.
- *List Box:* see prior description in Section 7.1.4.

- *Maximize:* an action choice which enlarges a window to the largest size possible for that work place (screen).
- *Mnemonic:* a single character which represents a choice and activates that choice the same as a mouse selection would. Usually the first character of the choice on a pull-down menu, for example.
- *Mouse:* multiple page guidelines on the use of the one-, two-, and three-button mouse, including action, direction, selection, and result.
- *Primary Window:* a window in which the main interaction between a user and an object takes place. A primary window is used to present information that is used independently from information in all other windows.
- *Object:* an item that can be manipulated. An object can be represented as text, image, graphic, video, or audio.
- *Options Menu:* a specific pull-down menu entry that allows a user to customize the functions of an application.
- *Push Button:* see prior description in Section 7.1.2.
- *Radio Button:* see prior description in Section 7.1.8.
- *Scroll Bar:* see prior description in Section 7.1.1.
- *Selection Types and Techniques:* multiple pages that describe methods that a user can use to identify objects to which actions are to be applied.
- *Shortcut Key:* key combinations which can be used to take an action instead of selecting a menu entry.
- *Size:* allowing the user to change the size of a window.
- *System Menu:* a pull-down menu from the menu bar that has choices that affect the window itself, such as the Size option mentioned above.
- *Warning Message:* a message that indicates that an undesirable condition could occur but that the user can continue to process.

7.3.2 GUI Component Definitions

Each of the components in *Object-Oriented Interface Design, IBM Common User Access Guidelines* is then defined, as follows:

- *definition:* the component is described.
- *graphic:* whenever possible an example in the form a graphic of an applicable GUI screen is given.

- *when to use:* a brief statement concerning the component's purpose.
- *recommended guidelines:* guidelines that apply to this component at all times.
- *suggested guidelines:* guidelines that are recommended but are optional.
- *essential related topics:* something that should be read in conjunction with this component.
- *supplemental related topics:* additional suggested topics.

The following are two sample components. They are included to give the reader a sense of the depth and comprehensive presentation available for each of the components.

7.3.3 Cursor Movement Guidelines

The following guidelines apply to the movement of the cursor in a window and access from the keyboard to any part of the window.

Essential Guidelines

- ALT Key—pressing the ALT key and a mnemonic assigned to push button, selects that push button.
- Cursor Movement
  * When the cursor is positioned on a push button, the Tab or Backtab key moves the cursor to another field on screen, not to another push button.
  * When the cursor is positioned on a push button, allow the ALT key and mnemonic to assign it to a different push button.
  * When the cursor leaves a field of push buttons, reset to the default push button.
  * When moving the cursor to a series of choices in a field for the first time, move the cursor to the first one selected. If none is selected, to the default. If no default, to the first in the list.

Guidelines to Assist in Ease of Use

- Provide a mnemonic for each choice in a window.
- Tab Key Movement
  * The Tab Key moves field to field left to right and top to bottom. After the bottom right it moves to the top left.

- Backtab Key Movement
  * The Backtab Key moves field to field right to left and bottom to top. After the top left, it moves to the bottom right.

7.3.4 List Box Guidelines

The following guidelines apply to lists of objects or setting choices.

Essential Guidelines

- In a scrollable list, do not allow the cursor to wrap.
- Provide horizontal and vertical scroll bars as appropriate when information is not visible.

Guidelines to Assist in Ease of Use

- Display the list in a meaningful order such as alphabetic, numeric, chronological, and the like.
- A list box should display at least 6 to 8 items at one time.
- List box should be wide enough to display most items in list. Create the box wide enough to minimally display the average-width item.
- If the user increases the size of the list box window, increase the items displayed.
- If the user decreases the size of the list box window, decrease the items displayed.
- Capitals should be used on the first letter of the first word of each choice unless the word is an abbreviation, acronym, or proper noun.

7.4 MICROSOFT WINDOWS DESIGN GUIDELINES

A second text that provides guidelines during the design process is Microsoft's *The Windows Interface, An Application Design Guide*, Microsoft Press. The text is focused on Microsoft's Windows GUI and provides guidelines for consistent application interfaces within this environment. Most of these guidelines have been incorporated in Microsoft's Windows operating system and in their application offerings. Additionally, other vendors who have developed applications that run under Microsoft's Windows generally adhere to these guidelines. As a result, if you plan to develop your applications to run under Windows and you adhere to these guidelines, your application will have the look and feel of other Windows products. This will minimize the need for additional user training.

These guidelines were developed in an attempt to be compatible with IBM's CUA. As a result, by following these guidelines you will generally be adhering to the design principles we covered earlier. Because these guidelines are focused specifically on the Windows environment, they tend to be more practical than the CUA guidelines. They can be used as the day-to-day programming guidelines and CUA can be used as a reference guide. The reader should note that since all GUI is a relatively new environment and is prone to change, these guidelines are applicable to the current versions of Windows and need to be revisited and revised as new interface issues develop.

Similar to the IBM CUA document, this text has three levels of guidelines:

- *recommended:* follow these guidelines in such a way that your application will have the minimal look and feel of other windows-based products.
- *optional:* these are extensions of the recommended guidelines. They provide the next level of common look and feel.
- *suggested:* use these where you can as long as they do not conflict with other needs of your applications or vendor-supplied applications that will be implemented on your client devices.

The text focuses on such topics as:

- *general techniques:* use of all input devices (keyboard, mouse, pen, etc.), navigation, user feedback, text editing, and so forth.
- *menus:* the types of menus you should be using, the components of these menus, the different techniques of interfacing with these menus.
- *dialog boxes:* what types of dialog boxes exist, what controls to use, what buttons to use, and common functions that they perform.

- *Object Linking and Embedding:* OLE concepts, OLE interface, handling objects, and so forth.

7.4.1 Basic Input Facility Guidelines

The following guidelines are based on Microsoft's *The Windows Interface, An Application Design Guide* and have been included here to provide the reader with additional design ideas as well as a sample of what this text is all about. They apply to the input facilities available on each client station, including the mouse and keyboard. In each case the appropriate facility is defined and then the guideline stated.

Basic Mouse Input Facilities

- *button 1:* the left side of the mouse. This selection button is involved in most mouse actions.
- *button 2:* the right side of the mouse. The guidelines recommend that it be used for context-specific actions and options.
- *point:* refers to the activity of moving the mouse pointer to the desired screen location in preparation for beginning another activity.
- *press:* is the operator activity of pressing and holding down the mouse button. This is used to identify the object to be selected.
- *click:* is the activity of pressing and releasing the mouse button without moving the mouse. It is used to select the insertion point or item or activate an inactive window or control.
- *double-click:* is the activity whereby the operator presses and releases the mouse button twice within a short time interval. It can be used as a short cut for multiple operations; for example, it may be used to activate an icon instead of performing two individual activities to select the icon and then maximize it.
- *drag:* is the activity whereby the operator presses the mouse button and holds it down while moving the mouse. This is typically used to move a window, object, etc. It is also used to resize items.
- *double-drag:* the operator presses the mouse button twice

and on the second press, holds down the button while moving mouse.

General mouse recommendations:

- Do not use or else limit the use of mouse button 2. Most Windows-based applications do not use this button; making use of it may confuse the user.
- Provide a "hot zone" big enough so that pointing the mouse is not difficult. This is a user-friendly consideration because that activity cannot be activated unless the mouse is pointing to the specific "hot zone" associated with it. Moving the pointer requires at least a minimum of dexterity and eyesight. Try increasing the speed of mouse movement significantly. You will find that manipulating the mouse is much more difficult.
- Limit double clicks and double-drags; again for reasons of dexterity. The timing required to distinguish a double click from two single clicks can be a problem for the user community. If they are used, provide alternative techniques for the user.

Basic Keyboard Input Facilities

Keyboard—Editing Keys

- *Del:* this key deletes an entire selection (for example, a field) or one character at a time to the right of insertion point.
- *Backspace:* this key deletes the entire selection or deletes one character at a time to the left of insertion point.
- *Ins:* this key toggles between insert mode and overtype mode.

Keyboard—Mode Toggle Keys

- *Caps Lock:* sets alphabetic upper and lower case.
- *Num Lock:* sets the keypad to numeric or cursor direction keys.
- *F8:* makes the keyboard behave as if SHIFT key is locked for all direction keys and mouse actions.

Keyboard—Modifier Key

- *Shift, Ctrl, and Alt:* each can modify the meaning of alphanumeric keys, mouse click, navigation keys, and function keys when depressed and held prior to the use of these keys.

Keyboard—Navigation Keys

- *Home:* moves to the beginning of line.
- *End:* moves to the end of line.
- *Page Up:* moves to the previous screen, same horizontal position.
- *Page Down:* moves to the next screen, same horizontal position.
- *left arrow:* moves left one unit (field or character).
- *right arrow:* moves right one unit (field or character).
- *up arrow:* moves up one unit (field or line).
- *down arrow:* moves down one unit (field or line).
- *Tab:* moves to the next field.

Keyboard—Shortcut Keys

- *F1-F12:* these keys by themselves and in conjunction with modifier keys (Shift, Ctrl, and Alt) provide 48 potential uses, many of which have already been assigned meanings. Many of the combinations of F1-F12 with the Ctrl modifier key have been assigned meanings. These should be reviewed and thoroughly understood prior to using them.
- General Guidelines
  * assign single keys for frequently performed small tasks
  * assign SHIFT+key combinations for actions that extend the use of the base key
  * assign CTRL+key combinations for infrequent actions
  * avoid assigning ALT+letter combinations
  * function keys should be a last resort as a choice for shortcuts

7.4.2   Dialog Box Guidelines

Similar to the previous section, the following guidelines are based on the Microsoft text. Dialog boxes generally do not contain menu bars, window scroll bars, split bars, or resizing buttons; instead they are a simple box which usually gathers additional information from the user relative to completing some other operation. For example, Microsoft uses a dialog box when you attempt to open a file; the box appears and requests the name of the file and where it is located. You either enter these pieces of information and complete the dialog or cancel the dialog.

Dialog boxes can be classified according to their use, as follows:

- *movable or fixed:* a movable dialog box has a title bar containing a control menu and a title, whereas a non-movable has no title bar. Movable dialog boxes are recommended so that they can be moved in case they are covering pertinent information on the screen. They are also preferable because the title explains their use.
- *fixed size:* dialog boxes have a non-sizable frame but the application may use two sizes. The small size would contain the basic controls; the larger size would include advanced options. The dialog box should first appear in the small size, with an indication that a larger version exists with an "unfold" button (for example, a command button such as "Options>>").
- *modal or modeless:* modal and modeless are explained in detail in a later section. For our purposes, modal forces a user response prior to continuing, whereas modeless allows them to continue some parts of processing. Microsoft describes four types of processing:
  * *application modal:* the user must respond to the dialog box before continuing processing in this application but can process other applications without responding. The dialog box remains on display.
  * *system modal:* the user must respond to the dialog box before running anything in the work place.
  * *application modeless:* the user can continue working in the current application without responding to the dialog box, which remains on display.
  * *application semi-modal:* the user can use the current application as a means of resolving or responding to the dialog box.
- *messages dialogues:* these are basically modal dialog boxes with error messages or other important information that requires a user response before the application can continue. If the message is critical at the system level, it should be a system modal dialog box, which would prevent the user from doing anything else until the problem is resolved. For example, during shutdown Microsoft Windows will prevent the shutdown if applications are currently running.

The user is forced to recognize this condition and respond prior to continuing.

Dialog boxes normally should be centered within the application window. An application may have a requirement to move the dialog box to a different location but these boxes should not overlay or be near the menu bar at the top of the window because this is the location that generates the most needs for the dialog box.

7.5 GENERAL DESIGN CONCERNS

One of the later chapters focuses briefly on prototyping. Considering what we have covered thus far concerning GUI design, the reader should appreciate that the best way to succeed in designing these applications is through an iterative prototyping of the application with user participation. This will identify the shortcomings early on and provide an opportunity to modify the flow and look and feel in such a way that the user can be more effective. As a result, be prepared during the design process to rework the user interface numerous times until it satisfies the user needs and the objectives and guidelines discussed.

7.5.1 Simple Do's and Don'ts

The following is a list of designer's temptations which fall into the do-not-recommend category:

- *design based solely on your knowledge:* you may get much of it right but there are too many considerations in the user interface of a GUI client/server based environment to attempt a design without input from other sources.
- *elegant design:* if some application component looks great, it does not necessarily make the user's task any easier. In fact, it may be a distraction.
- *additional features:* if there are too many features, the user will not know which to use. Good features are features that are used.
- *directing the user:* the designer should provide encouragement for user input and allow for trial and error during the design process. Suggesting how the system should be built

and then defending that suggestion will be an impediment to cooperative design.

- *documentation fixes:* using documentation to work around some application component that does not work properly is counterproductive. If it does not work properly, fix it or leave it out of the application.
- *next release:* the same applies to fixing a component in the next release. Fix it in this release or leave it out.
- *logical flow approach:* mainframe design often uses a logical work flow approach. All tasks that the user is to perform are reviewed and then listed in a logical sequence. The system is designed on this basis. Since the GUI client/server interface provides much more user control of the events, this logical work flow approach will not necessarily provide a good solution.

The following are simple recommendations to follow when designing the user interface:

- *group data functionally:* all of the data that the user requires to complete an activity should be available on one screen and within a window on that screen.
- *basic design principles:* be familiar with the basic design principles reviewed earlier. Feel comfortable with how they are to be applied to your application.
- *use CUA guidelines:* if a question arises concerning a specific implementation within the user interface, use IBM's CUA as a reference guide to help resolve the issue.
- *use Windows guidelines:* if you are designing an application for Microsoft's Windows, use the text mentioned previously to provide guidelines during the design.
- *avoid cluttered screens:* however, there is a fine balance that the designer needs to be aware of between all related data on a busy screen versus simpler screens with the need to traverse numerous screens to get the job done.
- *object placement:* place related objects near one another to reduce the need for eye movement.
- *data placement:* frequently accessed or entered data should be placed where it will be seen first. We are used to reading left to right and top to bottom.

- *use navigational diagrams:* diagram the sequence a user must follow to complete each task within the application. This will give you a sense of the number of levels and dialog boxes.
- *disable inappropriate choices:* if optional choices exist on a screen based on different selections made, disable (gray or eliminate from the screen) the inappropriate choices when the initial selection is made.
- *use defaults:* when defaults are used wherever possible, user error is reduced.
- *use lists:* when lists are used wherever possible, user typing errors are reduced.
- *data validation:* determine which approach you will use among the following alternatives: validate after each keystroke, after moving to the next field, and at the end of the screen, or when the user clicks on the OK button on the dialog box. The longer you wait to validate data items, the more that must be done at one time and the longer the response may be. Consider that the user response should be less than one second and consistent within the application.
- *font sizes:* 12 point fonts for menus and 10 point fonts for dialog boxes. Work out an acceptable standard for consistent application screens.

7.5.2   Modal Window Considerations

A modal window is a window that restricts the user by preventing user interaction with other open windows. It is a method that can be found in many different applications within Microsoft's Windows. There are different levels of modality, as follows:

- *full or absolute modality:* in this case the user can only interact with the modal window. All other windows are disabled until the modal window is closed.
- *partial modality:* in this case a modal window may only disable some of the related windows but the user can still interact with windows in other applications.

An example of a poor modal window sequence is one in which the user is prompted to answer a fixed sequence of questions, on each window. The user must answer each question before going on to the next window. There are no alternatives other than aborting the sequence and therefore the user is not in control. Modal windows put the system in control and so should only be used where necessary, for example, for parameter capture and object selection.

Generally, as the CUA guidelines suggest, the user should be in control; this applies to windows access as well. There are exceptional situations in which a modal style, non-object oriented interface is more usable. If the following apply, a modal interface design may be more effective:

- The user is only performing a very small number of different tasks.
- The tasks have to be performed using a fixed sequence of actions.
- There will be little or no opportunity to train or advise the users.

An example of a modal interface which many people have interfaced with is the Automated Teller Machine (ATM) for simple banking transactions. The user is prompted at each step and can only cancel the sequence. If you want to withdraw money the sequence might be:

- Insert Card
- Enter Personal Identifier: xxxxxx
- Select Transaction Type: W—Cash Withdrawal
                                      D—Check Deposit
- Enter Amount Desired
- Press ENTER to Confirm

Character-based full-screen systems tend to be modal (as in our example) and most GUI systems are relatively non-modal.

Figure 7.8 shows three different windows. The largest window is the standard Microsoft File Manager Window. The window inside it is for a specific directory called "C:\ABENDS*.*". The smallest window, in the center, is entitled "Select Files," which appears when you use the "File" pull-down menu and select the "Select Files" option. If you attempt to activate either the first window (File Manager) or the second window (directory of

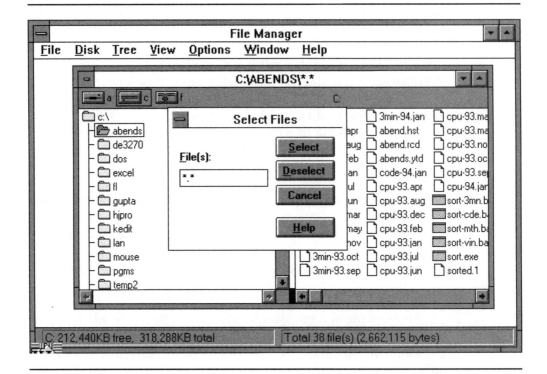

Figure 7.8   Example of Modal Window

C:\ABENDS*.*) nothing happens; you are completely locked out. The only window active in this work place is the small window (Select Files). You must either select a file or cancel the window.

7.5.3   Modeless Window Considerations

A modeless window is a window that does not restrict the user from interacting with other windows. Several modeless windows can be open and usable at once. The user can therefore perform several tasks in parallel. Modeless windows are the desired method of GUI design because they put the user in control.

Figure 7.9 shows three open windows: (1) the Program Manager window, (2) the MS-DOS Prompt window, and (3) the File Manager window. Each can be activated and worked on, therefore the user is in control of what will be done and in which sequence.

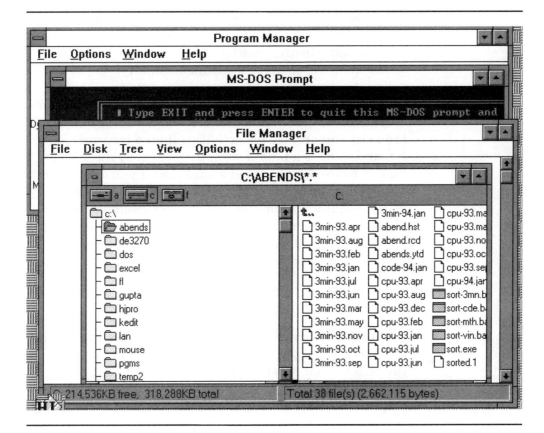

Figure 7.9   Example of Modeless Window

7.5.4   GUI Design by Task and Task Scenario

Generally, a task is a work activity carried out by an individual to achieve some goal as part of a business process. The task can be achieved by performing a real action or by using the GUI to perform a sequence of user interface actions on user objects. Each task has one or more associated user interface action sequences. Tasks are similar to what is commonly referred to as transactions, but they differ from transactions in the following ways:

- A task is a more encompassing term than a transaction. Examples of tasks include:

* preparing a document or letter on a word processor.
* preparing a spreadsheet.
* responding to an E-mail.
* telephone response to a customer inquiry.
* updating a customer address.

The last example is also a transaction but the first probably involves more than one transaction. They certainly are more comprehensive activities than a transaction.

• A transaction is a unit of work performed by the system. A task is focused on the user's goals and the user's actions. The task may involve numerous activities, some of which do not require a computer system. For example, responding to a customer inquiry involves communication with a customer and may or may not require use of the computer system to answer the question(s).

A task scenario is a specific task. The task scenario defines the details of the task, including:

• the business activity and/or event that triggers the activity.
• all associated input.
• the actions that must be performed.
• the status of existing information, as applicable. For example, if a loan is requested, the current debt would apply.

These task scenarios are then used to:

• guide the GUI design
• develop scripts for prototyping
• evaluate the applicability of GUI to the solution

An example of a task scenario might be the following:

• Correspondence received from a customer indicating that they have moved from Los Angeles to Panama City, Florida. Their new address is 12-45 Bay St., Panama City, FL. Their move from the West Coast to the East Coast implies that the salesman assigned to their account will also need to be changed.

The GUI design process requires that all the user tasks be identified and that each be provided with task scenarios. The scope of the application is determined from this set of tasks; they are evaluated to determine which can sensibly be supported in the application and which cannot. Some of these tasks will be identified easily but others may not be. Consider the following sources when identifying these tasks:

- *business design:* this consists of a model that defines the structure of the business processes, a description of each process, organization chart, defined roles and responsibilities of the staff, and a data model for the required business process data. This information can then be used to construct the tasks.
- *user interviews:* interview at least one user in each distinct area of the business process and ask them to define the tasks they perform and those that should be performed by the application. These users should include managers, remote site users, and support staff such as Help Desk.
- *current system procedures:* review existing procedures manuals, with a focus on defining tasks and restructuring the process. The designer should determine how these procedures and tasks will be processed in the new application.
- *business events:* examine all processes and data flow to determine when the event occurs and what triggers the event. Several types of triggers are found in most business processes, including arrival of data (mail, fax, information from another system, etc.), timed events (business processes that occur at the end of a week, month, quarter, etc.), and exception conditions (out of stock, overdrawn, overpayment).
- *data model:* examine the data model and check where each entity is created, updated, and deleted.
- *generic task list:* many tasks can be derived from common system requirements (for example, those tasks associated with data entry, inquiry, reporting, management and control, housekeeping, security access, and so forth).

7.5.5 GUI Initial Window Definition

GUI designs are influenced by the physical GUI platform environment. All client/server projects should start with a pilot to help define the usage of that platform and how it can be applied to the tasks you have identified. The next step is to define initial windows in this GUI platform, as follows:

First define the views required for the user objects. Multiple views of an object may be required because of:

- *excessive information:* too much related information exists to be displayed on a single view (window). Create several views that consist of associated objects presented coherently.
- *frequency of usage:* some information will be used rarely. If this information clutters the basic view, it may be better to create two views, one with the rarely used information and one without.
- *security:* certain information may be restricted to particular users.
- *contextual use:* if an object is used in different tasks, it may be purposeful to have the information appear in different views.

Whenever multiple views are required, the designer considers that each of these views must be consistent. The information should be presented in the same form. These views should be consistent relative to the content as well. For example, if a customer name and address can be viewed in two different windows simultaneously and one of these windows updates the name and address, the other window should be automatically updated or else the user is likely to be confused. Maintaining consistency between multiple views may make the design and implementation more complex but it is important.

The next step is to define the initial windows. This consists of various activities, such as:

- *allocate each object view to a window:* decide which window class to use for each view and create an initial outline of the window using a window painting or prototyping tool.
- *define dependencies between windows:* review the initial windows to identify dependencies which are normally used where one window offers a view of an object which is part of an object in another window. They can be identified by asking "If this window is closed, will any other windows be affected?" They can also be identified by determining which

window must be open prior to this window. These dependencies will define how the window responds to such events as closing a primary window; this closes all associated secondary windows.

- *define simultaneous instances:* define the number of instances of this window which will be open simultaneously. The simplest form is a single instance (occurrence) of a user object. There may be multiple-user instances, but each is viewed by itself and then the window is reused. The most complex is multiple-user instances and multiple simultaneous views. The recommendation is to use the third alternative as infrequently as possible because:
  * The fewer windows open simultaneously, the less confusing it is to the user.
  * The interface is less complex to develop.
  * Less memory will be required to run the application.
  * Fewer windows open means there are fewer windows to close upon completion.
- *define initial actions:* these initial windows are not just simply a picture of the window; they also include the actions to be accomplished in the window. These initial window actions are added to and modified during the prototyping process.

The next step is to express the task scenarios that have been defined as a sequence of window actions. This will identify missing window objects, ease of windows use, which user tasks cannot be satisfied by the application, and so forth.

At this point an iterative prototyping process should begin, involving the designer and the user. These windows will be refined based on user needs and desires. The interface will be reviewed for completeness and consistency.

8

Tools to Develop Application Solutions

Up to this point we have covered software alternatives that can provide client/server application solutions with a small amount of development effort. They are limited in most cases to the features offered by the product. Additionally, they do not necessarily take full advantage of the GUI platforms on which they can run.

8.1 TOOL INTRODUCTION

Let's focus on the broad range of GUI tools available and how they apply to the day-to-day business environment.

8.1.1 Why GUI and GUI Tools?

The GUI platforms provide facilities to meet all application requirements. They provide users with flexible access to information. They can perform multiple tasks concurrently or at least provide facilities to start multiple tasks and switch among them without losing information. They provide facilities that allow the user to decide what application path to take. However, the interface to these platforms is complex; development and maintenance in the native mode interface to the GUI platform is costly. As a result, the market place has seen a proliferation of GUI tools that make this development easier and the resulting application more maintainable.

Multiple GUI platforms exist, each with a significant base in the market place: IBM's Presentation Manager (runs under IBM's OS/2), Microsoft's Windows (runs under DOS and Microsoft's NT), Motif and OPENLOOK (use X-Windows under UNIX), and Macintosh (from Apple Corp.). Each of these environments provide mechanisms for creating and interacting with graphical images. If you build an application using the native mode interface of one of these platforms, you are responsible for porting the code to another platform. If instead you use a GUI tool, the tool vendor is responsible for building portability to other platforms. Let's consider some of the other overall reasons to use the GUI tools and GUI platforms:

- *PC graphic capability:* the PC hardware technology has been growing at an incredible rate. Monitor colors and resolution that are currently available are more than adequate to support GUI windowing. Supporting graphics can be easily developed, grabbed, or scanned. Large storage devices in LAN servers, in addition to CD-ROM and optical disk, make storage of these graphical images possible.
- *PC pricing:* all this hardware is now available to such an extent that cost justification for a GUI client/server solution is no longer hardware dependent. The next hot technology will soon be multimedia as the hardware pricing continues to drop.
- *supporting software platforms are in place:* Microsoft's Windows and IBM's Presentation Manager are available on a large installed base of PCs. Motif and OPENLOOK are in place on a large installed base of UNIX machines. They provide graphic primitives, a window manager, icons, and data exchange facilities.
- *GUI shrink-wrapped solutions:* desktop products such as OfficeVision, LOTUS Notes, and Microsoft's Office are setting the standards on starting applications and how these applications should communicate using DDE, clipboard, and drag and drop manipulation techniques. A basic object model is enforced so that the applications appear to work together naturally. This even applies to pieces of software

running under a single GUI platform, such as Microsoft's windows, although they are from different vendors.

8.1.2   Tools Applied to the Development Cycle

The GUI environment provides many tools to assist during each phase of the traditional development cycle: planning, analysis, design, transition (development and implementation), and production (running the application and maintenance). Consider the tool opportunities in each phase, as follows:

- *planning:* during this phase you examine the feasibility of the system to be undertaken, estimate the cost of development, the cost of running the system in production, the projected savings, length of time to develop, and so forth. Cost estimation is most accurate if it can be done using a modelling system. Specialized tools which use modelling techniques and historical project information in an artificial intelligence system during the planning stage exist. They are often mainframe based and expensive. A less expensive assist can be achieved through the use of PC-based basic tools such as spreadsheet and simple database tools which can assist in projections of time and cost. There are also PC-based artificial intelligence software products which can be used to model applications development and production costs.

  This book does not cover the use of these tools for this phase. However, it is important to note that estimations during this planning phase will be based on the development and production platform chosen. A complete definition of the platform will be required if you want accurate estimates. If you do not have prior experience with the platform(s) chosen, consider hiring a consultant with prior platform(s) experience to assist during the planning phase.
- *analysis:* during this phase we interview all users, managers, and operations personnel, review all existing systems, inputs, outputs, and procedures, and then prepare a statement of what the system should do and how. Case tools used to define requirements can be introduced at this time. Also prototyping tools should be introduced; they can be

used as a preliminary means of confirming the results of the analysis (for example, prepare limited sample screens to assist in the requirements definition).

- *design:* output of this phase will be detail specifications of what the system will do and how. All input, output, processing, database, and file requirements will be defined. Case technology tools have the most to contribute during this phase. Prototyping tools should be used to design all user interfaces: screens, window, and reports. The prototyping tool should be a tool that is integrated with the GUI development tool set; if the prototyping tool simply creates window images or pictures that must then be redeveloped within the GUI development environment, productivity has been lost. The third type of tool that applies during this phase is the database tool set; this includes the active data dictionary if it is available (see chapter on databases).

- *transition:* in this phase we develop and implement the application. This phase includes initial user training, unit, systems, and parallel testing. Case tools generate code for the application. Prototyping tools may be used to rework the application during this phase as required by the user who is using and testing the application as it is built. Prototyping tools may also be used to create training scripts for the user. The database tools will be used to define the database, generate application views, generate data, establish data security, and tune performance of the database server. EIS and 4GL tools can be used to develop part of the application. The most important role will be played by the GUI development toolset, which will assist in developing the main part of the application. These GUI development toolsets, which we discuss later in this chapter, sometimes provide EIS, 4GL, prototyping, and database tools in one integrated package. Automated testing tools can be used to record a series of actions, create a test script, and automate the iterative testing of an application in such a way that it can be delivered "bug free."

- *production:* in this phase we run the system, provide additional training, corrections, and implement enhancements to the application and system as required. Development tools are used at this point to provide system maintenance and enhancements; they also provide the "run time" version of the application. Software management tools provide software distribution facilities and controls (see last chapter). Performance tools assist in analyzing performance problems and providing solutions (see last chapter). EIS and 4GL tools provide the user with their own toolset to enhance the system by adding features, adhoc queries, and so forth.

8.1.3   Who Uses Which Tool?

The user will probably take advantage of the variety of tools which follows. Some of the tools advertised as user friendly require technical strengths that are not present in a large portion of the user community. However, these tools are useful to the PC-literate user community. All of these tools require some understanding of PCs and GUI interfaces because they are based in this environment, but all users should receive some basic education on the client/server platform prior to implementing any application on this platform. Generally, the following tools apply to users:

- *EIS tools:* these tools can be used to develop applications geared to management and non-literate PC users. They provide online reporting using graphics. They provide screens with "drill down" capability: choose one aspect of a screen object and request ("drill down") more detail on that aspect. At the subsequent detail screen, "drill" further for more detail. These EIS tools can extract data from various sources, such as mainframe and files and databases stored on the LAN.
- *spreadsheet, word processing, database software tools:* these shrink-wrapped software packages (covered in a prior chapter) provide the basis for PC-literate users to develop their own application enhancements. Users can easily write macros for spreadsheets and word processing that merge mainframe or LAN-extracted data into an application. The same data can be merged into a database software package to satisfy customized requirements. The only requirement of the developer may be to prepare data-extract facilities for the mainframe or LAN, which the user could then invoke. Although these tools can be used by a technical user (PC-

literate user) to develop applications, the casual non-PC-literate user will probably find them too difficult to use to develop applications.

- *4GL and query tools:* the tools which provide the user with adhoc query and reporting support are probably the most valuable. This places the user in control; he or she is not totally dependent upon data processing personnel to provide the data processing solutions.

The developer has all of the above-listed tools available. Although these tools are not as complex and sophisticated as the GUI development tool sets, they should not be ignored. If solutions can be provided more quickly using these simpler tools, requirements can be satisfied more quickly. With corporations focusing on "best bang for the buck" and "the bottom line" these simpler tools can be a valuable and time-saving asset.

The developer will be taking advantage of all of the types of tools described previously in the development cycle: CASE, prototyping, database, GUI development, testing, and performance tools.

Additionally, development may also be done using programming languages such as C and COBOL. The most common language used or integrated with the GUI development packages is C. This is the most common language for case tools as well. COBOL routine support is available in a few GUI development packages. However, a good GUI development package will drastically reduce the need to write any code, whether in the form of exit, routine, or snippet to be added to the generated code. Instead, many GUI tools have their own scripting tool or language which provides the means to develop more complex solutions.

8.1.4   Prototyping

Prototyping has been included in this chapter for several reasons:

- It should be part of any GUI design and part of any GUI development tool you intend to use in your client/server platform.
- It is an integral part of RAD.

Defining the problem correctly has always been one of the most significant development problems. Too often the analysis, design, and development of the system results in an application that does not meet user expectations. The classic cartoon describing this situation depicts the user requirement as a simple swing hanging from a tree limb. Everyone involved in the project envisions a different end product. If they had a picture of the result, it would be worth a thousand words. That's what prototyping is all about. During the design phase of a project, all screens, reports, and application flow are created. The user then works with the full "look and feel" of the application to clarify all potential points of misunderstanding.

Prototypes can range from simple sequences of graphical images or storyboards to actual working models. Since we are focusing on the prototype as an integral part of the GUI tool, it should be close to the latter. These prototypes are crucial to client/server development because they:

- help identify the gaps and flaws of a GUI application design. The errors and design flaws can be discovered before time and money are spent in actual development.
- provide a means of testing the design early in the development process.
- provide the project team an opportunity to build a design with a small investment and learn from the prototype what works and what does not.
- stimulate thought among the users and development community in the design stage and early in the development stage. Prototypes can be quickly changed to explore new task flows and different high-level design.
- provide substantive look and feel of the application to show to users and managers. This can be used as a marketing approach to encourage user buy in or perhaps expand the original scope.
- provide a means of communicating the design to users. The prototype provides a tangible visualization of the high-level design. The end users validate the system interface and system flow by using the application prototype as a functioning entity.
- provide an opportunity for user buy in to the new application. Because the user is involved in the building, modification, and finalization of these screens, windows, and reports,

the design is as much theirs as it is the developers'. As a result, you have user buy in, which is absent from systems designed, developed, and then presented to the user.

Interactive prototyping should play a major role in the user interface design. Prototyping can be used to:

- define initial windows
- express task scenarios as window actions
- explore alternative interface representations and sequences
- confirm usability for tasks
- confirm user understanding and acceptance of the interface specification

If prototyping facilities are not available, the user interface can be drawn on paper or flip charts, using sketches of windows and interaction sequences. However, this is a poor substitute for software prototyping. Users can understand the design on paper, but the actual GUI system when it is implemented has a different look and feel, which cannot be simulated on paper. Additionally, the paper approach does not easily accommodate the many iterations of prototyping that are required to properly satisfy the user and tune the design.

Prototyping does lead to some concerns that the designer and developer should watch out for:

- the developer, and even the user, can lose focus on central tasks issues while concentrating on the look, feel, and flow
- iterative prototyping can consume an excessive effort
- concentrating on the prototype can lead to inconsistencies in the interface

8.1.5   Rapid Application Development (RAD)

As a general concept in the development environment, RAD might best be understood as a set of techniques and tools to provide a faster and more on-target applications development. RAD in particular is a trademark of James Martin, the author and publisher of numerous books on a wide variety of data processing subjects.

In the ideal situation, a true RAD tool is one that makes a prototype that is good enough to use in a production environment. Additionally, once an application is developed, a RAD tool should be able to add new features with minimal effort. For example, if additional reports or screen views are required, the tool should make it possible to add a new menu item, code a few dialog boxes, and incorporate them in the existing application with little effort. The target benefits of RAD include:

- faster application development by validating business requirements before a detailed design model is constructed.
- generate detail design from the application prototype.
- provide the end user with the ability to validate the interface design and system flow by working with the application prototype.
- increase communication with the user through the prototype and thereby reduce the possibility of misunderstanding requirements and expectations.
- the ability to build an application prototype without specifying technical platform requirements. This allows developers to focus on the business requirements.

The five phases of the development life cycle are planning, analysis, design, transition, and production. Phases 2, 3, and 4 represent most of the time needed to prepare an application for its final state—production. If the time required for these three phases can be reduced significantly, you're on your way to rapid application development—RAD:

- *analysis:* if the analysis tool is integrated with a prototyping tool, the developer can build a prototype based on the data collected in the analysis phase.
- *design:* if the prototyping tool is integrated with the design tool, the prototyping tool will provide design constructs. Application flow and screen objects can easily be defined.
- *transition:* usable screen objects have already been built in the design phase. If CASE tools are part of this development environment, much of the code will be written as a result of the design phase. Since the application was validated in the analysis phase through prototyping, costly revisions are avoided during this phase.

Overall savings in the three phases of development lead to RAD.

Most of the GUI development tools discussed in this chapter provide prototyping capability. This means that the screen objects can be used in the production environment. In a loose definition of RAD, all of the GUI development tools in the following section provide RAD.

The more restrictive definition of RAD requires that the tool generate design specifications from the analysis phase. Currently this is done within the CASE environment. KnowledgeWare in the CASE vendors list referred to in a subsequent section of this chapter addresses RAD specifically with their ADW/RAD workstation component. However, even the current CASE environments do not solve all of the client/server development concerns.

Whenever we refer to "tool" here, the tool can be a series of tools that are well integrated. They may even be from multiple vendors (for example, Windows with an SQL database management system and a development tool with GUI capability).

8.2   GUI DEVELOPMENT TOOLS

Developing applications in a client/server environment requires Information System managers to focus on how to acclimate their mainframe-oriented developers. One approach is to take typical COBOL programmers and teach them C, and train them on the native APIs (Application Programming Interfaces) for the GUI, mainframe access, LAN access, and SQL server. This is an expensive and time-consuming approach. An alternative is to utilize a front-end tool that is designed to aid development of window-based applications in a client/server environment. You can reduce the training costs and cut the learning curve significantly.

8.2.1   GUI Development Tool Features

The following are some of the facilities available and concerns relating to these tool sets. They can be used as a basis for evaluation:

- *basic features:* the tool sits on top of the GUI platform. These GUI platforms have numerous facilities. The concern for the developer is to find out which of these facilities is supported within the tool set. Minimally they should support push buttons, radio buttons, check boxes, dialog boxes, list boxes, popup windows, entry field editing, message boxes, text box, OLE, DDE, and bit mapped images (BLOBS—binary linked objects).

- *additional features:* what special additional features does the tool provide? For example: forms support to create images of existing manual forms for data entry, draw editor, spell checker, multimedia support, audio/image capture and playback, libraries of screen objects, clip art, and so forth.
- *LAN software and distribution management:* does the tool include LAN software change management and distribution management? Is the tool compatible with and does it easily interface with the change management and distribution management software that will be running in your environment?
- *tool company stability:* will the tool company be in business tomorrow? Maybe this is the single most important point of evaluating one product against another. It is perhaps the most subjective, however. The cost of no longer having the tool vendor available to support your mission critical applications written under the tool is great.
- *windows platform support:* which tools are compatible with IBM's OS/2, DOS and Windows, UNIX, etc.? Does the tool provide for development in one platform (for example, Microsoft Windows) and then automatically convert to another platform for production (for example, IBM OS/2 Presentation Manager)?
- *CUA enforcement or conforming:* if you want your applications to be CUA compatible, enforcement can be tedious. If the tool does it and enforces CUA guidelines, developers and their management can direct more of their efforts to the application development. Minimally the tool should conform to CUA guidelines.
- *run-time component should be small:* the client machine's size requirements (both memory and disk) should be minimized so that the application can be run, for example, on minimally configured 386 machines. Some run time components require in excess of 1 meg memory, in addition to the Windows or OS/2 and application requirements.
- *no run-time license charges:* some of the best tools on the market require run-time fees of over $150 per client station. On large applications this can be expensive. Some of these products are based on an overall installation fee. Some of the products have no run-time license fee but the developer's workstation is very expensive. You need to review your pro-

duction and development workstation requirements in order to price the tool cost effectively.

- *low-cost development package:* this is a balancing act. A single developer's workstation can cost over $10,000 to set up, including hardware and software. However, if productivity increases dramatically, this can be cost-justified in less than a year.
- *conducive to reusable objects:* does the product simplify the use of object-oriented development and promote the use of reusable objects? One of the very desirable features in a client/server environment is that of producing objects that can be reused in many applications.
- *SQL access:* which SQL software engines does the software interface with? How does this interface work: through SQL code? through a special interface?
- *run-time speed:* how much overhead does the GUI tool interface have? How does this overhead impact the client or server? Some tools are adequate during development, but because they are interpretive, execution—especially in production—is too slow.
- *generate objects not inline code:* dialog objects should be separate from the code to make the objects more reusable and maintainable. Tools that create large amounts of inline PM or Windows code should be avoided because they are difficult to read, maintain, and so forth.
- *debugging and trace support:* does the tool provide a specialized debugging facility? Since the tool and its run-time components represent a very specialized environment, you need a debugging tool that is customized for this environment. The debugging facilities should also provide some type of trace facility so that a series of internal and external events can be logged for review.
- *C routine support:* does the tool support C code both as separate routines or modules and as modifications to code generated by the software?
- *COBOL routine support:* does the tool support COBOL code both as separate routines or modules and as modifications to code generated by the software?
- *report writer:* does the tool have a built-in report writer, 4GL, or query facility? How good is it?

- *CASE tool integration:* does the tool interface with any case tool vendors?
- *prototyping:* does the tool have a prototyping facility?
- *EIS:* does the tool have an Executive Information System facility?

8.2.2   Types of GUI Tools

GUI application development tools can be placed into four categories, each with some pros and cons, as follows:

Code Generators The tools in this category generate code that you can include in your program (usually C language). The tools usually provide a WYSIWYG editor so that you can define the screen objects you want to create. Then the tool generates the code necessary (for example, to interface to Microsoft's Windows or IBM's OS/2 Presentation Manager). The source code produced is merged into your program, where you can then edit and compile it. See Figure 8.1.

The pros include:

- *low-cost tools:* these tools are usually not expensive.
- *direct access to the GUI interface:* they are good for learning the GUI environment and interface itself. They can be use-

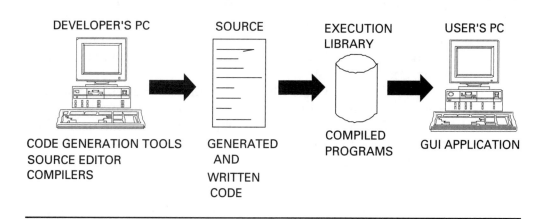

DEVELOPER'S PC   SOURCE   EXECUTION LIBRARY   USER'S PC

CODE GENERATION TOOLS
SOURCE EDITOR
COMPILERS

GENERATED
AND
WRITTEN
CODE

COMPILED
PROGRAMS

GUI APPLICATION

Figure 8.1   Code Generators

ful if you plan to be in only that environment and the application is small, or you are writing an architecture interface for your own development environment.

- *no run-time license:* they do not require a run-time license because you are producing the final version of the application code.

The cons include:

- *must code in GUI environment:* they generate some of the code but you must code at the GUI interface level. You must write the low end GUI interface functions; with other tool types you do not need to. You must write your own objects and in some cases use them as in-line code instead of objects.
- *must debug and maintain all programs:* you are responsible for maintaining and debugging the programs. After you have used the tools to create code and modified that code, you can no longer use the tool to maintain this code.
- *limited CUA enforcement:* any automated CUA enforcement is limited to the standards imposed by the tool. You will have to develop a rigorous set of standards that must be imposed manually.

Language-based Tools These types of tools provide the ability to manipulate external display objects directly from within language-based programs (for example, C, C++, or COBOL). You can specify which objects to display and when; the interface to screen objects is through an API. You display objects and wait for events to happen. There are control loops, event handlers, or GUI calls. See Figure 8.2.

One of the key areas which differentiates these tools from the prior tool types is that the tools determine the method of exchange of data with the screen objects and how the user selections and actions are returned to the program.

The pros include:

- *separation of the code from the screen objects:* this improves development because you can create a library of objects that can be used by all developers.

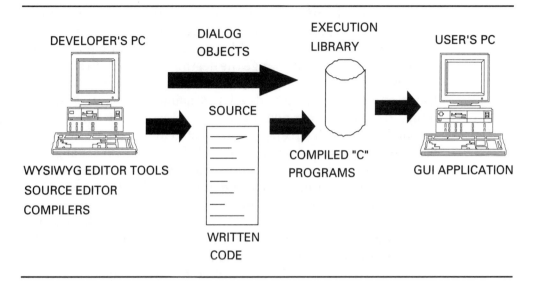

DEVELOPER'S PC · DIALOG OBJECTS · EXECUTION LIBRARY · USER'S PC

WYSIWYG EDITOR TOOLS
SOURCE EDITOR
COMPILERS

SOURCE

WRITTEN CODE

COMPILED "C" PROGRAMS

GUI APPLICATION

Figure 8.2   Language-based Tools

- *improved program maintenance:* it improves program maintenance, allowing the developer to focus on the logic of visual elements independently of code.
- *no run-time license:* these tools do not have a run-time component. Therefore, there cannot be a run-time license fee.

The cons include:

- *limited object development tool:* you are limited to the objects that can be constructed by using the screen object interface and the dialog with that interface.
- *restricted GUI usage:* if you have a need to use the full GUI facilities, you must code in the native GUI language interface. You can use the code generator tool previously discussed.
- *limited CUA enforcement:* any automated CUA enforcement is limited to the standards imposed by the tool. You will have to develop a rigorous set of standards that must be imposed manually.

Event-driven Tools The difference between procedure-driven and event-driven transactions or programming is important when applied to the client/server environment. Procedural transactions or programming predetermine a set of activities or tasks. The analogy sometimes used is that of riding a train. The train has a destination; the user cannot change the destination or the direction the train will travel to get to that destination. The majority of mainframe online processing is developed using procedural programming. Prompt the user and prepare for a response; when the user responds, all possible responses are tested for and an action taken based on the specific response entered. Then the next set of potential responses is developed and the transaction awaits a response.

Event-driven transactions and programs simply respond to an action by the user directly. The analogy used for event-driven applications is that of driving a car; the user can change the destination or direction the car will travel. Most of the client/server GUI applications are event driven. The path the user takes is not controlled as tightly as it is in a procedure-driven application. An event can be selecting a push button, keyboard input, clicking a mouse on a hot spot, jumping to another entry field, different dialog box, or window, and so forth. The programmer defines the responses to an event.

An example of procedural programming might be a series of menus which lead to a data entry screen. Each menu is a program that allows only certain selections, and passes control to another program which either controls a submenu or ultimately displays the data entry screen that is waiting for user input. Upon arrival at the data entry screen, the user must enter all appropriate fields on the screen and then depress the ENTER key to get a response. The sequence of processing is predetermined.

The equivalent event-driven activity is done by the user selecting from many other actions not necessarily related to this application; the menu and submenus are action bars and pulldown menus. An event-driven data entry screen may have help windows, list windows, and the like. The user can move to any portion of the screen and take an action (the event), which invokes a set of code. The actual data entry screen is flexible in such a way that the user can enter fields in any order; additionally, for each field entered the user receives a response because each field entry represents an event.

The event-driven tools are based on an event-driven environment in which you create events and code the responses to them.

A WYSIWYG editor is usually provided by the tool vendor to define the windows and dialog boxes in your application. The script associates event names with various window components. An event can be a push button selection, a keyboard input, a mouse click, and so forth. The editor will assist in generating a script of object definitions and the events they produce. The scripts are essentially a 3GL/4GL language with a limited vocabulary of commands. See Figure 8.3.

Most of the action statements will be coded in the language supplied by the tool vendor. This will allow you to take advantage of libraries of canned actions that are typically supplied with the tool. You can call C or C++ written functions from within the script.

The pros of these tools include:

- *debugging environment:* they generally include a debugging facility which enables you to run the program, set break points, and view the output from within the outline of your script.
- *code library and versioning system:* because these tools consist of many types of components, the tool facilities often contain a software library management and versioning component. If the tool does not, this can be a disadvantage.
- *good method of organizing the GUI application components:* these tools are well suited for GUI interfaces because the client/server applications in a GUI environment are event

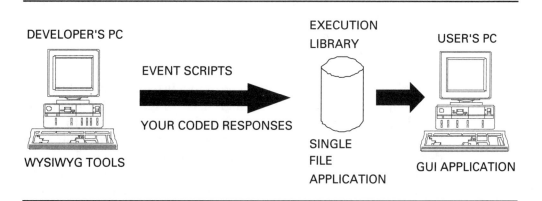

Figure 8.3   Event-driven Tools

driven. The event-driven application is a collection of responses to various kinds of inputs and stimuli.

- *you can reuse parts of scripts:* once you have a script, you can use it with minor modifications to create new applications. You can also create mini-scripts that can be stored and operate as objects.
- *CUA enforcement:* these tools are CUA compliant. Their included library of objects adhere to the CUA guidelines as well as their default options in the script creation process. If the tool is not CUA compliant, this is a major disadvantage.

The cons of these tools include:

- *new proprietary language and environment:* although it is like the English language, the script language is another new programming language that must be learned from scratch.
- *single file application:* some of these tools create application components that are compiled into a single file: for example, all screens may be stored in a single file. This may be too cumbersome for large applications.
- *the vendor's tool lags behind new functions provided by GUI platform:* this means you'll may have to program in the GUI and C whenever you need to create user interfaces that the tool vendor does not provide.
- *tools may be expensive:* they may cost $5,000 or more per developer workstation because they are much more comprehensive than the prior tool sets.
- *run-time license may be required:* a run-time license of $150 or more per client workstation may be required.
- *run-time components' memory requirements:* the run-time components have a significant memory requirement.

Object-oriented Tools This type of tool is event driven, but it is also "object oriented" to some degree. See Figure 8.4. Object-oriented programming can be explained by comparing it to traditional mainframe software. Traditional mainframe software design places code in one place (or multiple places) and data in another (or multiple other places). For example, in program validation for a zip code in a mailing address, the code is written to edit a specific zip code 5-digit field to be stored on a specific database or file. When zip codes increase in length from 5 to 9 digits,

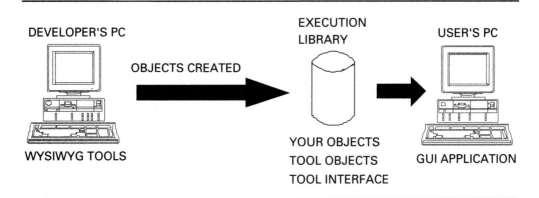

DEVELOPER'S PC

OBJECTS CREATED

EXECUTION
LIBRARY

USER'S PC

YOUR OBJECTS

TOOL OBJECTS

TOOL INTERFACE

WYSIWYG TOOLS

GUI APPLICATION

Figure 8.4   Object-oriented Tools

it is necessary to change database, files, and programs in multiple places.

The object-oriented approach joins a data structure more closely with the code that modifies it. The fundamentals of object technology include:

- *encapsulation:* the objects control access to data. The internal structure of data is not necessarily available to other modules and data can either be stored or computed as needed.
- *inheritance:* new classes of objects can be defined by how they differ from existing classes. Common behavior of the class is defined in place. Special behaviors are defined with affected data structures.
- *single message:* similar behaviors of different objects can be invoked with a single request: for example, the "PRINT" request. This improves consistency of user interface.

Applied to the zip code example, an application requesting the zip code talks to a black box. The calling program neither knows nor cares whether that code was retrieved as simple data or assembled on the fly: for example, is the zip code stored as a nine digit number or in two pieces, first 5 digits and last four digits. Properties about presenting the data (for example, a "-" between 5 and 4 digits) are also stored. This makes maintaining information much simpler.

A common example of a screen object (but not object-oriented programming) is a list box. The full function of the list box, including scrolling up and down the list an entry or page at a time and selecting an entry from the list, exists as an object. You simply provide the list of data and the rest is done by the object. Other list boxes can be created from this list box, for example, changing the size of the list box: increase or decrease the number of entries on the list shown at one time. The new list box inherits all of the characteristics of the original list box.

The pros of these tools include:

- *debugging environment:* they generally include a debugging facility that enables you to run the program, set break points, and view the output from within the outline of your script.
- *code library and versioning system:* because these tools consist of many types of components, the tool facilities often contain a software library management and versioning component. If the tool does not, this can be a disadvantage.
- *reusable code:* the tool provides libraries of reusable code. They can be used as is or customized. This code describes not only the object's structure but also its behavior and its interface to other objects.
- *tool provides the "glue":* the tool provides the glue that holds together the application and makes it work.
- *CUA enforcement:* these tools are CUA compliant. Their included library of objects adhere to the CUA guidelines as well as their default options in the script creation process. If the tool is not CUA compliant, this is a major disadvantage.
- *object tools have WYSIWYG editors:* these editors typically allow you to create screens from a library of predefined display classes. A class brings together data structures and the procedures that manipulate these structures. These methods are invoked by sending messages. When you create an object of a particular class you automatically inherit all of its methods and attributes.

The cons of these tools include:

- *the vendor tool lags behind new functions provided by GUI platform:* this means you'll may have to program in the

GUI and C whenever you need to create user interfaces that the tool vendor does not provide.

- *tools may be expensive:* they may cost $5,000 or more per developer workstation because they are much more comprehensive than the prior tool sets.
- *run-time license may be required:* a run-time license of $150 or more per client workstation may be required.
- *run-time components' memory requirements:* the run-time components have a significant memory requirement.
- *not fully object oriented:* although many of the tool vendors indicate that they are object oriented, they do not provide OOP (Object Oriented Programming) facilities.

8.2.3   Developer's Tools Available

The following pages contain a list of some of the client/server GUI development tool vendors. A comprehensive list would contain 30 to 40 vendors; however, since you will be developing mission critical applications using these tools, any vendor that will not be in business after the market settles down represents a major problem. The list concentrates on the vendors with the largest market share but it is not intended to cover all of the major players.

The first few vendors are also RDBMS vendors with a major database market share. They have a "complete" client/server solution set of tools from database to implementation. The remaining vendors focus on only development tools. All of these vendors interface with a variety of RDBMS, either directly or through gateways.

Each vendor has been listed with several of its products, the target development platforms, and so forth. The author has experience with several of these products and as a result makes the following observations:

- Most of these products can successfully support your client/server development needs.
- Choosing a product should be done carefully. Use the features check list earlier in the chapter as a basis for starting the evaluation.
- To evaluate your final few candidates, plan on using the full tool set for a minimum of 2 to 4 weeks. You should

develop the same application in each tool set environment to fully appreciate the differences in the development, debugging, implementation, change management and tuning facilities provided by the vendor.

Gupta Technologies, Inc.
1040 Marsh Road
Menlo Park, CA 92425
(415) 321-9500

SQL Windows	(complete GUI application development system)
Report Windows	(WYSIWYG report writer)
Quest	(user adhoc queries)
Express Windows	(application generator for SQL Windows)

Target Clients: IBM OS/2 PM, Microsoft Windows

Oracle
Redwood Shores, CA 94065
(415) 506-7000

ORACLE Precompilers	(SQL access code embedded in C, COBOL, Fortran across many client operating systems—UNIX, DOS, OS/2, etc.)
SQL Forms and Menu	(screen forms/windows and menu building support for applications development)
SQL Text Retrieval	(text retrieval capability—interface to applications)
SQL Report Writer	(report writer)
SQL PLUS	
Oracle Data query	(user adhoc queries)

Target Clients: IBM OS/2 PM, Microsoft Windows, Unix MOTIF

Informix Software, Inc.
4100 Bohannon Drive
Menlo Park, CA 94025
(415) 926-6300

Informix 4GL   (4GL application development tool)

Target Clients: Unix

Ingres
1080 Marina Village Parkway
Alameda, CA 94501
(415) 748-2668

    INGRES/Windows   (GUI object-oriented 4GL
                                development facility)
    INGRES Query by Forms   (user adhoc queries)
    INGRES Report by Forms (user report writer)

    Target Clients: IBM OS/2 PM, Microsoft Windows, Unix
                         MOTIF

Microsoft Corp.
One Microsoft Way
Redmond WA 98052
(800) 227-4679

    Visual Basic   (GUI object-oriented development facility)
    Visual C, C++ (GUI object-oriented development facility)

    Target Clients: Microsoft Windows

Easel Corporation
25 Corporate Drive
Burlington, MA 01803
(617) 221-2100

    Easel/2 &
    Easel/W   (complete GUI application
                              development system)
    Manager's Portfolio EIS (EIS software)

    Target Clients: IBM OS/2 PM, Microsoft Windows

    Note: Easel is an IBM International Alliance Partner.
          Their orientation is to provide a more comprehensive
          interface to many IBM products than the other GUI
          tools vendors provide.

Borland International, Inc.
1800 Green Hills Rd.
Scotts Valley, CA 95067
(408) 438-5300

ObjectVision   (complete GUI application
                             development system)
Turbo Reports for Windows   (report writer)

Target Clients: IBM OS/2 PM, Microsoft Windows

Powersoft Corporation
70 Blanchard Road
Burlington, MA 01803
(617) 229-2200

PowerBuilder   (complete GUI application
                             development system)
Dynamic DataWindow   (report writer)

Target Clients: Microsoft Windows

Enfin Software Corp.
6920 Miramar Road, Suite 307
San Diego, CA 92121
(619) 549-6798

Enfin/Windows &
Enfin/3 PM   (complete GUI application development
                     system)

Target Clients: Microsoft Windows, IBM OS/2 PM

8.2.4   GUI Automated Testing Tools

An additional concern in developing mission critical client/server applications using these development tools is thoroughly testing the resulting application. Testing these applications traditionally can be done by using several different methods or combinations of methods, as follows:

- have the programmers run a thorough test, saving the results (before and after images) for review by a team of end users and QA personnel (people intensive option).

- put together a QA team to enter and evaluate all results (people intensive option).
- develop test scripts using the development tools' macro or script writing capability. This is an expensive programming effort and requires programmer modification every time the application is modified.
- use an automated testing tool. If this is available for your development platform and toolset, it represents the best alternative.

Automated testing tools can generally automate tests for GUI-based applications, simulating the input from a human user and recording results. Some of them can try every permutation that is possible in a feature set, reproduce tests many times over, or test a program continuously. Using this last option, it is possible to do volume tests with only a few developers or users.

These tools are typically limited in their scope of interface with products and platforms. Some of these products include:
QA Partner (Windows, Macintosh, Unix)

Segue Software
Newton Centre, MA 02159
(617) 969-3771

Microsoft Test (Windows)
Microsoft Corp.
One Microsoft Way
Redmond, WA 98052
(800) 227-4679

SQA TeamTest (Windows, Gupta's SQL Windows, and
Powersoft's Powerbuilder)
Software Quality Automation
Woburn, MA 01801
(617) 932-0110

WinRunner (Windows, Gupta's SQLWindows, and
Powersoft's Powerbuilder)
Mercury Interactive
Santa Clara, CA 95054
(408) 987-0100

8.3   OTHER GUI TOOLS

Other tools are important to the GUI client/server environment. They provide the means for developers and users to take full advantage of this new technology.

8.3.1   Query Tools and Report Writers

A good complement of query tools and SQL report writers can ease the data processing development load by taking data queries and report generation out of the developers' hands and placing them in the hands of end users. To easily extract data from an SQL database server (or other PC-based databases or mainframe data) you need a powerful report writer or query tool. The client/server LAN environment has numerous tools to provide reporting. These can be both developer designed and user designed. The report writers operate on mainframe, database, SQL, and flat file data. They can run on the client machine or on a server of their own. They can print on a printer attached to the client, a print server on the LAN, or simply be a print image presented on the screen.

The term 4GL is usually associated with report writers provided today to meet the needs of client/server environments. James Martin published a book in 1982 entitled *Application Development Without Programming,* in which he coined the term fourth-generation language (4GL) to describe a simplified type of software development language. 4GLs were supposed to provide higher developer productivity, greater user involvement in the development cycle, and code that was easier to maintain when compared to the existing 3GLs such as COBOL and C. Although 4GLs have advanced significantly since that time, they have not replaced 3GLs such as COBOL. However, their current state is such that they can meet the targets of a 4GL as outlined in Martin's text.

The 4GL tools provide facilities such as:

- choosing a report format from many predefined report layouts, including columnar field per line, record entry, mailing labels
- placing fields, system variables, and calculated variables anywhere on the report

- specifying any number of group breaks on fields or variables
- calculating fields to be used to perform lookups, compute totals, and combine columns

You can create reports using the database packages previously covered. Again, these reports can be generated by a developer and be available on a report server, or be generated by users on their client machine by using the client/server environment as data servers and print servers. Often the "report writer" is simply preparing a report for online use instead of being printed. Since the data can be more easily gathered and presented, permanent hardcopy may not be necessary.

The EIS software covered in the next section can also be categorized as report writing software.

A second type of inquiry/reporting tool which should be available to both the developer and the user in the client/server environment is the query tool. These tools offer a simple, uncluttered interface to the data online. Pull-down menus offer the user available functions such as create a new query or run an existing query. Defining new queries is simplified by an interface that lists the information available (for example, all tables available and the data within each table). You can click on to each item desired in the query and entire conditional searches via a simplified interface (the interface will construct the necessary SQL to retrieve the data). More complex features are available so that you can write your own SQL to retrieve the data. The results of the query can also be printed so that it can be used as a real-time inquiry and a report.

The following list of report writer and query tools are in some cases from SQL database vendors that can provide a complete GUI development environment. The other software vendors specialize in report writing and query tools.

Oracle Data Query

SQL ReportWriter
    Oracle Corporation
    500 Oracle Parkway
    Redwood Shores, CA 94065
    (415) 506-7000

Informix 4GL
Informix Software, Inc.
4100 Bohannon Drive
Menlo Park, CA 94025
(415) 926-6300

Object Oriented 4GL
Ingres
1080 Marina Village Parkway
Alameda, CA 94501
(510) 748-2668

Momentum 4GL
Sybase Inc.
6475 Christie Avenue
Emeryville, CA 94608
(510) 596-3500

Quest
Gupta Technologies, Inc.
1040 Marsh Road
Menlo Park, CA 94025
(415) 321-9500

FOCUS
Information Builders, Inc.
New York, NY 10001
(212) 736-4433

Crystal Reports
Crystal Computer Services
Vancouver, British Columbia, Canada
(604) 681-3435

R & R Report Writer
Concentric Data Systems
Westborough, MA 01581
(508) 366-1122

8.3.2   Executive Information Systems (EIS)

In general, EIS is based on a simple approach. Executives don't want to spend time learning to use complicated and cumbersome software, not even traditional software like word processors and spreadsheet. They want to know what the bottom line is as quickly as possible without having to dig through many screens or many papers and reports. An EIS ties into these sources as well as many different databases, extracts the valuable data, and presents it to the executive in a simplified form; the executive then can identify any problem and take appropriate action.

The EIS is simple to use and assists the executive in the decision-making process. Information is prepared in such a way that the executive can drill down to any level to research a problem. Icons, graphics, and text are used to display the information. Hotspots are identified on each screen which the executive can select and then drill down for more detail.

The following criteria should be met to make an EIS useful to executives:

- *self-explanatory system:* generally, executives have no spare time for training. They cannot afford time to read manuals, notes, and help screens, nor do they often have that kind of patience. The executive should simply be able to look at the screen and know what to do.
- *graphic displays:* graphs and charts give an excellent instant broad picture of data turned into information. Intuitive icons should identify the features and functions available. Color can be used to simplify the message. For example, a map of the United States with each sales region delineated might then have the sales regions that have not met their sales quotas highlighted in red while all the regions that have met their quotas are colored in green.
- *minimum use of keyboard:* executives may have limited keyboard skills. The system should not require that they learn these skills. Instead, they could use a mouse with simple single click selection or a touch screen. Either input device can be used to choose from menu items or activate hot buttons.
- *response must be fast:* response time of less than a second is desirable; however, this may not always be feasible when displaying complex graphic images driven by dynamic data. On the other hand, executives are both busy and easily distracted. Therefore, each response must be immediate; if a response will take more than one second, consider plac-

ing a message on the screen indicating exactly how long it will take.

The EIS software tools generally provide many of the following capabilities:

- *NOS and GUI compatibility:* they operate on all of the established LAN network operating systems: Banyan VINES, IBM LAN Server, Novell Netware, Microsoft Lan Manager. They run on various GUI platforms: Microsoft Windows, IBM OS/2 Presentation Manager.
- *data access:* they can interface with most LAN-based SQL servers: Oracle, Microsoft, and Sybase SQL Server. You can tap into data in external database or spreadsheet sources such as dBase, Paradox, and Lotus 1-2-3 by using Dynamic Link Libraries bought separately or built on your own. They can access mainframe data through product interfaces.
- *live connections to internal and external data:* Dynamic Data Exchange (DDE) and Dynamic Link Libraries (DLLs) can make live connections to internal and external data on LAN or mainframe, which can then be automatically updated based on a designated time.
- *draw capability:* choose among the shapes such as rectangle, line, ellipse, polygon, and so forth and then change the size and proportion.
- *text handling:* can be used to create titles or other static information. You can justify text, choose colors, fonts, and type sizes.
- *document handling:* you can bring in live data, both text and numeric.
- *include images:* include photos of people, products, floor space, promotional displays, and so forth. You can include images from PCX or bitmap file from clipboard, DDE request, or DLL connection, as well as from symbol library or clip art package.
- *point and click navigation:* the mouse is used to point and click on any hot spot item you identify, and then the tool will display the next layer of more detailed information.

Many of the full GUI development tools covered earlier in this chapter claim to provide EIS building tools. Certainly many of them can be used to build EIS applications. However, building these applications may be as significant an effort as building a full-blown client/server application. Other tools in the market place specializing in EIS-like solutions probably provide a better alternative. Some of these vendors include:

Lightship
Pilot Executive Software
Boston, MA 02109
(617) 350-7035

Forest & Trees
Channel Computing
Portsmouth, NH 03801-3872
(603) 427-0444

FOCUS/EIS for Windows
Information Builders, Inc.
New York, NY 10001
(212) 736-4433

8.3.3 CASE Tools

This section is not intended to be a comprehensive review of CASE (Computer Aided or Assisted Software or System Engineering) technology as it applies to the client/server environment. The following is some background information as it applies to CASE technology in general.

CASE is made up of a combination of tools such as data flow diagrammers, screen painters, and code generators. CASE provides a method for using these tools in the strategic planning, analysis, and design phases of applications development. CASE technology improves the development process during the analysis, design, and programming activities. The purpose of CASE technology is to improve the process of systems design and implementation.

The ideal CASE environment can facilitate the following:

* *speed up the system development process:* CASE tools can be part of a RAD solution.
* *more flexible systems:* change the input from the analysis stage and the CASE tools should automatically generate the new design.

- *quality control:* since the CASE tool is in control, quality can be controlled uniformly by the tool.
- *assembly line components:* parts of systems can be defined, generated, and assembled similar to manufacturing on an assembly line. This means that many people can work on the system components simultaneously.
- *component sharing:* since the system is built using components, these components can be shared across the system.
- *database definition:* the database definition is integrated with the development process.
- *generate code:* the target result of CASE input is generated application code. Ideally, applications can be generated without any need for programming; the reality is different.
- *generates documentation:* since CASE is driven by data gathered in the analysis stage and generates the design as well as application code, the information exists within the CASE database to generate the appropriate documentation at both the system and component level.

CASE tool sets consist of:

- *project management tools:* these are used to organize and control the project. They may be off-the-shelf Project Management shrink-wrapped solutions or software integrated with other components from the same vendor.
- *analysis tools:* these tools model the business information requirements.
- *design tools:* these tools use the results of the analysis phase to develop system specifications and define the databases and files.
- *expert systems:* these tools ease the analysis process. The analyst therefore requires less experience; this can translate to less overall analysis experience or less experience with the new client/server platform.
- *programming tools:* these tools take the output of the analysis and design phases and then generate application code.
- *implementation tools:* these tools are used to test the system, monitor performance, and provide version control.
- *maintenance tools:* these tools support existing applications. They include program analyzers, code restructuring, and reverse engineering tools.

There are three types of generally accepted CASE environments:

- *I-CASE:* Integrated CASE is soup-to-nuts software, automating the entire system development process. Usually it is a single large purchase of a set of tools from a single vendor, including all of the above plus training.
- *C-CASE:* using Component CASE, you select pieces of CASE software from different vendors and integrate them yourself. The idea is to find the best components and work at integrating them; these components are typically referred to as front-end or back-end tools.
- *R-CASE:* Repository CASE is based on a data dictionary that you populate with information gathered in the analysis stage. You then use this data dictionary to drive all development. It is usually the first step in all CASE-driven applications development and often only requires training as an expense to get started.

One of the problems with all CASE technology is that it ideally takes you from planning to implementation via code generation. This code generation creates two major concerns in the client/server development process:

- *no GUI interface:* CASE solutions generally do not have built-in GUI prototyping in the analysis and design stages and, as a result, do not currently generate the GUI interface required in client/server applications.
- *code generation:* CASE tools generate code to build the application. They are for the most part not object oriented. CASE tools vendors are just beginning to address event-driven, object-oriented solutions.

The list of vendors below has been included to provide a variety of vendors that address the different types of CASE environments. You can consider various vendors as sources that provide the individual components for the full CASE environment, such as ADW (used for analysis) and BACHMAN DBA (used for design). Also, the reader should note that some of these products do address generation of GUI code; for example, Caseworks generates GUI code interfaces for Microsoft's Windows in C and for IBM's OS/2 Presentation Manager in both C and COBOL.

Foundation (I-CASE)
Foundation for Cooperative Processing (C-CASE)
  Anderson Consulting
  Chicago, IL 60602
  (312) 580-0069

HyperAnalyst & DBA (C-CASE)
  Bachman Information Systems
  Burlington, MA 01803
  (617) 273-9003

CASE:W & CASE:PM (C-CASE)
  Caseworks Inc.
  Atlanta, GA 30338
  (404) 399-6236

Excelerator (C-CASE)
  Intersolv
  Rockville, MD 20852
  (301) 230-3200

ADW—Application Development Workbench/Workstations
(C-CASE)
  Knowledgeware
  Atlanta, GA 30326
  (404) 231-8587

ProKit Workbench (C-CASE)
  McDonnel Douglas Information Systems Int.
  Hazelwood, MO 63042
  (314) 233-2635

CASE Products (I-CASE)
  Oracle
  Redwood Shores, CA 94065
  (415) 506-7000

IEF—Information Engineering Facility (C-CASE)
  Texas Instruments
  Houston, TX 77251
  (713) 274-2000

9

Special Considerations

The client/server architecture flexibility and cost advantages have attracted both end users and corporate management. They envision data on a server on the LAN, and desktop workstations that provide all possible services imaginable. They want complete access to existing mainframe data, connectivity to all existing platforms, and applications with the same high level of system availability they currently have with the mainframe. Storage management, change management, backup, and security should all be "taken care of" without user participation.

Data center managers who have been requested to provide this environment and these facilities quickly find that comprehensive tool sets that provide these facilities do not exist or are not yet mature in the client/server environment.

9.1   CHANGE MANAGEMENT

Within the client/server environment development and modifications (see Figure 9.1) take place on multiple platforms (individual PCs, multiple LANs, mainframes, and minis). This is different than the mainframe, where there are limited machines and sites and typically library management is the central point for all changes. Two copies of the same program can be controlled through library management and a system of program checkouts.

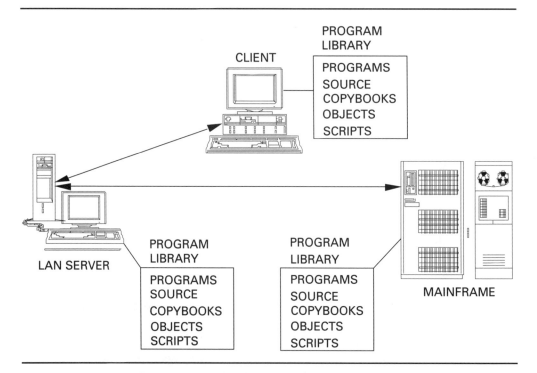

Figure 9.1   Change Management Client/Server Complexity

Since many PCs will be used in the development environment and can operate as independent development stations, the management problems can grow exponentially.

9.1.1   Client/Server Concerns

The following are some of the special considerations that exist in the client/server environment:

- *monitoring changes across multiple platforms:* the change management software has to bridge the platforms in use (for example, mainframe, mini, LAN, PC). Therefore, if development in a project is divided between a mainframe and several LANs, the software must be capable of tracking and controlling in all of these environments.
- *LAN software inventory:* the first step in managing the soft-

ware is to inventory the software across all platforms. Determine where inventory currently resides and where it will need to reside to satisfy all development needs. This includes an inventory by application, by routines/module, and by copy book, especially file and database definition.

- *inter-program dependencies:* a typical program interdependency is a copybook shared by numerous programs. To modify the copybook it is frequently necessary to recompile or change all programs using it. Minimally, all programs using it must be reviewed. In an environment with multiple platforms (for example, LANs and PCs), this is made more difficult by each additional station which stores source code.

- *migration path:* A typical promotion/migration path is unit test, integration test, QA, production. In the client/server environment, unit test may be done on a PC, integration test on a LAN, and QA on the LAN and mainframe or different combinations of these platforms. Software used to assist must be flexible enough to accommodate these paths.

- *version control:* Where is the current version of a particular program? It can be on any platform, including on any PC. This information should be available online; therefore a comprehensive multi-platform-based change management system is required.

- *parallel program changes:* Changing the same program for two different projects is always a problem. Single thread these changes with one programmer at a time and you still have a problem with scheduling test and promotion of multiple changes. Parallel development, where two versions of the program exist, solves the resource and scheduling problems but creates a "version" problem. The best way to manage the versions is to have software to compare versions, identify conflicts, and merge changes. This is simply made more complex by the addition of multiple development platforms.

- *emergency fixes:* the program has extensive changes being tested but production requires an "emergency fix" immediately. How do you control the change to production being incorporated in the test version? This problem is similar to the parallel program change problem and can be handled similarly, but in a client/server environment emergency override libraries do not exist, as they do on the mainframe.

9.1.2 What Should Change Management Provide?

Currently there is probably no single software package available to meet all your requirements for controlling the specific multi-platform and vendor software-based development environment that will become your client/server development environment. Some may come close, and they must minimally meet the following requirements:

- *manage all platforms:* does the software operate on a PC, LAN, mini, and mainframe? If it uses the mainframe as the only repository, development on individual PCs or LANs cannot be controlled properly. It must run on all platforms and be integrated. It should be LAN-based because most development will take place with the LAN platform as the focal point.
- *compatible with development tools:* is the software compatible with existing development tools? If code is written using COBOL, for example, Microfocus and Realia are the two main providers of a COBOL-based development environment. This includes their own library scheme per workstation. Will the change management tool be compatible and easily interfaced? If development is taking place in a GUI environment using scripts, objects, and pieces of code to build the application, does the software interface with this GUI development product or must you use the GUI software's own library manager?
- *compatible with network software:* the change management software must minimally work with your network software (Novell Netware, IBM LAN Server, Banyan VINES). It should probably work with all or most of these to provide you with maximum flexibility, especially in a large corporate environment where different LAN-based development solutions may be instituted.
- *version control software:* the challenge of multiple versions of the same program being developed simultaneously is typical of most corporate environments. Therefore the change management software should minimally have a compare,

merge, and potential problem set of software to combine different versions of the same program.

- *user friendly:* Is the change management software user friendly? Does it take advantage of GUI? Since it must integrate multiple environments and is by nature complex, it should be GUI based.
- *source to executable synchronization:* change management should assist in the identification of source and executable across platforms. An automatic stamp containing information such as system, sub-system, version, level, date, and time is desirable. This stamp should be in both the source and the executable so that control can take place across all platforms.

Several software tools which can assist in change management are covered in Section 9.3 Software Management.

9.2 DEVELOPMENT ENVIRONMENT AND TESTING

Mainframe applications development takes place in a mature environment. The software languages in use are defined, and the development tools have been integrated into that environment. There usually exists a document describing this environment and the procedures necessary to interface with it for both online and batch development. Certainly there are existing production applications that one can draw upon as an example. The client/ server platform, on the other hand, is either not defined or loosely defined.

The challenges in this environment require that developers think in a new way:

- They can no longer separate application issues from the platform.
- They should make data distribution decisions based on volatility of data and response time.
- They should be flexible, especially concerning the GUI that provides the user with his or her interface to the application.

9.2.1 Client/Server Approach

Even if you have a client/server development environment, the following should be considered:

- *define platform:* define the production and user requirements so that the platform can be properly selected. The platform should include standards and guidelines. Select the SQL server, GUI, programming languages, LAN environment, development tool set, and so forth.
- *configure environment:* purchase the hardware and software that are required and assemble the client/server development environment. This effort can be substantial in terms of elapsed time because the hardware and software must be ordered, purchased, delivered, set up, and tested.
- *integrate vendor software:* although the vendor-supplied components may advertise total integration, the reality is that they often need tuning to run together efficiently. The components may consist of GUI, development tools, spreadsheet and word processing software, LAN printers, gateways, and mainframe connectivity. This combination of products will need customization and user-written code to operate as an integrated environment.
- *simulate production environment:* the development environment may be five workstations and an SQL server on a simple LAN. The production environment may have 20 workstations and a single SQL server. How do your systems test simulating volume? You should consider creating the production environment with all its devices and test on it. Also consider creating test scripts with predefined keystrokes and run a volume test with these scripts, each having multiple transactions and running on the multiple development machines simultaneously. In this manner you can simulate the traffic of many more devices.

9.3 SOFTWARE MANAGEMENT

As previously discussed, in a distributed development environment, the same program may exist in sundry states on different platforms. Developers and project leaders should be able to determine the status of all copies of programs across the environment at any time. They need to know who has which version of a program, on what platform the version resides, what changes have been made and by whom. This requires a change in strategy.

Manual software management procedures, which are difficult on a single platform like the mainframe, become extremely difficult on a multi-platform environment. By automating these procedures and eliminating human error, you can achieve the degree of accuracy and reliability required.

Software systems are comprised of many development objects, including:

- source code in multiple languages
- data and files
- graphics
- screen picture files
- design specs and documentation

The development team must track a multitude of development tools as well as including compiler versions and parameter settings.

A piecemeal approach to software management by using different software on the host and on the PC platforms can work, but not well. The products are usually not designed to work together cooperatively. The single best approach is a change and library management software product that operates across all platforms.

9.3.1 Library Management Software

Such is the case with ENDEVOR, a software product from Legent Corp., Vienna, VA. It addresses the change management platform problems we have discussed and provides software that covers the mainframe, LAN, and PC development environments.

Products also exist that address the PC development library management needs. Both of the following companies offer a suite of integrated change management and library management products:

PVCS from Intersolv in Beaverton, OR 97006.
 (800) 547-7827

ENDEVOR from Legent Corp., Vienna, VA 22070-5226.
 (703) 708-3000

The Intersolv suite of software uses the PC or LAN as the controlling point but can interface with the mainframe through gateway software. They provide source locking facilities and run under DOS and OS/2. Their version control software is comprehensive and provides the following features:

- *reverse delta storage:* a specific technique used by Intersolv (not all vendors use this technique) to archive every change made to a module. The current version is kept in its entirety for quick access; all deltas or changes made to arrive at the current version are kept in reverse order to re-create prior versions by applying the prior differences in code one at a time from most current to oldest.
- *change history:* All changes are time stamped with the author for a complete change history.
- *genesis of the module:* this technique provides for a complete recovery path to the oldest version and all changes as they were made.

The ENDEVOR family of automated software management products provides an integrated environment for controlling the entire software development cycle. ENDEVOR supports the key development platforms with IBM's SAA. It manages COBOL, PL/I, C, ADA, other structured languages, advanced 4GL, DBMS facilities, CASE generators, specialized third-party applications, and workstation environments. They can link to mainframe library management products such as Panvalet, The Librarian.

9.3.2   Distribution Software

Software distribution is usually not an issue on the mainframe because multiple mainframes usually share the production libraries at a single site and software procedures are usually in place for propagating that software to the limited other mainframe sites that may exist.

The client/server world is different, because promotion to production is not to one set of libraries but may be to 100 sets of libraries, one for each workstation or server on a single LAN and the same to all LANs on multiple networks (see Figure 9.2). How do you coordinate an update of a new version of software (in-house written or vendor) to numerous stations throughout the country? By diskette through the mail? Mailed well in advance?

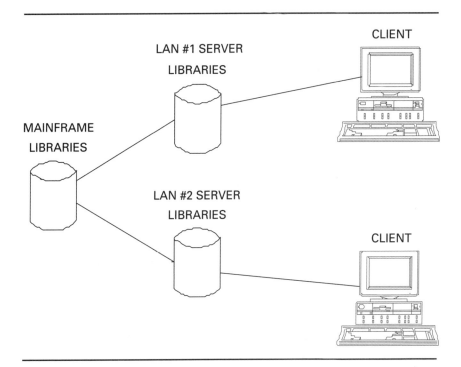

LAN #1 SERVER
LIBRARIES

CLIENT

MAINFRAME
LIBRARIES

LAN #2 SERVER
LIBRARIES

CLIENT

Figure 9.2   Software Distribution

What if diskettes are damaged? Do infrequent updates to avoid user frustration? By downloading software to each station from the mainframe?

A comprehensive software distribution system should be capable of interfacing with components that reside on your mainframe, workstations, and LAN servers. The software should work on all of these platforms to prepare packages of software and data for distribution, store the packages on a central repository, send them electronically to remote sites, install them automatically at a specified time, and verify that installations have been completed.

Products exist that address these needs:

SYNCHRONY
Telepartner International
Farmington, CT 06032
(203) 674-2640

AM:PM
Tangram
Raleigh, NC 27606
(919) 851-6000

SUDS
Frye Computer Systems Inc.
Boston, MA 02111
(617) 451-5400

NORTON ADMINISTRATOR for NETWORKS
Symantec Corp.
Cupertino, CA 95014
(800) 441-7234

NETVIEW DISTRIBUTION MANAGER & OS/2 CID
IBM Corp.
Kingston, NY 12401
(800) 426-3333

DISTRIBULINK & XCOM
Legent Corp.
Herndon, VA 22070-5226
(703) 708-3000

NETWARE NAVIGATOR
Novell Inc.
Provo, UT 84606
(801) 429-7000

HERMES
Microsoft Corp.
Redmond, WA 98052-6309
(800) 426-9400

These products are LAN based, mainframe based or some combination thereof. The mainframe based products integrate with mainframe security and provide PC level security, Generally, they can schedule distributions and retrievals from PCs and LANs as attended and unattended activities. They support EDI (Electronic Data Interchange). Because they can function in distribution or retrieval mode on data as well as software they have further uses. The retrieval function can be used as a data collection facility or file upload facility; together with the scheduler, you can, for example, collect data from multiple LANs or PCs throughout the country overnight or once a week. Similarly, reports can be distributed nightly or weekly on a scheduled basis. Some of these products can collect directory listings and view and modify workstation configurations. This helps audit LAN devices and provides a facility that could be used to do backup to a host instead of local LAN devices.

The cost of any of these products may be a concern because the vendors can charge not only for the mainframe component but for each PC in the distribution network as well. However, for large companies that must distribute software and control software inventory on thousands of devices on a frequent basis, these types of initial costs can easily be justified.

9.4   SECURITY

Computers are of course vulnerable, and loss of processing capability could be costly to any organization. PCs and LANs are particularly vulnerable. However, total protection is very costly and by no means 100 percent effective. A common-sense approach focuses on two elements: economical security measures to provide a reasonable level of protection and detailed emergency procedures for quick recovery for equipment, software, and data.

9.4.1   Physical Security

For those readers who have not been exposed to personal computers, it must be emphasized that personal computers differ from dumb terminals in that each can operate independently. Dumb terminals connected to a mainframe cannot function if the mainframe is not operating. Mainframe security systems are fully developed and mature. Since the PC operates as an independent device, security is necessary for each individual device.

This security can start with physical security. Consider servers, gateways, repeaters, and bridges as mainframe equipment. Therefore, they should be separated from other equipment and made secure (for example, in a locked room). They also should have special climate and electrical facilities. Consider 24-hour air conditioning because they will remain on all the time, unlike workstations that will be turned off when not in use. Also consider a UPS (Uninterruptable Power Supply) for this equipment since it is critical to all users.

For the workstations themselves, consider the use of individual PC keyboard locks that some computers are equipped with; these locks disable the PC keyboard.

9.4.2   Software Security

The PC/workstation itself presents a unique problem. You can, for instance, use the security facilities built into network operating systems. Typically the AUTOEXEC.BAT file on the PC, which is executed at startup, points to a LAN logon procedure which in turn requires an id and password. However, a "boot diskette," which starts up the PC in stand-alone mode, can be used to bypass that security.

Software products are available which, after installed, will not permit a boot diskette to bypass its security. As with any security product, your id and password are the only "key" to the system. Bypassing the security is extremely difficult, as you would expect. However, if you forget your password, gaining access to your own system may be difficult. Combination hardware and software products are available that provide the same facilities.

Dial-in security breaches are often the most frequent form of security breach. Since networks of LANs and WANs have substantially increased the number of sites at which companies have intelligent computers in operation, dial-in facilities should be a major security concern. These LANs and WANs provide access to E-mail and legacy systems. Hardware provides the access via modems, for example, but software must provide security protection. Before any remote access (such as modems) is provided, a comprehensive security system should be in place.

9.4.3   System Security—Single Sign-On

Many security requirements exist in the client/server LAN environment:

- access to the LAN itself
- access to each application on the LAN

- access to individual functions within the application
- data access and modification authorization by file (table), record (row), and field to data available on the LAN

Additionally, there are requirements that must be met in order to access existing mainframe applications:

- access to each application
- access to individual functions within the application
- data access and modification authorization by file (table), record (row), and field of mainframe files and databases

The mainframe applications are probably fully defined and at many user sites already have problems with multiple sign-ons and security requirements driven by individual user-written interfaces and system security software that is installed. Add to this environment the LAN-based security requirements and the result can be debilitating.

Users should not have to sign on multiple times in order to do their job, nor should they have to remember multiple sign-ons and passwords. Therefore, an integrated security facility that encompasses both mainframe and LAN is required.

For those applications that require screen scraping (gathering information from various mainframe screens and presenting that information on a single PC screen, all done behind the scenes), there are additional security considerations. The screens that are to be traversed to gather the information may be in different applications, each of which requires a sign-on. To make the screen scraping transparent, the sign-ons and passwords have to be built into the screen-scraping script that is run behind the scenes. This means that the security data information is stored on the client or server station and is therefore vulnerable.

9.4.4   Available Security Software

LAN client/server security software solutions do exist, but they are usually limited in scope. SQL server software usually provides robust data security facilities. However, this is limited to the use of that SQL server.

Network operating systems offer LAN access security; however, they often have flaws. For example, network operating systems encrypt passwords stored on the LAN. But during the authentication process for the password, they may not be encrypted at all times. Utility software exists to capture and play back user activity on the network, including log in. Therefore, the users' passwords can be read. Also, LAN administrator privileges are often such that they can change all passwords, user system rights, and data read-write access without getting approval or leaving records.

The security environment should be defined as part of the initial development process. If it is installed at a later date, it can be much more expensive. In addition to network operating system security and SQL server security, add-on security packages exist that provide the following:

- an audit trail of user activity
- boot control via passwords
- encryption of files as well as data
- encryption of data and files on diskettes
- screen blanking and locking based on absence of activity
- screen blanking and locking on user request
- special security for LAN password access

Most literature written about client/server security indicates that currently there are no commercially available integrated security products that address all of the concerns. Most of the time the developer has to custom program a solution in order to meet auditing requirements.

Companies such as IBM and Computer Associates International Inc., which provide mainframe security software, are developing security products that will run across a wide spectrum of platforms and that will give IS the ability to secure a workstation and tie that security all the way back through the mainframe.

9.5 THE VIRUS PROBLEM

Perhaps the single most visible security concern in most organizations are the viruses that are easily introduced to a single workstation and then begin to encroach upon the LAN, the workstations on it, and all the other CPUs that the LAN accesses (for example, other LANs and mainframes). Since the workstations are intelligent, simply loading or running an infected piece of software can start the problem. Virus detection and removal programs exist and some computer installations run the virus detection as part of their daily start up.

Computer viruses are programs designed to reproduce and attach themselves to other codes to perform unwanted actions. In many cases, the virus writes itself into memory and then attaches itself to other programs.

Some viruses are just nuisances, but many are destructive. Some have trigger dates that act like time bombs, as is the case with the Jerusalem (any Friday the 13th) or the Michelangelo (March 6) viruses; other viruses are triggered by an operator action—an example is the Yankee Doodle Virus, which is activated with a reboot (Ctrl-Alt-Del) of the PC.

There are two types of viruses: those that infect the disk boot sector and those that infect files. The boot viruses can infect the boot sectors of hard drives or floppies. The file viruses affect executable files, usually EXE or COM extensions.

Examples of boot infectors are the Stoned, Joshi, and Michelangelo viruses. Examples of file infectors include the Jerusalem and Cascade viruses.

9.5.1   Virus Infection and Spreading

Most frequently these viruses are transmitted from "freeware" diskettes (software that is available for free on bulletin boards or passed among friends). Sometimes even a "shrink-wrapped" piece of software that you have purchased will contain a virus.

The following is a list of "high-risk" activities that have been identified in virus infection:

1. Downloading software from bulletin boards. People who wish to spread viruses often place infected "freeware" on these bulletin boards.
2. Demo diskettes can be another source. Even though most software vendors carefully check their software prior to distribution, instances of "shrink-wrapped" software with viruses have occurred.
3. Having a PC repaired usually requires that software be loaded

to diagnose or fix problems. This is an opportunity for a virus to gain access no matter how unintentionally.

4. Diskettes from a "friend." Illegally copied games and software often are carriers of viruses.

Typically, viruses spread most frequently because the user ignores strange symptoms on his or her PC and continues to operate.

9.5.2   Identifying an Invasion by a Virus

It is likely that you have a virus on your machine if one or more of the following occurs:

1. A file suddenly appears that you cannot identify.
2. Data stored no longer has integrity: for example, numbers appear truncated or their order is changed.
3. Files or parts of files disappear but you know that you did not delete them.
4. Your hard disk or diskettes run out of space too quickly.
5. Your system begins to run very slowly.
6. Your system runs out of memory and, as a result, software that had been running without a problem now will not execute.
7. Lights on your floppy drive are on even though you are using your hard drive exclusively.

9.5.3   Recovery

If a virus has been identified on your system, stop operating the system and leave it turned on. Next, note the exact symptoms including messages, graphics, and so forth. Finally, begin the recovery process by either contacting an expert to assist you or by purchasing a virus detection/removal program and apply it to your system and diskettes.

Virus removal can be as tedious as reinitializing the hard disk and then reloading all software from original diskettes.

Data reload is another matter. Most likely a virus will not attach itself to data; it will, however, sometimes tamper with the data. In this case it is necessary to find the last backup of your data which is not infected by the virus.

9.5.4 Prevention

The best prevention is caution in the use of the PC. Purchase virus detection software and run it regularly (for example, once a week) on your machine and on each diskette you receive for the first time, including shrink-wrapped software. If your machine is located where it may be publicly accessed, consider locking the machine (see Physical Security). Use discretion when you receive diskettes or software from nonstandard sources.

Software in the market place includes virus software from numerous vendors, including IBM, Central Point Software, Norton, and Microsoft's DOS 6.0. It is important to review their virus detection and correction capabilities. Additionally, consider the frequency and cost of new releases of this software. Since new strains and types of viruses are being released with increased frequency, the software you choose must remain current in order to be effective.

9.6 UPS

Power surges and interruptions have plagued many PC users. Mainframe computer room designs take into account the electric supply, how "dirty" it is and how frequently there is disruption of service. Often a special electrical environment will be designed to minimize any disruption of service or equipment damage. This includes an uninterruptable power supply or UPS.

UPS consists of batteries that hold power for a period of time in case of electrical loss. The UPS simply keeps the batteries charged and the computer runs off the battery power. This is one way to eliminate outages and problems due to surges or brown outs. A second type of implementation uses the UPS as a backup only. The primary source is the electric company power. Protection from brown outs and surges are accomplished by electronic equipment.

The electric circuits themselves are specially wired to avoid interference from any other source. For example, they may be wired directly to the electric company as a separate source. This is not the case with most client/server environments where the servers and clients are distributed about the office and most of them are on different electrical circuits with potential problems.

9.6.1   Power Problem Symptoms

Any one of the following list of symptoms is a good indication that there are power problems at your site. In most cases a UPS will provide the solution. Since this is not affordable at each individual workstation or client, review and modification of the electrical circuitry or quality surge protectors will help.

1. *flickering lights*—usually indicates split-second outages or temporary voltage drops.
2. *unexplained system (client or server) lockup*—software problems can cause this system lockup but low voltage can cause RAM failure.
3. *premature component failure*—I/O cards and motherboard die without notice. Although a manufacturer defect is often blamed, the problem can be damage caused by a spike in electric power.
4. *hard drive crash*—sudden power loss can damage a disk during read or write operations.
5. *data loss or corruption in CMOS*—if your computer no longer can identify its own hardware configuration (amount of memory, ports available, etc.), the CMOS chip may have experienced an electrical surge, including electrostatic discharge. Each workstation should be properly grounded.
6. *aborted modem transfer*—could be caused by a telephone line-related problem outside the organization or surges within that affect the unshielded wiring used in most cases.

9.6.2   UPS Considerations

If you are designing a client/server environment that has any of the following considerations, UPS should be implemented for the critical components:

- the application is critical
- the data is not replaceable or replaceable at a high cost
- downtime is totally unacceptable
- the hardware is an expensive high-end system
- you have experienced power problem symptoms
- the location of your system has special considerations, for example, remote, mobile office, heavy industrial equipment (perhaps an elevator, motor) nearby

In all cases the recommendation is that *all* servers be protected by UPS equipment.

Several factors should be considered in purchasing UPS equipment. First, there are three basic kinds of UPS equipment:

1. *online UPS*—the AC electrical power charges the UPS batteries and the batteries always power the connected equipment.
2. *standby UPS*—the AC electrical power charges the batteries and powers the connected equipment. When the AC power fails, batteries become the source of power. The switch-over time may be a concern.
3. *line interactive*—the input AC electrical power charges the batteries and powers the connected equipment the same as the standby UPS. However, since a regulating transformer provides power during the switch over, no switch-over time is experienced at the PC.

Second, UPS software is available that will provide an orderly shutdown of your equipment if required. If the power fails in the server room and is not reinstated within an hour or two, the batteries in the UPS will run out. Therefore, especially for unattended equipment (equipment that is up 24 hours per day, like servers), UPS software should be integrated with the servers to automatically shut them down when the battery supply is getting low. Check to see if the UPS software interfaces with your network operating system.

Additionally, UPS software sometimes tracks power quality. This may be of great value when negotiating with a landlord or solving electrical problems in your own building.

9.7   BACKUP AND RECOVERY

The mainframe environment is mature and, as a result, backup and recovery utilities and procedures are in place. They provide the necessary facilities for all users: programmers, analysts, managers, and users. They have satisfied audit requirements.

The mainframe has all data, program libraries, and software centralized. Even though there may be more than one CPU at a single site, DASD is centralized and normally shared between machines at that site; most companies have a limited number of data centers where backup and recovery procedures must be in place. This makes instituting backup and restore procedures for all development and production data and programs simply a matter of running a predefined set of jobs. Vendors supply backup and restore software that manages libraries (programs), databases (for example, DB2), and all other data files stored on DASD.

Batch processing has checkpoint restart to limit restarting long-running jobs to the last checkpoint taken. Online system software has built-in backout and recovery tools (for example, IBM CICS Dynamic Transaction Backout) at the transaction level and journal facilities to recover databases that have been corrupted.

9.7.1   Client/Server Backup and Recovery Concerns

Within the client/server environment, there are concerns that are not inherent in the mainframe environment:

- *number of locations requiring backup and recovery*—each individual workstation within the client/server environment can be considered a mini mainframe. Each has operating systems, system software, application software, and may contain data files. Even if the client stations are not included in the centralized backup and recovery plans, each server on each LAN must be backed up. Where should this backup be done? At each individual server or centralized? If centralized, how can it be done?
- *diverse operating systems*—in an enterprise network, backup and restore should be independent of the operating systems on the network. As a result, backup and restore software must be capable of dealing with a variety of data storage techniques. For example, if Macintosh and Unix/NFX files stored on a Novell NetWare network have different file-naming conventions (different numbers of characters), different file attributes, and different file permissions (access rights), the backup and restore software must be able to handle the variety of data storage techniques involved.
- *large volume of data*—consider networks with many servers and workstations. Network backup is typically done to magnetic tape, but with cartridges that do not operate at mainframe tape facility speeds. Also, the tape cartridge

facilities do not store large volumes of data; it is possible that a single file will span many tape cartridges.

9.7.2   Client/Server Backup and Recovery Approach

Ideally, backup and restore facilities could be done from a central point, for example, the mainframe. All components (each LAN, each server, and each workstation) would be backed up daily (overnight) as part of a corporate regimen. This would take advantage of high-volume data backup facilities, as well as procedures for offsite and disaster recovery already in place.

However, this is impractical given the current state of the technology. High-speed data transmissions for backup and restore that is integrated with automated backup software by individual device is not currently available. Moreover, the diverse LAN operating system environments provide problems for a vendor who wishes to write a mainframe-based integrated backup facility.

Client/Server vendors are beginning to offer backup recovery products that are LAN-based but address some of the concerns. These products typically assign the backup recovery facilities to a server or set of servers that have adequate tape backup facilities and cataloging software to manage the entire LAN or multiple LANs. These products are relatively new but may provide enough functionality to satisfy corporate operational and auditing requirements.

The most commonly used approach is a combination of individual backup facilities coupled with manual procedures. When this approach is used, only servers are backed up. The user must keep critical data or information on a server to be part of this backup process. The user is then responsible for his or her own PC's backup of any data or programs kept exclusively on the PC.

The servers are backed up to magnetic tape, with automated procedures in place to run the backup overnight (to reduce disk contention and file conflicts that would occur during the day). The automated process can only work if the data to be backed up is limited to one tape; alternatively, backups must be done by the LAN administrator and probably done off hours. Individual backup software components may be required to satisfy diverse LAN operating system environments. Procedures must be instituted that are similar to those on the mainframe to satisfy backup cycles (daily, weekly, monthly, etc.), as well as offsite and disaster recovery requirements.

Online transaction processing backup and recovery processing requirements are often left to the vendor who is supplying the SQL server software and applications developer who must write software to adequately take care of backward or forward recovery for transactions and recovery of databases that may have been corrupted.

If you use a combination of hardware and software you may find LAN based backup solutions which can handle most needs. The first concern is hardware based LAN backups that can hold large amounts of data on a single tape. The following vendor provides large storage capacity tape backup to 25 gigabyte capacity per tape:

Cybernetics
Newport News, VA 23606
(804) 873-9000

The following software is available:

ARCADA (Windows NT Advanced Server)
Arcada Software Inc.
Lake Mary, FL 32746
(407) 262-8000

NORTON ENTERPRISE BACKUP (DOS, Windows)
Symantec Corp.
Cupertino, CA 95014
(800) 441-7234

PROSERVE CA (NLM for Novell's NetWare)
Rexon Inc.
Manhattan Beach, CA 90266
(310) 545-4441

9.8   **PERFORMANCE**

Performance of a mission critical client/server application is as important as it would be on a mainframe. Performance tuning in the client/server environment, however, is more complex.

The main components of mainframe response time measurement are CPU (amount of CPU usage), I/O (time waiting for I/O to complete), and transmission time on the network (amount of data versus transmission speed). For those applications that are too large to be totally resident at all times in the computer, paging is the other important factor (time spent retrieving pages).

9.8.1   Performance Considerations

In the C/S environment each intelligent node in the environment should be viewed as a mini-mainframe with all the inherent response time components.

To accomplish meaningful response time information, each server requires a review of CPU, I/O, and network time back to client. Paging may also be a component that requires measurement; for example, OS/2 applications and applications running under windows can take advantage of paging facilities built into these environments. It may be necessary to log intervals at the component level, for example, time spent within SQL server code separate from the time spent retrieving data.

Each client requires a review of CPU, I/O, and—if in use—also paging (OS/2, Windows, etc.) components of response time. At the client workstation overall response time measurement takes place, capturing the start (user depresses an action key) and stop (response arrives to the user) of each user activity or transaction. The response time measurement facility must therefore be resident on the client workstation.

The network represents a major factor influencing response time. Both the client workstation and the server machines individually may provide excellent throughput, but the overall response time may be poor due to a poorly tuned or problem-prone network. The two concerns are:

- *traffic on the network.* Based on the types of applications being run on the same network, the network speed may become a factor. If, for example, you are running an imaging application whereby an image server will transmit pages upon pages of documents to clients at 50,000 bytes per page, it is possible to congest a network with that application alone. All other applications running on that LAN will be affected.

- *error traffic on the network.* This was covered briefly in the chapters on LANs. Essentially, shorts and malfunctioning components can cause noise on the network. This noise or electronic interference travels the network along with the good message traffic. If it is frequent enough, noise can degrade or debilitate a network.

If you access the mainframe in your applications (for example, in a cooperative processing application), this is an additional response time component. The time spent on the mainframe should be logged separately from the transmission time to the client or server.

One product exists which addresses some of these needs:

LANSPY from Legent Corporation in Vienna, VA.
(703) 734-9494

This product is a component of the mainframe product called NETSPY, which is also from Legent Corp. It provides end-to-end response time measurements and statistics for token ring LANs. The statistics include the number of errors on workstations and LANs. Unfortunately, no comprehensive response time measurement software exists at this time.

9.8.2   Tools to Use

If you had the tools to assist in the performance tuning process, they should measure:

- overall response time for each transaction on the client machine
- CPU, I/O, and paging on the server
- CPU, I/O, and paging on the client
- start and stop time for each server transaction or activity
- start and stop of each vendor component on the LAN (for example, separate GUI presentation overhead from user code)
- start and stop time of network transmission
- start and stop time of mainframe transmission
- volume of network traffic

Once you are armed with this information, bottlenecks and response time problems can be analyzed and addressed.

Mature performance-monitoring tools exist on the mainframe. IBM, Candle Corp., and other vendors provide enough tools to monitor most operating systems, system software packages (for example, CICS, IMS, DB2), and networks. Within the client/server LAN environment a comprehensive set of these tools is not yet available. However, tools exist that can measure some of the response time components.

Network tools exist: for example, LANSpy (from Legent), a component of their mainframe product called NetSpy. This software reports token-ring LAN performance and error statistics to NetSpy on the mainframe.

Some SQL servers provide transaction logging and response time facilities that can help tune the SQL server.

Candle Corp., which specializes in performance and bottleneck monitoring and reporting tools for IBM mainframes, is addressing the problem. Candle is developing a new generation of performance monitors and automated operations products that can be ported to any platform and that can all report back to a central focal point: the focal point being a mainframe or any workstation on the system. In a joint development with IBM, Candle is building the first of its new toolsets for the AS/400.

Be prepared to provide your own tools. Log the start and end time of each component on your client machine and then write some simple reports to assist in the data analysis.

9.9   STANDARDS AND GUIDELINES

Mainframe standards and guidelines in most cases are comprehensive. They are usually integrated into the development process and are familiar to the developer. But they do not necessarily apply to the client/server LAN-based environment.

9.9.1   Client/Server Considerations

The client/server environment provides many special considerations:

1. *user interface*—a common user interface should be based on common screen design, definition of function keys, messages, action bars, pop up windows, colors, and so forth. The user should not have to learn a whole new interface from one ap-

plication to another. Differences in application interfaces burden the user with additional training requirements and take away from their day-to-day proficiency.

2. *windows interface*—if one chooses one, and only one, GUI for all client/server platforms, the user interface will, by default, be "standardized." Client/server environments should take advantage of existing shrink-wrapped software (for example, word processing, spread sheet, etc.). This, however, leads to problems; these software packages each have potentially different user interfaces. Additionally, there are many vendors who produce shrink-wrapped software for applications such as word processing, spreadsheet, and so forth. If more than one word processor is implemented, for example, you end up with yet another user interface. If these products can be purchased and run under one common GUI, they will look and feel more alike. It is even better if they were built to interface with that GUI.

3. *programming standards*—programming languages must be chosen and then standards defined. In many cases client/server architecture will require new languages (full languages, scripting languages, etc.). Standards need to be defined for coding in these languages. Application programming interfaces for such facilities as connectivity to mainframe and SQL server routines require definition and standardization.

4. *documentation*—because a programmed function in this environment may consist of many components (screens, objects, scripts, routines, etc.), document standards should be revisited.

In addition, if applications standards and guidelines are added to this GUI interface, the user and maintenance programmer will have commonality running throughout the application.

9.9.2   Client/Server Approach

The following simple recommendations should be considered.

1. Review applicable mainframe standards and guidelines. Some may still apply and there is also a comfort level with the existing development environment.

2. Choose one graphic user interface (GUI), such as Microsoft

Windows or IBM Presentation Manager, to provide the common user interface for all applications.

3. Run all of the vendor software under the GUI chosen. This will provide a common look and feel at the highest level.
4. Minimally, set simple standards and guidelines. Detailed standards and guidelines should be considered for APIs, GUI, and data security. Use both texts identified in the chapter on GUI design to assist in the definition of GUI standards.

Retroactively enforcing standards will be even more costly and time consuming than on the mainframe because many more software components and languages are involved. Standards and guidelines must be prepared for each platform chosen; if at all possible, do not implement multiple platforms.

9.10   PROBLEM MANAGEMENT

There are three concerns that should be addressed: debugging tools available, trouble shooting tools, and hardware and especially software vendor relations. In each of these three areas we will compare the current mainframe solutions to the client/server environment.

9.10.1   Debugging Tools

Debugging tools are mentioned here because they are part of the problem management picture. They are used to assist in developing a quality piece of software and can be a major factor in programmer productivity. Additionally, if there are still "bugs" in the production environment, these tools can be used in the trouble shooting arena. Debugging tools available on the mainframe are at best only adequate, despite the number of years of opportunity to improve them. The developer is not as productive as possible.

Debugging tools in the client/server environment are generally excellent. Most compilers, GUI script processors, and so forth provide excellent debugging facilities for stepping through a program, viewing data as you go, and the like. Products such as Microfocus' Workbench provide a comprehensive debugging toolset for PC development in languages such as COBOL; these tools can be used to solve run-time problems. Although mainframe software exists that can assist in resolving run-time abends, they are not as comprehensive.

9.10.2   Trouble Shooting Tools

Most mainframe software provides run-time diagnostic messages that help in trouble shooting. Additionally, vendors also supply software for both batch and online processing that the data center can use for real-time problem resolution, as well as debugging aids for the applications personnel to use in isolating the problem and providing a snapshot for quick diagnosis that can be used after the abend has taken place.

Trouble shooting facilities in the client/server environment are not as comprehensive. Since there are usually numerous software packages in the final production configuration and you have a whole new technology to deal with in the LAN and its components, identifying the source of a problem is too often complex. Also the software versions change frequently.

Network administration is assisted by basic tools of the trade: cable testers, protocol analyzers, and vendor applications designed to monitor and manage the network. These can provide the following: traffic flow over the network, server and workstation monitoring, alarms, application monitoring, network load analysis by workstation and applications.

Hardware diagnostic software has replaced highly specialized equipment: for example, Norton Utilities from Symantec Corp. of Cupertino, CA and Central Point PC tools from Central Point Software Inc. of Beaverton, OR. These provide facilities to fix hard disk system errors, reset lost machine configurations, defragment disks, provide system analysis, and provide diagnostic advise.

Software trouble shooting tools are often limited to the vendor supplying that piece of software. There is no comprehensive tool that will assist in trouble shooting a multi-vendor software platform.

9.10.3   Vendor Relations

The number of hardware and software vendors that comprise the mainframe environment is usually less than those in the client/

server environment. Relationships with these vendors is well established. Often there is a maintenance agreement in place. Additionally, each mainframe hardware or software manufacturer has fewer customers, which should mean easier access to the manufacturer and better service for the customer.

The client/server vendor issue is not as clear. The first concern is the number of components in the client/server environment and the resulting number of vendors. Each piece of software can be from a different vendor: for example, word processing, spreadsheet, database, SQL server, network operating system, server and client operating system, development tools, GUI interface, mainframe connectivity, library management, version control software can each be from a different vendor. Each has its own hotline or help desk telephone number and procedures. This applies to hardware as well: client, server, network interface card, emulation cards for PCs and gateways, and so forth may all have been purchased from different vendors.

The second concern relates to the price and volume of client/server components. The number of users of PC-based software is many times more than the mainframe; therefore, there is less support to go around. Also, since the price (and the profit margin) of each piece of hardware or software is low, full-service technical support is not always cost justifiable.

Be prepared to use vendor-supplied documentation and manuals to do your own debugging. Be prepared to purchase books written about the software other than those provided by the vendor. Be prepared to join user groups to share information. Be prepared to wait 24 hours for an answer to a question when you use the technical support "hot lines." Be prepared to use "trial and error" to work around problems.

The situation is not that severe overall. Many vendors provide excellent technical support; they either respond while you are on the phone or within several hours after you have placed the call.

9.11   AUDITING

The auditing process involves two approaches: passive and active. Passive controls and processes audit systems after they have completed processing; this type of audit would include sign-on facilities, data security, and accuracy of data changes. Active facilities audit systems during their processing. The client/server environment presents new concerns in both of these areas.

9.11.1   Passive Audit Concerns

There are several concerns related to auditing within the client/server environment.

1. *Security access*—as we covered in the security section, the LAN client/server environment presents many new challenges to those responsible for making it a secure environment.
2. *Training*—all the new software components in the client/server environment create a challenge to the auditor. To successfully audit a system, knowledge of these components is necessary; for example, to review data integrity, the auditor must now be knowledgeable about the new database technology and the language used to interface with it.
3. *Data security*—once data leaves the mainframe and resides on clients and servers, all the challenges that apply to the mainframe also apply to each client and server node.
4. *Additional equipment*—normally, auditing of production data is done by taking a copy and then using that copy to perform the audit. In the client/server world this may require additional server hardware and software to accommodate that copy.
5. *Policy data compliance*—the design of a client/server system should focus on placing much of policy editing (tables and table-driven algorithms that define the data content and limits of fields) on the database server. Again, the auditor must be knowledgeable about the database server product in order to audit policy compliance. Knowledge of the application tools used to maintain the data is required as well, to be able to understand what and how tools can be used to "tamper" with production data.

Access to the client/server systems presents another challenge. The following should be reviewed in the client/server environment:

1. *software manuals*—determine vulnerability.
2. *software defaults*—such as E-mail, electronic fax, and so forth should be changed.

3. *hacker bulletin boards*—good source for ideas about how an intrusion may take place.
4. *system access*—identify all entry points (physical dial-in ports—every modem) to your systems, including stand-alone PCs, all dial-in points including LANs.
5. *random dial-in*—attempt to blindly enter your system as a hacker might.

9.11.2   Active Audit Concerns

An active security routine for detecting and diagnosing intrusion attempts in progress is sometimes used in critical financial applications that run real time. This routine would independently validate an update and then compare the results to the application itself. If the results differ, the original transaction may be aborted and an alert generated. On the mainframe where the terminals are non-intelligent and the applications run on that mainframe, a single active security routine can provide the active auditing desired.

There are several concerns related to auditing within the client/server environment.

1. Since the client/server environment data, programs, and processes can reside at the client and at the server, a single active security procedure may not be practical. Individual active security systems may be required for each LAN, workstation, and perhaps each server. Another approach makes these critical transactions cooperative with the update component on the mainframe. A single active security procedure could do the job.
2. *Training*—all the new software components in the client/server environment create a challenge to the auditor. To develop an active routine within this environment would require a thorough knowledge of this software.

9.11.3   Security Versus Performance

Scrambling devices are a combination of hardware cards and software that can be used on the LAN to secure transmission and residency of data. This can provide data security outside the application while it is resident on the server or client. However, there may be a response time concern. If each data access requires an unscramble and, in the case of an update, a scramble, the additional processing may be a concern. Active security software also has a potential impact on performance at both the server and workstation level.

9.12   TRAINING

Additional training that specializes in the new platform (hardware and software) is essential to the success of client/server applications development and implementation. Because the hardware, software, and user interface is so different, the cost of training is often underestimated.

9.12.1   User Training

Minimally, the user will require the following:

- *technology introduction:* an introduction to the concepts and facilities in the client/server environment geared to the platform in use.
- *LAN support:* in addition to the GUI interface and other unique characteristics of the workstation, the user should understand the LAN hardware he or she is working with. The user will probably have to be responsible for much of the equipment, especially if there are many LANs at remote locations. Fully qualified LAN administrators at each location would be too expensive, so designated users must be knowledgeable about the basics and must be backed up by phone support.
- *application:* training every user is normally required, but even if this is an existing legacy system, retraining will be required because the user interface is completely different. The applications will have a whole new look and feel. The user needs training to develop a comfort level with this technology.
- *GUI (mouse):* the GUI interface that uses mouse technology is a new physical and logical concept. Training should be geared to making the transition a comfortable one. Simply learning to traverse windows technology by using a

mouse, clicking, dragging, opening and closing windows, and so forth should be hands-on training.

The recommendation is that before the first client/server application is rolled out to the user community, their workstation is installed with the same platform together with a shrink-wrapped software product (e.g., Word Processing, E-mail) and mainframe access. This should be done three months in advance so they can become acclimated to the new workstation hardware and software platform independent of the application they must learn to use.

9.12.2   Developer Training

The following is a brief statement of the skills that each type of developer must acquire:

- *DBA (DB2):* relational database design as it relates to the SQL server chosen.
- *COBOL programmer:* event-driven programming, call-level SQL, relational database design, and skills at all of the selected development tools.
- *PC database programmers (for example, Paradox):* analysis and design methodology, event-driven programming relational database design, SQL skills, skills at all of the selected development tools.
- *systems analysts:* joint application design (JAD), prototyping skill, user interface design skill, platform introduction.
- *business analysts:* platform introduction, user interface introduction.
- *project manager:* platform introduction, user interface introduction.

All of the above require a basic or in-depth knowledge of the project management tool and the standards and guidelines in use. Also note that the development tools that require training include the GUI, gateway interface and communications software, programming languages and scripting languages, shrink-wrapped software to be utilized, and so forth.

Retraining of the development staff can be done by using one of three alternative approaches. Listed below are the pros and cons:

- retraining: *pro*—long-time employees are seasoned, loyal, and knowledgeable about the business and systems.

  con—if there is an unwillingness to learn, the training effort is expensive and will be unsuccessful.

- replace workers: *pro*—younger employees cost less and have more of the required skill set.

  con—new workers are unfamiliar with the business and do not have loyalty to the organization initially.

- outsourcing: *pro*—immediate results; potential reduction in operating (development) expenses.

  con—loss of control over systems and creates dependency on service provider.

9.13   HELP DESK

For reasons similar to those already covered in the Auditing and Training section, specialized training will be required for Help Desk personnel if these client/server applications are to be covered by a Help Desk facility. The client/server environment involves not only new applications but also a new hardware platform, as we have discussed. The user community will probably require more assistance initially per person than for any existing mainframe environment. This means that the Help Desk volume will increase. At the same time the range and depth of questions that will be asked will increase. Consider some of the following approaches:

- *sample software:* provide some of the Help Desk personnel with all of the types of software made available to the users in the client/server environment. This will enable them to mimic the user's problem and therefore provide a better explanation of how to resolve the problem.
- *hands-on experience:* the Help Desk personnel will need training and hands-on experience with each piece of client/server software in place.
- *hardware overview:* provide the Help Desk personnel with

training and hands-on experience with the LAN and client hardware.
- *intermediate experience:* consider providing the Help Desk personnel with intermediate-level experience instead of just basic experience so that they can provide in-depth assistance for the users across the many different client/server solutions that will be available.

The following Help Desk client/server solutions vary in price from $995 to $45,000 and run under some combination of Unix, Windows, DOS, OS/2, Macintosh, and Windows NT as shown.

ACTION REQUEST SYSTEM (Unix, Windows)
Remedy Corp.
Mountain View, CA 94043
(415) 903-5200

APRIORI (Unix, Windows, DOS, Macintosh)
Answer Computer Inc.
Sunnyvale, CA 95113
(408) 739-6130

COMMAND HELPDESK (Unix, Windows)
IsiCAD Inc.
Anaheim, CA 92803-6122
(714) 533-8910

DKHELP DESK for WINDOWS (Unix, OS/2, Windows, Windows NT)
DKSystems Inc.
Chicago, IL 60611
(312) 876-3042

EXPERT ADVISOR (OS/2, Windows, DOS)
Software Artistry Inc.
Indianapolis, MN 46268
(317) 876-3042

LANDESK RESPONSE SOFTWARE (Windows, DOS)
Intel Corp.
Hillsboro, OR 97124
(800) 538-3373

PARADIGM (Unix, Windows)
Legent Corp.
Bellevue, WA 98004
(206) 646-1850

TAKE CONTROL CUSTOMER Support/Help Desk (Unix,
Windows, DOS)
Brock Control Systems Inc.
Atlanta, GA 30339
(404) 431-1200

UTOPIA HELP DESK (Windows)
Corporate Software Inc.
Canton, MA 02021
(800) 786-4778

VANTIVE SUPPORT (Unix, Windows, Macintosh)
The Vantive Corp.
Mountain View, CA 94043
(415) 691-1500

Trademarks

Trademark or Registered Trademark	Corporation
1-2-3	Lotus Development Corp.
ADW	KnowledgeWare, Inc.
APPC	International Business Machines Corp.
Apple System 7	Apple Computer, Inc.
AppleTalk	Apple Computer, Inc.
Application Control Architecture	Digital Equipment Corp.
Application Development Workbench	KnowledgeWare, Inc.
AS/400	International Business Machines Corp.
Banyan	Banyan Systems, Inc.
CA-Realia COBOL	Computer Associates International, Inc.
cc:Mail	Lotus Development Corp.
CICS	International Business Machines Corp.
COBOL Workbench	Micro Focus Inc.
Customer Information Control System	International Business Machines Corp.

Trademark or Registered Trademark	*Corporation*
DB2	International Business Machines Corp.
Digital	Digital Equipment Corp.
Distributed Relational Database Architecture	International Business Machines Corp.
DRDA	International Business Machines Corp.
Dynamic Data Exchange	Microsoft Corp.
EASEL	Easel Corp.
Forest & Trees	Channel Computing
Gupta	Gupta Technologies, Inc.
IBM	International Business Machines Corp.
IBM Information Warehouse	International Business Machines Corp.
IEF	Texas Instruments, Inc.
IMS	International Business Machines Corp.
Information Engineering Facility	Texas Instruments, Inc.
INFORMIX	Informix, Inc.
INGRES	Ingres Corp.
LAN Manager	Microsoft Corp.
LAN Network Manager	International Business Machines Corp.
LAN Server	International Business Machines Corp.
Lotus	Lotus Development Corp.
Lotus Notes	Lotus Development Corp.
LU6.2	International Business Machines Corp.
Microsoft	Microsoft Corp.
Motif	Open Software Foundation
MS DOS	Microsoft Corp.
MVS	International Business Machines Corp.
NetWare	Novell, Inc.

Trademark or Registered Trademark	*Corporation*
NetWare Message Handling System	Novell, Inc.
NFS	Sun Microsystems, Inc.
Novell	Novell, Inc.
Open Database Connectivity	Microsoft Corp.
OpenLook	Sun Microsystems and USL
ORACLE	Oracle Corp.
OS/2	International Business Machines Corp.
OS/2 Communications Manager	International Business Machines Corp.
OS/2 Data Base Manager	International Business Machines Corp.
OS/400	International Business Machines Corp.
Paradox	Borland International Inc.
PowerBuilder	Powersoft Corp.
Powersoft	Powersoft Corp.
Presentation Manager	International Business Machines Corp.
Professional Office System	International Business Machines Corp.
PROFS	International Business Machines Corp.
PS/2	International Business Machines Corp.
Quest	Gupta Technologies Inc.
SAA	International Business Machines Corp.
SQL Bridge	Microsoft Corp.
SQLBase	Gupta Technologies Inc.
SQLNetwork	Gupta Technologies Inc.
SQLWindows	Gupta Technologies Inc.
Sun	Sun Microsystems, Inc.
SunOS	Sun Microsystems, Inc.
Sybase	Sybase, Inc.
SYBASE SQL Server	Sybase, Inc.

Trademark or Registered Trademark	*Corporation*
SYBASE SQL Toolset	Sybase, Inc.
Systems Application Architecture	International Business Machines Corp.
Systems Network Architecture	International Business Machines Corp.
UNIX	UNIX System Laboratories, Inc.
VAX	Digital Equipment Corp.
Visual Basic	Microsoft Corp.
VM	International Business Machines Corp.
VSAM	International Business Machines Corp.
VTAM	International Business Machines Corp.
Windows	Microsoft Corp.
Windows for Workgroups	Microsoft Corp.
Windows New Technology	Microsoft Corp.
Windows NT	Microsoft Corp.

Other company and product names listed in this book may be trademarks of the respective company. Wherever possible the author has attempted to identify all of the registered trademarks in the public domain. Casual use of product and company names in this book does not imply that they are or are not trademarks.

List of Abbreviations

3GL	Third-Generation Language
4GL	Fourth-Generation Language
ACK	Acknowledgment
ADW	Application Development Workbench (KnowledgeWare)
ANSI	American National Institute of Standards
API	Application Programming Interface
APPC	Advanced Program-to-Program Communication (IBM)
ASCII	American National Standard Code for Information Interchange
ATM	Automated Teller Machine
BLOB	Binary Large Object
CASE	Computer Aided Software Engineering
CICS	Customer Information Control System (IBM)
CMS	Conversational Monitor System (IBM)
CPU	Central Processing Unit
CRC	Cyclical Redundancy Checking
CSMA	Carrier Sense Multiple Access
CSMA/CD	Carrier Sense Multiple Access/Collision Detect
CUA	Common User Access (IBM)
DBA	Database Administrator
DB2	Database 2 (IBM)

DBMS	Database Management Systems
DDE	Dynamic Data Exchange (Microsoft Windows)
DLC	Data Link Control (layering)
DLL	Dynamic Link Libraries
DOS	Disk Operating System
DRDA	Distributed Relational Database Architecture (IBM)
DSS	Decision Support System
EDI	Electronic Data Interchange
EISA	Extended Industry Standard Architecture
E-mail	Electronic Mail
EMI	Electromagnetic Interface
GUI	Graphical User Interface
HLLAPI	High Level Language Application Programming Interface (IBM)
I/O	Input/Output
IEEE	Institute of Electrical and Electronic Engineers
IEF	Information Engineering Facility (Texas Instruments)
IMS	Information Management System (IBM)
IMS/DC	IMS/Data Communication (IBM)
IP	Internet Protocol
IPX	Internet Packet Exchange (Novell)
IS	Information Systems
ISO	International Standards Organization
JAD	Joint Application Design
LAN	Local Area Network
LU	Logical Unit
LU1	Logical Unit 1 (IBM)
LU2	Logical Unit 2 (IBM)
LU3	Logical Unit 3 (IBM)
LU6.2	Logical Unit 6.2 (IBM)
k	Thousands of bytes
Kbps	Thousands of bits per second
km	kilometer
m	meter
MAN	Metropolitan Area Network
Mb	Megabyte (1 million bytes)
Mbps	Millions of bits per second

MHS	Message Handling Service (Novell)
Mhz	Megahertz
MIPS	Millions of Instructions Per Second
mm	millimeter
MVS	Multiple Virtual Storage (IBM)
NetBIOS	Network Basic Input/Output System (IBM)
NFS	Network File System (Sun Microsystems)
NIC	Network Interface Card
NLM	NetWare Loadable Modules (Novell)
NOS	Network Operating System
NT	New Technology (Microsoft)
ODBC	Open Database Connectivity (Microsoft)
OCR	Optical Character Recognition
OLE	Object Linking and Embedding
OLTP	Online Transaction Processing
PBX	Private Branch Exchange
PBAX	Private Automatic Branch Exchange
PC	Personal Computer
PF	Program Function (key)
PM	Presentation Manager (IBM)
PROFS	Professional Office System (IBM)
RAD	Rapid Application Development
RAM	Random Access Memory
RDBMS	Relational Database Management System
RISC	Reduced Instruction Set Computing
RM/OSI	Reference Model/Open Systems Interconnection
SAA	System Application Architecture (IBM)
SNA	Systems Network Architecture (IBM)
SOR	System of Record
TCP/IP	Transmission Control Protocol/Internet Protocol
TP	Teleprocessing
TSR	Terminate and Stay Resident (program)
VM	Virtual Machine (IBM)
WAN	Wide Area Network
Windows NT	Windows New Technology (Microsoft)
WOSA	Windows Open Services Architecture (Microsoft)